*Use ancient Chinese wisdom to unlock your Digital-DNA
and discover your true character*

HON SHŌ

本性

A MODERN MANUAL
FOR DIGITAL DIVINATION

DR KEVIN WILSON

CONNECTIONS
BOOK PUBLISHING

*To the unfathomable force which binds
my family together with love.*

The Hon-Shō logo is written in English, Japanese and Chinese and means
'your true character'. In Mandarin it is pronounced 'ben-xing'.

A CONNECTIONS EDITION
This edition published in Great Britain in 2012 by
Connections Book Publishing Limited
St Chad's House, 148 King's Cross Road
London WC1X 9DH
www.connections-publishing.com

Text copyright © Dr Kevin Wilson 2012
This edition copyright © Eddison Sadd Editions 2012

British Library Cataloguing-in-Publication data available on request.

ISBN 978-1-85906-340-8

1 3 5 7 9 10 8 6 4 2

Phototypeset in Warnock Pro and Post Antiqua BE using InDesign on Apple Macintosh
Printed in China

CONTENTS

Everything existing in the universe is the fruit of chance and necessity.

DEMOCRITUS

An Oracle for Our Time

We live in a world of frantic change in which our activities depend increasingly upon technology. Our working and personal lives are transformed regularly by the latest gadgets and only the youngest can keep pace. We watch programme repeats on television and are aghast at how they become out of date so quickly. We seem to be accelerating through time at a speed with unknown consequences, and few of us stop to think where it is we are heading. We just don't have the time.

The old covenant between man and nature has been broken. Science, through technological advancement, has brought undreamed-of wealth to many, and previously cherished traditional values have become redundant and been jettisoned. Conventional religions are struggling to cope with the pace of change and many of us are seeking something else to fill the void. Modern Western societies, living on the products of scientific progress, have become dependent upon materialism, technology and economic growth, and no one knows what effect this will have in the long term.

Even in this 'modern' age, it is difficult to improve upon the observations made by Carl Jung more than fifty years ago:

> *We are very far from having finished completely with the Middle Ages,*
> *classical antiquity and primitivity, as our modern psyches pretend.*
> *Nevertheless, we have plunged down a cataract of progress which sweeps*

us on into the future with ever wilder violence the farther it takes us from our roots. ... it is precisely the loss of connection with the past ... which has given rise to [our] 'discontents' ... We rush impetuously into novelty, driven by a mounting sense of insufficiency, dissatisfaction and restlessness.

Memories, Dreams, Reflections C. G. JUNG

You could view the financial collapse felt throughout the world since the summer of 2008 as a warning. It should serve as a reminder of the fragile nature of our way of life. The domino effect in the destruction of many financial institutions, watched by us all with a powerless fascination, arises from the interconnectedness of the lives of all humankind. Unrestrained economic 'progress' brought our civilization to the brink of destruction through the reality of mutual contagion. This would be no surprise to Jung.

That we need to find a way to reconnect with nature is beyond argument. Hon-Shō is a small step in the process of rebuilding that bridge. By harnessing the earliest known method of divination, employed by the ancient Chinese diviners using oracle bones, Hon-Shō accesses pronouncements delivered by their sages and philosophers concerning our fate, using metaphors from nature.

The early oracle-bone diviners recognized the need to find mythical explanations to illustrate what happens in our world by drawing parallels in nature. Just as our genes are driven purposely to select each other through a bio-molecular process, our ancient predecessors possessed an aching desire for an explanation of their own existence. We have followed in the footsteps of these people. We can still draw lessons from their experiences.

Consulting the oracle is a practice that has featured throughout the whole of European civilization – from the Neolithic 'oracle holes' discovered in the ancient ruins of Malta to the Greek Delphic oracles and their Roman equivalent. I have come to believe that the Chinese may have been the first to employ an oracle process as a formal part of their government administration. When it comes to consulting the oracle, the parallels across various civilizations at different points in history are remarkable. There appears once to have been a widely accepted universal resonance accessed by an unknown mechanism which modern-day science believes it has discredited. It's only now, in our own time, that there is no room for what some believe is irrational speculation on messages received from a mysterious authority. We may come to regret this oversight.

An oracle can be viewed as a detection device which explores the unknown and presents to us a set of alternative images about what may or could befall us. Our minds are conditioned to choose the image that suits our circumstances best and gives us comfort in certainty. This is why, throughout ancient history, oracle reading was used as an aid to decision-making at turning points in people's lives – and sometimes in the fortunes of whole civilizations.

Drawing instruction from coincidences and observing how we interact with nature is entirely sensible and, arguably, genetically necessary. This is the rationale behind Hon-Shō. It compresses our specific Digital-DNA into a personal label. Our digital fingerprint is then used to observe how our character interacts with chance each day. It acts like a tuning fork to detect resonance in a set of daily random numbers which produces a unique personal reading relevant to our lives each day. It's consulting the oracle using a digital mechanism.

Shaped by synchronicity

I didn't choose to become interested in the fascinating subject of oracle reading. Time and again the role played by coincidence or 'synchronicity' in shaping our lives was revealed to me, and brought me to the readings and messages contained in the ancient Chinese Book of Changes, or 'Yi Jing' (*see Introduction*).

Over the last decade, numerous students from the Far East have lodged with my family while studying at college in England. This provoked an interest in the origins of Japanese and Chinese language and philosophy and their shared ancient history. I developed an inquisitiveness regarding the core traditional values inherited from those ancient cultures and the different perspective this sheds on what's important in our lives. We in the West have a lot to learn from their traditions and, to some extent, they too have lost touch with their own traditional values and could benefit enormously from their rediscovery.

I have always retained a fascination with numbers and the workings of probability and chance. During my research it became apparent that the ancient Chinese believed our everyday existence is shaped by chance but that our future depends on our choices. They believed in synchronicity as a guiding principle. The future results from the fusion of chance and coincidence colliding with our personal choices. We can do nothing about the events which unfold around us every day, driven by the twin effects of randomness and nature. But the choices we make still shape our lives. Much of ancient Chinese philosophy appears to revolve around this single concept.

It has also become evident to me, after thirty years teaching finance at business schools, that numbers – even those generated at random – frequently contain recognizable patterns. Numbers are used to express everything in our lives. The patterns they produce remain mostly unpredictable, but they influence outcomes and frame the picture of our existence. In the same way that we are affected by the weather, just because we can't predict how the numbers will fall doesn't mean they won't dictate our lives. Hon-Shō uses our unique personal numbers to harness probability and set the scene of our life at a point in time. It uses the inheritance from our families and the knowledge from our predecessors to provide a glimpse into how our character interacts with the natural world. Once this is exposed to us, the rest is down to personal choice. Our fate remains – always – in our own hands.

Hon-Shō is available to everyone and this handbook explains simply how it works for daily use. There are also digital versions available for those who want to access it that way. The internet and access to the World Wide Web could be regarded as the rediscovery of what we once had but have lost. It can be viewed, not as a threat to our civilization, but as an opportunity to reconstruct the unknown universal mechanism which our ancestors naturally possessed and which lies embedded and dormant within us all. While many regard modern digital technology as further distancing us from nature, quite the opposite may be true. The detection of synchronicity could be harnessed to become a means of discovering more about ourselves – and for rediscovering the things we may have lost.

This philosophy has been around in Western thought from time immemorial:

> *Synchronicity is religion without dogma, wherein all are free to draw their own conclusions from personal experience ... No religion could want for anything more, and few have ever attained so much.*
>
> *The Power of Coincidence* FRANK JOSEPH

There are many theories about the natural geometry of nature and how, in ancient times, our predecessors may have possessed knowledge regarding the earth and its place in the cosmos which came to influence the positioning of many ancient monuments – monuments about which we still know so little. This knowledge is said by some to be responsible for humankind's many and varied civilizations, scattered far and wide across the globe yet sharing, for example, commonly adopted systems of weights, measurement – even musical harmonies.

In our time we may be forced by some hidden hand to build a physical replica of this natural human attribute which we have lost in our rush to become 'civilized'. To the surprise of many, digital technology could become the bridge by which we rebuild the community of the unconscious between us all once more.

*Coincidence is a dormant event
waiting for its chance.*

INTRODUCTION

Capturing Coincidence

I came upon the subject of Chinese oracle reading entirely by accident. I lost my job nine years ago and, with more time on my hands, developed an interest in ancient Chinese history and its fascinating philosophy. This led me to an understanding of how the early Chinese captured and passed on their knowledge. I discovered the Book of Changes during this time – a book that, for many years during the first millennium BCE, was statutory reading for all aspiring government employees in China. I can recall vaguely hearing of the book at university forty years ago, and associating it with the hippies who were around at the time.

I now have little doubt that one does not accidentally stumble across this book. There appears to be a mysterious operation by which it reveals itself to those with an open mind and at a pivotal point in their lives. Anyone who goes through this experience will find their life enriched and their capacity for considered and beneficial introspection greatly improved. Millions worldwide will testify to this fact. It stimulates a process of self-discovery in those it touches. And it has done this for me. I developed the Hon-Shō oracle system so that this knowledge would be available to everyone; it holds a mirror to our fate and contains a rich tapestry of meaning for those who are willing to listen.

Ask anyone to give an example of a personal coincidence and they will tell you about something that happened to them which was both unpredictable and mysterious – travelling thousands of miles only to bump into a neighbour from home, for example, or having an experience that relied on the occurrence of a number of scarcely believable accidental meetings. Indeed, both our relationships and our careers appear to depend crucially upon such coincidences taking place on a regular basis.

Coincidences in a series of unrelated events are quite common, and are interpreted by some as premonitions, warning signs or a form of divine guidance. Dreams have a special place in this regard because, in our sleeping state, our minds are uncorrupted by the flux of everyday life. Things that come to us in a dream and remain in our heads when we wake often have a lasting effect on our conduct. And there's ample evidence that we are keen to share this knowledge with those close to us in order to interpret its meaning. Yet, if the same peculiar coincidences had occurred to us while we were awake, our conscious minds would simply dismiss them as fabrications or, alternatively, just miss them completely.

The discovery of a dramatic coincidence in our lives that lies beyond conventional explanation is what synchronicity is all about. By detecting this using an objective and incorruptible oracle method such as Hon-Shō, we can spark an insight into the resonances taking place around us every day. The Chinese represented this by inscribing images on bone, which ultimately gave birth to their written language, the oldest on earth in continual use. The early authors of the Book of Changes used specific images known as hexagrams – a series of six solid (━━━) or broken (━ ━) lines – to indicate different outcomes. These hexagrams reflected the changes taking place in their lives. This was because their language had not yet been formalized and they needed a way to represent events that would be recognizable by everyone. As the world turned, a new set of circumstances generated a fresh pattern of hexagrams which brought changes in circumstances for everyone.

Everyday choices

The messages we receive through using Hon-Shō can convey the same special meaning to us that no one else will experience, because the recipient of the synchronicity is in a unique position to experience it. All we are doing when consulting the oracle with Hon-Shō is holding a mirror to our lives. It enables us to discern signals from everyday events to improve our choices. Detecting coincidence alerts us to warning signals and provides insight but we are still free to decide our own fate. This is never taken from us.

To the early Chinese scribes this was entirely obvious. They believed every man and woman contains the universe replicated inside them. Our whole being should balance, expressed through the combined forces of Yin and Yang. They viewed life not as a straight line of cause and effect, taking us from birth to death, but as a gift from nature whose course was determined by the choices we make every day in the face of unpredictable circumstances. They viewed life as a temporary journey because we are not here for ever. Our final goal rests somewhere else in the universe, and to seek our ultimate happiness here on earth is a grave mistake.

Some modern writers in the West have come to share this view:

You could see the universe as one single, complex, infinitely interconnected potential event: waiting only for you and me to touch it here and there in passing.

The Human Touch MICHAEL FRAYN

The ancient Chinese philosophers mapped the sky rather than the earth so they could instruct the population when to sow, harvest and store their crops. As the sun rises each day its light paints a picture within which we make such decisions. We decide what we want to do each day in the context provided by our natural surroundings. Our fate is always in our own hands, but coincidence drives our range of choices and the decisions we make determine how each of us navigates our way through life's trials and tribulations.

The evidence gleaned from the earliest Chinese archaeological discoveries points to the widespread expression of this pattern of thinking from around 4,000 years ago in the Shaanxi region, where Chang An (now Xian) was the ancient capital of China. Much of the early natural philosophy which still colours Chinese thinking originated in this area situated in the middle of the Chinese land mass. Both the Yellow River and Luo River are located here. The earliest evidence of writing, measurement and mathematics in China was discovered here, and today this is still reflected in the symbol of a rectangle ⊏⊐

bisected by a line 中 which indicates 'the middle kingdom', or China.

Consulting the oracle was developed by these people to detect clues from everyday events and provide guidance for major decision-making. It harnessed the laws of probability to identify coincidences and gain a clearer picture of how events might be unfolding, always determined principally by nature. Hon-Shō does the same. It uses personal number coincidence in precisely the same way as they did in ancient China. It also accesses a body of knowledge which the earliest Chinese scribes and sages believed was gained from their ancestors. For thousands of years the scribes kept a record of readings undertaken at important decision points, from engaging in battles to approving a marriage. Initially passed on through oral tradition, this body of knowledge was later inscribed onto oracle bones, which many believe represent the earliest expression of writing in China (more on this in Chapter One). Later still this body of knowledge was coded, formalized and documented and became known as the Book of Changes ('Yi Jing').

The Book of Changes

Around 900 BCE, during the Zhou dynasty, the oracle readings were first assembled together in a book then called the 'Zhou Yi', before being discovered much later by the West, after which it became known universally as the 'Yi Jing' (pronounced 'E Jing'). The Yi Jing, translated in English as 'The Book of Changes', is said to be the second most reprinted book in the world after the Bible.*

Jesuit missionaries from Belgium, seeking to convert the Chinese to Christianity from the 1580s, are believed to have been the first Westerners to come across the Yi Jing and reveal its contents to sceptical Europeans. For a hundred years the Roman Catholic Church accepted that the pronouncements in the Book of Changes were consistent with Christian teaching, and allowed it to circulate freely. But controversy raged, since some traditionalists refused to accept that such 'uncivilized' people could have developed ideas such as this before Christ was born. This culminated in investigations submitted to the Vatican on the instruction of Louis XIV of France in 1688. The result was a furious debate which lasted for a hundred years – and, to some extent, still continues to this day – concerning the compatibility of ancient Chinese philosophy with Christian belief. The original papers remain in the Vatican library (*see bibliography, no. 4*).†

The most famous Jesuit missionary, the Italian Matteo Ricci (1522–1610), who was also the first Westerner known to have been officially buried on his own plot of land in China, retained no doubts on this subject. He saw parallels between Christian beliefs and the ancient Chinese philosophies of Taoism and Confucianism, and regarded them as compatible:

> *... since the essence of their doctrine contains nothing contrary to the essence of the Catholic faith, nor would the Catholic faith hinder them in any way.*
> *The Memory Palace of Matteo Ricci* JONATHAN SPENCE

Despite the revelations contained in the Book of Changes, it was not until 1876 that Thomas McClatchie (1814–1885), a young Irish curate from Midsomer Norton in Somerset, published the first English version of the book, before ending his days as Bishop of Shanghai. This was shortly followed by a publication by the Cambridge professor (and reverend) James Legge – and many others thereafter (*see bibliography, no. 5*).

---

* Some readers may be more familiar with the term 'I Ching', but in recent years the more acceptable pinyin version – 'Yi Jing' – has been adopted throughout the world, just as Peking is now more commonly known as Beijing.

† The debate focused principally upon hexagram 15 to do with 'humility'. Humility has always been central to Chinese thought, which is why today greeting with a low bow remains very important in Far Eastern culture. This action represents the oceans standing physically lower than the rivers and mountains, yet the oceans are the most powerful force of all and shape the earth. Interestingly, this practice still remains commonplace in Japanese culture, which has not experienced the same dramatic political change in recent memory as mainland China.

The raw information in the book, which contains a series of complicated pronouncements and commentaries on a variety of matters, is difficult for most of us in the West to understand because of its arcane terminology. It has been at times reinterpreted, sometimes lost then found, reinvented then corrupted and violently suppressed, always to withstand the test of time. It survived the 'burning of the books' during the Qin dynasty in 231 BCE, as information on divination was considered too important to lose. In 605 CE the Sui dynasty second Emperor Yang Di ordered the destruction of all 'occult' books to 'lessen the hold of superstition on the Chinese people', but still the book endured. Its core content is delivered by the Hon-Shō oracle process in language familiar to us all.

The Book expresses coincidence through a series of sixty-four hexagrams, each of which is a combination of solid or broken lines, as mentioned earlier. These were used as a simple device to show the uneducated how the swirling mysteries of the cosmos and nature combine to influence our lives – how our existence is dictated by the cycle of nature as it unfolds. At any point in time we can take a snapshot of this scene to take a peek at what's happening to us all within heaven's canopy. This is what happens when we engage in Hon-Shō oracle reading – we receive a daily reading to guide our decisions.

The readings and messages delivered by Hon-Shō draw faithfully upon this material, retaining the Chinese imagery to protect the integrity of the procedure yet offering no-nonsense statements that are clear and easy to interpret. The daily readings we obtain relate to a personal question posed on that day. The question should be very intimate and result from a few moments of quiet reflection (more on how to frame your question in the next chapter; *see page 29*). In our highly pressured lives this may represent a rare and welcome opportunity for us to explore our innermost world.

When you obtain your daily Hon-Shō reading, you are engaging in a process which is thousands of years old, and which has been used throughout history to influence life-and-death decisions. Use it carefully – it could change your life.

There's a divinity that shapes our ends.
FAY COMPTON

CHAPTER ONE
The Origins of Hon-Shō

Hon-Shō is a method of reading the oracle designed for the digital era. It brings focus to our fate by using our Digital-DNA. Its mechanics are based upon an ancient Chinese method of divination originally using alternative even and odd numbers, or pluses and minuses, to produce an outcome on a particular day. Its pronouncements were originally passed on orally by the population to their children through myths and legends.

Some of the earliest divination methods used by the Chinese involved the use of sticks to produce a set of numbers or a code to deliver messages from their ancestors. The messages resulting from the earliest oracle readings were then inscribed on turtle shells and the shoulder blades of cattle (scapulae) and kept as records. The examples shown in the back of this book (*see Appendix, page 241*) reside in the British Library in London, and are thought to originate from the Shang era around 1200 BCE. Even earlier oracle readings tended to use heated turtle shells:

These objects were probably used because they provide a flat surface for writing. In Shang rituals, the objects were deliberately weakened through the small notches in the back. Diviners then applied a hot object to the notches, until the surface cracked. The cracks were interpreted by the King and other diviners, and echoes of their statements can be found in the inscriptions.

Oracle Bones PETER HESSLER

Being largely dependent on hunting and gathering, the Chinese oracle-bone diviners – and, later, sages – generated their oracle numbers by using Yarrow stalks (more properly described as milfoil or *achillea millefolium*), a type of vegetable plant commonly grown in China. It was obviously produced from the earth and is reliable and pliable enough for use as a counting measure, and as such qualified for use as an oracle device. As civilizations developed, coins became more commonly used, as did dice and gemstones, to produce numbers for detecting coincidence. Hon-Shō uses twenty-first-century technology and Digital-DNA in the same way the oracle-bone diviners used their own methods in order to capture coincidences from a set of sixty-four random numbers generated every day. The process is, to all intents and purposes, identical.

Various archaeologists and writers on anthropology have unearthed extensive evidence of oracle reading extending to the late Neolithic Longshan Culture (2900–2000 BCE), and the Hsia (2205–1600 BCE), Shang (1600–1027 BCE) and Zhou (1027–475 BCE) Chinese dynasties. There is strong evidence of the existence of even earlier Chinese cultures. The earliest traces of divination using scapulomancy, for example, are from 4000 BCE – although it is believed that modern Chinese writing evolved from the script employed by diviners during the Shang period (*see bibliography, no. 6*). The Shang were a complex Bronze Age civilization. Many thousands of inscribed cattle bones dating from 1200 BCE and much earlier have been discovered which clearly contained predictions and pronouncements. Some have also been found inscribed on early bronze vessels, with an impressive collection available to be viewed today in Shanghai Museum.

zhān bǔ: *'to read the oracle' or 'fortune telling' in Mandarin.*

The crack on an oracle bone used in divination. This became the origins of the word 'oracle'.

According to one of Britain's greatest Sinologists, Joseph Needham, the nineteenth century saw a dramatic reappraisal of ancient divination in China. Farmers tilling fields at Anyang (the former Shang capital before it was moved) kept turning up curious fragments of bones. These were sold in local markets as 'Dragon Bones' and kept as lucky charms until, in 1899, Chinese scholars discovered that they were inscribed with ancient writing. They were in fact the earliest discovered inscribed oracle bones, and this immediately pushed back our knowledge of Chinese history by more than a thousand years.

Needham produced a monumental scholarly work which transformed the West's understanding of Chinese civilization and its science, having studied Chinese culture from ancient times to the advent of the Jesuits and modern science in the seventeenth century. Others have made valuable contributions to the whole subject area by streamlining and interpreting much of this work. The Institute in Cambridge which bears his name remains as a testimony to Needham's priceless contribution to our knowledge in this whole field of study.

Oracle bones numbering tens of thousands which date from much earlier have since been unearthed in China. Many are on public display, and the earliest are said to date from 6000 BCE. Oracle bones have provided vast amounts of new information, particularly about the Shang period and the subjects for divination, ranging from astronomy, climate, planting and farming to military expeditions, marriage and religious beliefs.

Most scholars have come to accept that oracle-bone divination during the Shang dynasty is where the modern Chinese written language originated:

> *... it was the Shang who adopted the custom of engraving alongside each cracking a written summary of the divination, including the date and the name of the diviner, and of then storing – one might almost say 'filing' – the completed 'documents'.*
>
> Zhouyi: The Book of Changes
> RICHARD RUTT

The early Chinese sages sought a natural order which they observed by studying living organisms and patterns in nature. They analysed nature's processes, from the swirling stars to the tiniest flowers, and concluded that all events were interwoven. This philosophy is known as the 'Canopy of Heaven', which recognizes that the ever-changing universe nevertheless has its natural laws which should always be adhered to.

This is reflected in the balance of Yin and Yang. In order to explain the function of nature and its crucial role in all our lives, the concept of the determined male (Yang) combining and co-operating with the reconciling female (Yin) was described as a gift from heaven. They believed all the elements of our lives are interconnected – not by mechanical causes, but by a kind of resonating influence we in the West are only now beginning to appreciate. Nature is the overriding influence but cannot be tamed. It follows that, when consulting the oracle, if an opportunity to assess our position in the maelstrom of existence is missed at a point in time then it ceases to exist and has gone for ever. They believed that a given set of human circumstances can never be repeated precisely, since our existence is just too complex to replicate as if it were some kind of simple scientific experiment in a laboratory.

THE YIN-YANG SYMBOL *Also known as the 'egg of chaos', it represents opposing but complementary forces which are universal truths. Each flows into and contains the seed of the other.*

Divinatory devices

Divination has, throughout history, taken many and varied forms. But ancient Chinese divination appears exclusively to have started through the use of devices to produce numbers and records kept for future reference. As Chinese civilization progressed and the movement of the stars was accurately recorded, the two ancient disciplines of divination and astrology became inextricably linked to provide an all-encompassing cosmic system which governs our existence.

This view of the world was not restricted to the Chinese alone. Oracles at Delphi in ancient Greece were used frequently for a thousand years before the birth of Christ. The procedure involved an elaborate ritual which resulted in a priestess whispering a message from the gods to the recipient. The common theme in all oracle consultations is a secret process which results in a spoken or written outcome said to come from a higher authority. In ancient Greece this higher power came from the gods, while in ancient China they believed such wisdom came from their ancestors. It is a grave error, stemming from a deep arrogance common among the doubters in our modern world, to believe that oracles are the preserve of the naive and gullible. Some of the greatest thinkers who have lived on our planet and formed the basis of our current civilization entertained the notion of oracles as a critical element in their daily decision-making.

The 'Canopy of Heaven' philosophy touches all aspects of Chinese life and patterns of thought and has been around for many generations. An early Chinese manuscript (which can be found in the British Library) depicting the night sky and used for divination dates from the eighth century CE, while animals of the Chinese Zodiac, feng shui diagrams and lucky days are also depicted on a printed almanac dated 877 CE. These are quite late in the scheme of ancient history, but they are valuable evidence of the far-reaching and permanent nature of this way of thinking.

The legacy we have been left by the ancient Chinese is priceless:

> But the irony of Chinese archaeology is that the earliest known writings attempt to tell the future. Nobody knows precisely what kind of tool was used to create the notches in the back [of the oracle bones]. The Shang writing and carving implements have never been found. The artefacts have been completely disengaged from the act of creation, like a book sent from heaven.
>
> Oracle Bones PETER HESSLER

For those wishing to explore the depth and breadth of the whole subject of ancient Chinese history, a selective reading list is provided in the bibliography (see page 255).

It is clear that some of the most important

developments in early Chinese philosophy are inextricably linked to oracle reading and the Book of Changes, and there is strong evidence the Book was widely used as a manual for divination long before the time of Confucius (551–479 BCE). Both Taoism and Buddhism have links to its underlying philosophy, and the teachings of many other world religions contain remarkable parallels with its pronouncements. The daily readings and messages delivered by Hon-Shō, drawn from the original Chinese commentaries made by the Book's ancient philosophers and scholars, reflect faithfully this inheritance.

In our time many people seek refuge through being cynical and dismissive about anything labelled 'unscientific'. It protects them from confronting the unknown, and this is the only way they know how to deal with it. They point to the ambivalence of oracle reading or its equivocation as a form of deception, and conclude that it could mean almost anything. But sometimes we are forced by life to confront an uncomfortable reality which may present itself as a conundrum because our brain simply won't 'get the message'. This, too, is reflected in Hon-Shō. When consulting the oracle you may receive two messages that appear to be in conflict – but, in fact, the oracle may be speaking to you about two aspects of the same thing. Remember: you are holding a mirror to your fate, and contradictions abound inside every one of us. After all, 'Nothing is just one thing', wrote Virginia Woolf in *To the Lighthouse*, just as quantum physics has discovered that all matter is both a particle and a wave.

How the hexagrams came about

Your daily oracle reading always comes in the company of a hexagram. As we discovered in the Introduction, these are made up of six solid or broken lines, and there are sixty-four in total. The hexagrams are derived from a set of eight three-lined figures called trigrams (again, each consisting of a combination of solid and broken lines), known collectively as the 'Bagua' (literally, 'eight symbols'). The trigrams reflect the never-ending cycle of movement and change in the universe, and are central to the culture of the Far East; even today the number eight is accorded great significance in the Chinese psyche and is generally associated with good fortune. (In addition, trigrams also feature on the flag of The Republic of South Korea – further testament to their importance; *see Appendix, page 252*.)

The trigrams are said to have originated as a gift from the cosmos to a mythical leader, Fu Xi, before 3000 BCE. They represent heaven above, earth below and humanity in the middle, connecting them both. He purportedly received this wisdom on a map setting out the numbers which became the source of Chinese natural philosophy, measurement and mathematics. It also contains the code by which divination operates and which seeks to connect humankind to nature and the cosmos. The Yellow River Map is explored further in Chapter Six (*see also Appendix, page 250*).

The trigrams are usually depicted in a circular formation, reflecting their cyclical nature. The original order of these trigrams, known as the Early Heaven sequence, was subsequently refined during the Zhou period by the legendary King Wen, and has become known as the Later Heaven sequence (*see panel below*). Commercialization has since corrupted their depiction and it's now difficult to achieve consistency at all times, but the Later Heaven sequence is the one that is commonly used in books about Yi Jing.

Moving clockwise through the sequence you will notice how each trigram is different: the lines change until a cycle is completed, and then the process begins again, reflecting the renewal of life and nature. There are eight situations and seven phases of change. The sequence acts like a clock with an inbuilt capacity to return to the beginning and start again.

This is the earliest known representation in China of nature's action, devised by a civilization

Early Heaven sequence

Later Heaven sequence

which had not then invented writing or numbers as we know them. Yet the original map which displays how this mechanism works contains a remarkable symmetry. And symmetry necessarily forms the basis of all modern science, whether East or West.

Three solid (Yang) lines ☰ represent a man (and heaven), and three broken (Yin) lines ☷ represent a woman (and earth). The remaining trigrams were described as six offspring (three boys and three girls), representing all the changes in between, linking the man and woman. According to King Wen, heaven and earth mated and gave birth to everything in the world. Comparing the trigrams to a perfectly balanced family was the most effective way of then communicating difficult concepts to an uneducated population.

Many people know the terms 'Yin' and 'Yang' but aren't really clear what they represent or where they came from. Most people also cite the attraction of opposites without knowing where this originated. Yin and Yang reflect nature's action through ever-changing positive and negative forces, which produces outcomes varying from the growth of plants to the movement of planets and changes in human biology.

During the Zhou dynasty the eight trigrams were expanded to sixty-four hexagrams. According to one of the most renowned translators of the Yi Jing, Richard Wilhelm:

A strong [▬▬▬] and weak [▬▬ ▬▬] line were manipulated together (till there were the 8 trigrams) and those 8 trigrams were added each to itself and to all the others (till the 64 hexagrams were formed).

I Ching or Book of Changes RICHARD WILHELM

And this produced the sixty-four hexagrams we now use, while the same principles of heaven above, earth below and ourselves in between were maintained:

In correspondence with the principle of duality in the universe, the original three line signs are doubled; thus in the hexagrams (six lines) there are two places each for earth, for man and for heaven. The two lowest ... are earth, third and fourth ... of man and the two at the top .... of heaven.

I Ching or Book of Changes RICHARD WILHELM

The ancient Chinese believed that divination could access the knowledge of their ancestors, who were better tuned in to the views of heaven and could confer (or otherwise) the mandate of heaven on the ruling emperor. Successive emperors gained their authority from heaven and needed this reinforcing regularly through oracle reading. But they never abdicated final responsibility for making decisions. Divination was an aid to decision-making but not a substitute for it.

If you look at how the original trigrams graduated to become the six-lined hexagrams, you can see the changes or (messages) moving through a hexagram like waves in water, reflecting the influence of chance and coincidence on all our lives (*look at the Appendix, pages 244–5*). This is a startling early representation of the relationship between particles and waves, something which is now very familiar to Western physicists.

And why stop at the six lines in the hexagrams? Why not manipulate the numbers further and create ever larger and more complex diagrams to detect fate and manage our lives? The short answer is that six is perfection, and the six lines of a hexagram are sufficient to encompass all the universal laws. Each person contains a universe inside themselves and, according to the ancient Chinese philosophy, we are all governed by a set of fixed principles through which the universe operates. The eight trigrams sit at the root of this process, and six lines are all we need.

The best authority to quote on this occasion is St Augustine:

> *Six is a number perfect in itself, and not because God created all things in six days; rather the inverse is true; God created all things in six days because this number is perfect. And it would remain perfect even if the work of the six days did not exist.*
>
> The Loom of God CLIFFORD A. PICKOVER

A test of character

In ancient times Far Eastern mysticism and philosophy focused upon individuals and how they interacted with the world around them. All the major world religions contain elements which are directly comparable with one another and reflect upon how we should conduct our lives. Hon-Shō helps to build on this inheritance by adopting a mechanism for generating outcomes that can be traced as far back as 8,000 years, according to recent evidence unearthed by archaeologists in China.

Consulting the oracle is often described as divination. Hon-Shō engages in divination by detecting resonance in the world around us through connecting our characters – expressed in numbers – with chance. Detecting this synchronicity – the simultaneous coincidence of unrelated events – is like water-divining. If you watch a water-diviner perform, even sceptics don't doubt their capacity to locate water using just a couple of sticks. For many it works unquestionably, and some of us have observed it in action. Something natural, innate and unscientific is being accessed by the water-diviners; the sticks are simply a device for displaying discovery and signalling synchronicity in a way we've never quite grasped or, more likely, that humankind has simply forgotten. But it may still be there, lying dormant somewhere in our subconscious, ready to be retrieved from a deeply embedded but unused corner of the neural networks in our brains.

Hon-Shō detects synchronicity. Your date of birth and name are converted into numbers in the most simple and understandable way. This is your unique Digital-DNA and it never changes: it reflects your inherited character traits formed at birth. It's like a biological label which can be tracked as you progress along life's path. This information is then used to access a different oracle reading every day which is specific to you. It's not rigorously scientific, but it works.

Most people are familiar with the term 'DNA'. We are used to reading about court cases and disputes being settled using DNA-based evidence. This is because it is commonly accepted that our genetic codes are unique and inherited, and that we can trace our genetic history through a series of gene-sequences that allow us to draw conclusions based on probabilities. This is what biological mapping does. It converts our personal genetic data into a set of probabilities, which enables us to demonstrate that we've inherited particular biological characteristics. This information is then used to make statements about our health prospects. No one questions this thinking any more.

Probability is a measure of the likelihood of something happening which pervades the whole of Western civilization and, some argue, distinguishes Western civilization from those which preceded it. For thousands of years Chinese philosophers and sages occupied themselves with the study of coincidence rather than the Western scientific preoccupation with cause and effect. Coincidence was their equivalent of probability. And they believed that the information gained from detecting coincidence and reading the oracle came from their ancestors rather than from gods: the oracle provided information about people's lives based on detecting coincidences from their natural surroundings.

Hon-Shō builds on this approach by fusing this ancient philosophy with modern probability. It seeks to reconcile Eastern analogue thinking with modern Western digital technology. By measuring coincidences from apparently unrelated events, it detects helpful information about our current circumstances. Any event has an infinity of possible causes. As Taleb says:

The world is more non-linear than we think, and than scientists would like to think.

The Black Swan NASSIM NICHOLAS TALEB

What Hon-Shō does is allow you to scrutinize your character, attitudes and motivation by locating resonance using the unique pattern of your Digital-DNA. Your Digital-DNA structure reveals your Life Numbers, and these are used to access your personal character profile using a method set out in the Book of Changes. While your character profile was formed at birth and cannot change, your personal conduct *can*, of course, alter throughout your life. Your digital label is then used to detect a daily resonance in sixty-four random numbers, identifying the likelihood of coincidences occurring around you and from which you may want to draw inferences and take guidance. It produces a daily reading and attendant messages directly relevant to a question you have posed about your life on any particular day. The more attention you devote to considering your question, the more relevant your reading will be (*see opposite page*). The outcome possesses genuine psychotherapeutic value by shedding light on your innermost world.

In 1920 Carl Jung began to experiment with the Book of Changes. Being a rational scientist and a medical practitioner, he was determined 'to make an all out attack on the riddle of the book'. So he sat under a hundred-year-old pear tree with a stack of sticks and, using the old Chinese method of divination, tested its outcomes over and over. His conclusion was unambiguous:

> *All sorts of undeniably remarkable results emerged – meaningful connections with my own thought processes which I could not explain to myself. Time and again I encountered an amazing coincidence which seemed to suggest ... synchronicity, as I later called it.*
>
> *Memories, Dreams, Reflections* C. G. JUNG

Whether we are inclined to spiritual matters or not, it is entirely natural that we search for guidance as to how to deal with everyday events – what issues surround us and what our choices are. This is what the daily Hon-Shō oracle reading achieves: it reveals what's in store for you today by measuring how your character will interact with events unfolding around you and over which you have no direct control. You cannot predict what will happen around you at any point in time as events unfold, but you *do* have choices as to how to live your life. Hon-Shō is therefore not a horoscope; it's a helpful guide which enables you to make your own decisions with confidence. In this way you can take responsibility and influence the outcomes in your life, rather than abandoning yourself hopelessly to fate.

Bringing focus through Digital-DNA

So, despite the extensive information that exists concerning the ancient art of oracle reading, the vast majority of people in the West still have no idea what it's all about. The pace of technological change and the pressures of life appear increasingly to distance us from what really matters, disconnecting us further from our past. Hon-Shō seeks to help reverse this trend. By embracing the most advanced digital technology, it reconnects us once more to the knowledge and experience of those who preceded us. It genuinely accesses a font of ancient knowledge which was drawn from observing parallels in nature.

There's no magic or mystery about how Hon-Shō works – the daily scores your personal Life Numbers produce reflect coincidence and allow access to your oracle reading – but the outcomes can be dramatic, and sometimes shocking.

The elements of Hon-Shō

The three key constituents of the Hon-Shō oracle method are as follows:

- **Your Digital-DNA** This is generated from your date of birth and both your first and last names expressed in numbers using the natural ordering of letters in the Roman alphabet (where A is 1, B is 2, and so on). This is your unique digital fingerprint or genetic code.
- **Your Life Numbers** These are the three totals of the above, line by line.
- **Your Daily Scores** These are achieved from the number of times both your age and your Life Numbers appear, along with that day's date, in a set of sixty-four numbers randomly generated each day. This gives a score which occurs only on that day and is exclusive to you. This score retrieves your personal oracle reading for that day.

All this is done by inputting your personal details and is simply explained in the next chapter. This produces your character profile (found in Chapter

Three) and is accompanied by your personal hexagram and the Chinese symbol always associated with your character. This is equivalent to your Chinese birth sign. You can then use Hon-Shō on any day to access the oracle using the readings and messages set out in Chapter Five.

Framing your personal question

When framing your personal question it's important to recognize that you must interact with an oracle reading to get the most out of it. It's best to confine yourself to a situation which is very personal to you. It's also a good idea to write your question down; it's amazing how many people try to remember their question only to discover that it wasn't a question at all – just a statement about themselves. There is also little point in asking a question to which you already know the answer. If, after a period of thought, you can't think of anything specific to ask, then just consult Hon-Shō and ask what information about your current circumstances it wants to give you on that particular day. You will receive unequivocal commentary which will give you peace of mind. After all, this is one of the objectives of reading the oracle.

Take time to frame your question carefully. Don't do it in a hurry, and try not to let someone else tell you what it should be (though it's uncanny how often you can produce a reading for a close friend or partner you know is under pressure, which precisely reflects their current situation even though they played no direct role in accessing the reading). Remember that you are consulting the oracle using a procedure based on the earliest method known to be created by humankind, so take your time to get the most out of it. Your question should ideally be written during a period of stillness when you've set aside time to really consider your situation.

Our brains have developed in a way which forces us to simplify things so our decision-making is made easy and comes naturally to us. But the inferences we draw often cannot cope with the complex information presented to us daily. Real events don't unfold in a neat straight line for our convenience. A slight modification in the wording of your question can have profound consequences in the way you interpret the daily reading and messages, so it's worth giving it your full attention.

Examining your innermost world provides the opportunity for mature reflection in an introspective manner. In our increasingly pressured lives we need an outlet to allow us to access our subconscious thoughts. Framing your personal question gives you this opportunity.

We all know people who make the mistake of seeking happiness by gathering material possessions or distracting themselves with fruitless pursuits – more often than not in a desperate effort to avoid a reality check. This is a mistake. True contentedness can only be achieved by exploring our innermost world in an *honest* way – by finding our inner truth. There are therefore some key points to bear in mind when asking your question.

Your question should:

- be emotionally relevant to you and as specific as possible in order for you to honestly assess your current situation.
- not require you to be told what to do. The reading you receive reflects a set of images created through the interaction of your Digital-DNA with chance. You will be given guidance or advice to enable you to make more considered, better informed choices. But you will not be told what to do.
- avoid alternatives, like 'Should I do this or should I do that?' But you may want to disclose your preferred or intended course of action in order to test it, or to check whether a decision you've already made was correct. The reading, and any accompanying messages, will then be more meaningful.

It's worth bearing in mind that the ancient Chinese sages consulted the oracle before making major and sometimes dramatic decisions such as engaging in military campaigns and making sacrifices. It was frequently used to render pronouncements on matters of life and death and was never taken lightly.

Interpreting your daily oracle reading

The original Chinese diviners regarded the oracle numbers as coded representations of hidden cosmic connections between all phenomena in the universe. The Chinese symbol, and hexagram, which accompanies the daily reading is important because it reflects the current influences exerted by the world on your choices. The oracle reading provides an insight into your own situation that day and enables you to consider your circumstances more fully: there's nothing better to remind you of what's really important in your life than to receive a reading which is uniquely yours that day.

The pronouncement you obtain represents a field of vision within which the influences on your character are revealed. Regard this as independent wisdom reflecting your current situation, resulting from a correspondence between you and chance that day. It's an objective view of where your life stands at that point in time.

Your reading will usually be accompanied by a specific message or messages, which means there is an immediate change taking place in your life. The messages are embedded in your hexagram on that day and revealed by using the Chinese Code, which identifies them as represented by either the number six or the number nine (*see Chapter Four*). If you have any messages delivered that day you should pay special attention to them. If you have more than two messages, your life is likely to be hectic. Some believe they are more potent than the daily reading itself. On balance, most people will receive between one and three messages on any day, but you could receive more – or even none at all, if your life is relatively calm.

For thousands of years debate has raged regarding the interpretation of oracles. An oracle reading should be capable of more than one interpretation; if not, then it represents an omen not an oracle. As we learned earlier, there's always more than one aspect to any situation, so it's entirely possible that two messages received appear contradictory; this should simply prompt you to readdress your question. Your situation may have changed in emphasis, or another aspect – previously hidden from view – may have now revealed itself.

If you don't receive any messages on a particular day then there are no specific or dramatic changes taking place in your current situation and your life has become stable. The Chinese diviners regarded this as a period of resting before the world turns and another set of circumstances collide with chance to alter your life choices. It doesn't mean there's nothing happening – it's just that any dramatic twists and turns in your life are not fully formed.

Treat the reading as practical advice, reflecting the issues impacting upon your life on that day and how you are interacting with the world around you. It should focus attention on what's on your mind, even if you weren't aware of it at the time of making the consultation. It may be reassuring and encourage you to renew your energy in a current pursuit. The significance of a reading often becomes clear with time and on deeper consideration.

On the other hand, your personal reading may discourage you from doing something you were about to embark upon and lead you to change direction completely. Sometimes, it may invite you to do absolutely nothing and just allow things to develop at their own pace. The one thing your Hon-Shō oracle reading should always give you, however, is hope. It is honest but never defeatist. It can be a useful mechanism for discovering healing and wholeness. It is never dismissive because that would be tantamount to resigning ourselves entirely to fate, and the early oracle readers knew that life is the result of a two-way process between the decisions made by human beings and the influences of nature.

But beware! There is no point in performing the consultation again on the same day just because you don't like or understand the reading; you can't fool yourself, and your reading won't change in any case if you're doing it correctly and using the same data on the correct day. Your situation cannot change until a full revolution of the earth has taken place, allowing nature and chance to reset themselves in order to produce another coincidence of unrelated events. It's the

daylight which exposes our reality. So if you're not happy with what you've received, the solution may lie inside yourself.

Authors based at the Eranos Foundation, an institute for the investigation of self-discovery in Ascona, Switzerland, explained this whole process as accessing a universal compass. My personal search for this Foundation is described in the Epilogue (*see page 237*). The hexagram which on any day is obtained through consulting Hon-Shō taps into coincidence to produce a reading which is personal to you:

... [it] triggers an inner process that will lead you to your answer. The Chinese saw the 64 hexagrams as an exhaustive catalogue of all possible processes between heaven and earth.

The Original I Ching Oracle
R. RITSEMA AND S. A. SABBADINI

Whatever pronouncement you receive from the oracle, always to try to make the best out of your present situation. Change, harmony and the search for balance in our lives is the driving force behind the readings and messages. We are naturally free to choose whether to follow its advice or not. Our free will is never taken from us; Hon-Shō assists us in crystallizing the issues we are forced to confront every day and indicates how contentedness and fulfilment might be achieved. It often invites us to reassess a familiar predicament from an entirely different perspective.

Some people feel they are naturally lucky or unlucky. There's an increasing body of evidence that this is simply not true. The outcomes in our life spring from our interpretation of everyday events driven by our attitude, which can be conditioned or changed completely. We may have no influence over chance events but we do exercise choice as to how to deal with their consequences. Chance you can do nothing about, but you can to some extent make your own luck by changing your behaviour (*see bibliography, no.17*).

Navigating through life

In ancient times oracles were used across different civilizations, from China to Greece and Rome, in order to consider momentous decisions. As a result they have often been associated with great turning points in history:

> *A decision to go to war for instance or dispatch a colony, had normally been made by the state before approaching the oracle. What was sought was divine sanction.*
> The Road to Delphi MICHAEL WOOD

So never be afraid to consult the oracle if you're uncertain about a decision you've already made. We often need reassurance, and the consultation provides a valuable second opinion. By refining your decisions, the daily Hon-Shō consultation will help you navigate a route through your emotional life and achieve a better balance. This is why some have claimed that reading the oracle can be beneficial in treating stress and depression. What it frequently does, through its psychotherapeutic value, is allow you to resolve the painful uncertainty of indecision.

When you use Hon-Shō to consult the oracle you are engaging in a process which has stood the test of time – but you are harnessing the most advanced methods yet devised in order to do so. This is the only technique available to detect synchronicity in your life by linking your unique digital fingerprint to chance and coincidence. The person best qualified to elicit meaning from the daily reading is, of course, yourself:

> *Just as we would rather not have someone else read for us the letters we receive from loved ones, so we are quite capable of reading the communiqués of meaningful coincidence without outside assistance ... The final word on interpretation rests with the person to whom the synchronicity has been given.*
> The Power of Coincidence FRANK JOSEPH

The rest is up to you.

The further you explore the less you know.
To grasp all beneath heaven, leave it alone.
Leave it alone, that's all,
and nothing in all beneath heaven will elude you.

LAO TZU

CHAPTER TWO
Your Character Profile

In this chapter you will discover how to create your Digital-DNA by converting your date of birth and name into numbers. This digital label identifies your inherited character traits, and is also used to obtain your daily oracle reading (which we will come to in Chapter Four). The example set out over the following pages will guide you through the steps as you create your character profile.

First, photocopy the templates included in the pocket at the front of the book. You will be filling in Template 1 to complete your character profile. Once you are familiar with the steps, you can then go on to identify the character profiles for your friends and family too.

Finding your Life Numbers

Let's take Samantha Smith as an example. Samantha was born on 17 September 1969, and her name and birth date are as shown on her birth certificate. Her Life Numbers are calculated from her date of birth, her first name and her surname, with letters of the alphabet expressed according to their place in the Roman alphabet – so, A scores 1, B scores 2, and so on, through to Z, which scores 26 (see panel **A**, below).

Let's look at the birth date first. Here we employ a simple rule to split the numbers up. Because no letter in the alphabet may exceed 26, any number in your birth date which exceeds 26 is split into two digits. So, in Samantha's case

A

A	B	C	D	E	F	G	H	I	J	K	L	M
1	2	3	4	5	6	7	8	9	10	11	12	13
N	O	P	Q	R	S	T	U	V	W	X	Y	Z
14	15	16	17	18	19	20	21	22	23	24	25	26

her birth year – 1969 – is split into 19, 6 and 9. Similarly, if you were born on a date after the 26th of the month, this number is also split into two digits (for example, the 29th of the month would split into a 2 and a 9). This rule only applies to the first line of your Digital-DNA, as the numbers in the second and third lines are derived from letters of the alphabet and cannot exceed 26.

Samantha then fills in the numbers that equate to the letters in her name, adding up the numbers in each line to reveal her three Life Numbers (see panel **B**, below).

Now do the same for yourself. Just complete the boxes at stage **1** on Template 1, filling in your details from your your birth certificate (use your full name even if you're more commonly known by a shortened version). Allocate numbers to the letters in your name by using the alphabet number-grid on page 35. (If your name is longer than the space allowed – if you have a double-barrelled name, for instance – just add more boxes, or write it out on a separate piece of paper.)

This is your Digital-DNA. It is your unique signature expressed in numbers. Add up each line to get your Life Numbers, and fill in the boxes to the right on the template. Your Life Numbers are personal to you and will never change. You will need these numbers whenever you want to obtain your daily Hon-Shō oracle reading.

Identifying your personal profile

Having revealed your digital fingerprint, Hon-Shō now uses your Life Numbers to disclose your Chinese character reading. This is called your personal profile. It describes your inherited character traits using an ancient method set out in the Book of Changes. Your Life Numbers are converted into a series of six broken (━━ ━━) or solid (━━━━) lines to create a hexagram, and, as we now know from Chapter One, there are sixty-

B

DIGITAL-DNA

									LIFE NUMBERS
Date of birth: 17/09/1969	17 +	9 +	19 +	6 +	9			=	60
First name: Samantha	S	A	M	A	N	T	H	A	
	19 +	1 +	13 +	1 +	14 +	20 +	8 +	1 =	77
Surname: Smith	S	M	I	T	H				
	19 +	13 +	9 +	20 +	8			=	69

four possible combinations.

Your hexagram reflects your character. You cannot avoid it – in the same way that you adopted a particular zodiac sign by being born on a certain day. The method used to create your hexagram is simple. It is based on how the Life Numbers fall and whether they are odd or even, as this determines whether a line is solid (Yang) or broken (Yin). We will come to this shortly.

Oddly enough, in biochemistry there are four core chemicals which combine in all living creatures to create their DNA. These are called nucleotides, which combine together in what biologists call 'triplets'. And how many possible combinations are there of these chemicals? The answer is sixty-four. Maybe this is just a coincidence, but there are many who are convinced this is no accident:

From the 20th Century people have come to realize that our genetic codes are determined by four chemicals in groups of three combinations, or 64.

Zhou Yi: Bagua XU KUN

This correspondence between the genetic code and the Book of Changes has been identified by others and, according to Walter:

ZHUN
Overcoming early obstacles

▲ *An example of a hexagram with its associated name and Chinese symbol.*

Your life's events are patterned similarly yet different each day. The way you find out what's going to happen today – exactly – is by watching it happen. Days cycle again and again, but in subtly new formulations. Every once in a while there's a big shift. Then it settles down again.

Tao of Chaos: DNA and the I Ching
K. WALTER

It's all down to the shifting patterns of probability which result from the collision between biochemical laws and nature's influence. (If you would like to explore this connection further, see bibliography, nos. 7–10.)

Creating your own personal hexagram

Let's look at how Samantha Smith obtains her Hon-Shō personal profile and hexagram from her Life Numbers. As we can see from her Digital-DNA opposite, her Life Numbers are revealed to be 60, 77 and 69. She then follows these next three simple steps to identify her hexagram:

Step 1: *Using the Life Numbers*
The ancient Chinese philosophy contained in the Book of Changes describes us all as emanating from the cosmos (or heaven) above and rooted on the earth below our feet, while our lives connect

	Cosmos	6 0	*These two numbers are said to represent the **cosmos** (heaven).*
Samantha's Life Numbers:	Life	7 7	*These two numbers represent her **life**.*
	Earth	6 9	*These two numbers represent the **earth**.*

the two for the time we are alive. It is this philosophy that Hon-Shō uses to produce your personal profile and hexagram at birth. So, by taking Samantha's Life Numbers and setting them out in a vertical line, we can see which numbers relate to which aspect (see panel **C**, above).

Note: If you have a three-digit Life Number (the name 'Rosemary', for example, produces a total of 114; double-barrelled names will also most likely produce a three-digit Life Number), the numbers are split into two according to the rule dictating that no number may exceed 26. So, in

Rosemary's case, 114 would be split into 11 and 4, when setting the numbers out vertically.

Step 2: *Rearranging the Life Numbers*
The next step is to take Samantha's two middle numbers (77) and add the adjacent number from heaven above (0) to create one set of three numbers, and the adjacent number from earth below (6) to create another set, and arrange them in a vertical line (see panel **D**, below).

The reason the Book of Changes takes an adjacent number from above and below is because

38

these two numbers connect our lives to the power of both the cosmos and the earth. This new set of numbers, sometimes referred to as 'natal numbers', is used to produce our hexagram at birth (sometimes called natal hexagram) using an ancient Chinese method devised before writing was invented, which we now come to in Step 3.

Step 3: *Creating the hexagram*
Odd numbers denote Yang (━━━) lines, while even numbers (or zero) represent Yin (━ ━). This produces the following hexagram for Samantha (see panel **E**), using the final numbers as shown in panel **D**. This is Samantha's hexagram at birth. It is associated with her character profile and is connected to an attendant symbol in Chinese.

If we turn to Chapter Three we can locate this hexagram in the table on page 43: simply find the upper three lines of the hexagram across the top of the table and the lower three lines down the side,

and where they meet gives you the number of her hexagram. You can then look up the relevant page in that chapter. Samantha's hexagram is number 28, the character profile for which can be found on page 57, along with the associated Chinese symbol and its English-language interpretation.

Now you can turn to stage **2** on the template and fill in your own details, following Samantha's example, to create your own personal hexagram. You now have all the information you need to complete your own Digital-DNA certificate.

The Digital-DNA certificate

Your Digital-DNA certificate is an incorruptible record of your 'fingerprint' formed at birth. It reveals your own character and it will never change. Samantha's completed certificate is shown overleaf. We now know where her Digital-DNA originated and how her Life Numbers were used to produce her hexagram at birth.

E

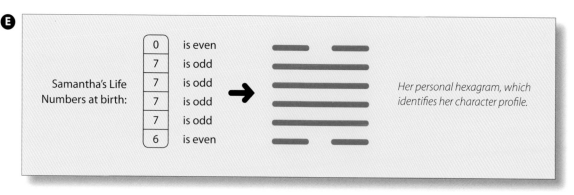

Samantha's Life Numbers at birth:		
0	is even	
7	is odd	
7	is odd	
7	is odd	
7	is odd	
6	is even	

Her personal hexagram, which identifies her character profile.

▶ *Fill in the numbers relating to your date of birth and name, and add up each line to find your Life Numbers.*

▶ *Rearrange your Life Numbers into a new set of 'natal numbers', then convert these into Yang or Yin lines to find your personal hexagram.*

YOUR **DIGITAL-DNA** CERTIFICATE

Name: Samantha Smith

Date of birth: 17 September 1969

DIGITAL-DNA

Date of birth:

17 + 9 + 19 + 6 + 9 + ☐ + ☐ + ☐ = 60 LIFE NUMBERS

First name:

S A M A N T H A ☐
19 + 1 + 13 + 1 + 14 + 20 + 8 + 1 + ☐ = 77

Surname:

S M I T H ☐ ☐ ☐
19 + 13 + 9 + 20 + 8 + ☐ + ☐ + ☐ = 69

This is your personal

DIGITAL-DNA

It never changes

Your personal hexagram   Chinese symbol

Name: Daguo   Interpretation: Critical Mass

Notes from your Hon-Shō Character Profile:

My determination increases my chances of success, but I must make sure I channel my energy in the right direction. I give great support to others, but must be wary that I don't take things too far. Know when to retreat.

THE FUTURE IN YOUR HANDS

Using the natural ordering of letters in the Roman alphabet, this certificate provides your Digital-DNA and your resulting Life Numbers. These are unique to you and were formed when you were born. They will never change. You will need your Life Numbers any time you want to obtain your daily reading.

◀ *Look up your hexagram in Chapter Three to discover your inherent character profile.*

Her hexagram, on the left of the certificate, carries the Chinese word 'Daguo', and this is visually represented by the Chinese symbol on the right of the certificate. The English-language interpretation of this symbol is 'Critical Mass' and Samantha has added key notes taken from her personal Hon-Shō profile in Chapter Three. Once you have determined your personal hexagram, it's easy to look up your own profile with its associated Chinese symbol, using the table on page 43.

Of course, you may not be in the best position to determine whether the personal profile accurately describes your character. Ask a friend for their objective opinion – though prepare yourself for the fact that it may not always be complimentary!

While your inherent character never changes, you do have choices to make every day when confronted by events and coincidences spinning all around you and over which you have no control. And you are always in a position to make your own *decisions* when confronted with those choices. The decisions you make change every day, and this is why it's important to consult the oracle regularly for guidance. The procedure for daily consultation is explained in Chapter Four.

Note: Hon-Shō is also available to download as an application for the iPhone, iPod touch or iPad. This gives instant access to your Digital-DNA certificate and daily reading, should you wish to receive your oracle readings digitally.

... it is impossible to imagine an experiment which could prove the nonexistence anywhere in nature of a purpose, of a pursued end.

... living organisms ... pursue a purpose. In fact the central problem of biology lies with this very contradiction (between chance and necessity).

JACQUES MONOD

CHAPTER THREE
Hon-Shō Profiles

Having identified your unique Digital-DNA in the previous chapter, you can now locate your birth hexagram in the table to the right. Find the top three lines of your hexagram (the upper trigram) along the top of the table, and the bottom three lines (the lower trigram) down the side, and where they meet gives you the number of your hexagram. Then simply turn to the relevant page in this chapter to discover your character profile and associated Chinese symbol. You can then add key character notes to your Digital-DNA certificate.

Don't forget that, once you've discovered your own profile, you can then go on to look up the profiles for your friends and family too.

UPPER TRIGRAM

	1	34	5	26	11	9	14	43
	25	51	3	27	24	42	21	17
	6	40	29	4	7	59	64	47
	33	62	39	52	15	53	56	31
	12	16	8	23	2	20	35	45
	44	32	48	18	46	57	50	28
	13	55	63	22	36	37	30	49
	10	54	60	41	19	61	38	58

LOWER TRIGRAM

No. 1
CREATIVE ENERGY

QIAN

You are blessed with an innovative power which can be boundless. Leadership and perseverance are your strongest characteristics. You can act like a light switch which ignites others into action. There is an inherent balance in your nature, but you do not like to be distracted by trivia or diverted from what you see as moral or just causes. You will assume positions of authority with wisdom but must retain your humility. Dragon stars were associated with your character by the ancient Chinese; these display strength and constancy. Qian is often associated with the sun as the source of power and life. In the wrong hands, however, this power can be immensely destructive. It is how this power is unleashed through your own free will which decides your fate. Trust your instincts at all times.

No. 2
PATIENTLY POWERFUL

KUN

Adaptability and sensitivity are your dominant characteristics. Healing and comfort are natural aptitudes and working with others is the context within which you are most comfortable. You are not a natural leader but rather a facilitator and visionary, without which leaders could not achieve their aims. You are open-minded to change but need clear guidance. You reflect all earthly characteristics of balance, being receptive to change, but you may have a tendency to go up blind alleys and should always take a deep breath before acting. Quiet and unassuming, your character often achieves success in mysterious ways by rising above the ordinary in life.

No. 3
OVERCOMING EARLY OBSTACLES

 ZHUN

Your inherent potential is not easily released. The ancient Chinese recognized that the germination of seeds is always an uncertain process, yet their potential is enormous. This applies to your character and manifests itself in career and personal relationships. You will always be forced to surmount obstacles to achieve even the smallest success, and you may experience an identity crisis at some point. Within you is the capacity to excel, but it has to be worked at in order to be uncovered and realized. You are open to new ideas, but you must develop a caution in your actions in order not to be blocked in your endeavours. You may need others in your life to point out the obstacles before you grasp where they are. Only then can you achieve your full potential.

No. 4
WINDING PATH TO SUCCESS

 MENG

Struggling to find meaning early in life is a feature of your character. Experience, sometimes painful, plays a pivotal role in your development. As a process of discovery, the journey of life rarely runs smooth, but in your case it is a necessary part of your character's development. You get there in the end, but the path is often rocky and uncertain. You were not born hard-wired with common sense; your capacity for experimentation and observation allows you to unravel the mysteries of life and learn by your mistakes but you will need a trustful teacher. You do, however, regularly enjoy beginner's luck. You are destined to live an interesting life with many twists and turns.

No. 5
WATCHING AND WAITING

 XU

You are frequently at the centre of the eternal flux of change. An inner strength and purpose is held in check by your unexplained caution; you often feel that you can't quite get there in life. You are not as in control of events as you would like to be, and are destined to spend what seems an inordinate amount of time struggling to comprehend what's happening around you. The ancient Chinese likened your character to being imprisoned before escaping to restore order and improve people's lives. Only act after careful consideration; your character does not lend itself to taking huge risks or rushing things. Like observing clouds rushing across the sky, your character knows what is coming but is destined to have to wait until the time is right. When change does come, it produces an interesting career and fulfilment in relationships.

No. 6
STRENGTH THROUGH CONFLICT

 SONG

Your character does not take too kindly to criticism. You are blessed with drive and forcefulness but not a reconciling nature. You tend to laugh in the face of adversity and get on with things. This results from an innermost conviction that your chosen path is correct. You are, however, capable of recognizing what's coming and avoiding the conflict it may bring – but not always. This could lead to disillusionment on occasion, as your experience teaches you difficult lessons. Your greatest challenge in life will be to yield to others and learn to enlist their help, and to keep your nerve under pressure. It is only by containing your natural instincts that you can thrive in harmony. Sometimes it may seem as though nothing is going right, but things usually fall into place in their own time.

No. 7
WINNING OVER OTHERS

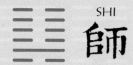

SHI 師

You possess an inherent ability to reconcile the needs of different people and a capacity to tune into a given situation and see what is required. It has long been understood that large masses of people, through collective force, can achieve great things, but not everyone perceives this. The original Chinese oracles described your character as possessing the power of an army – but you need to be in good fettle to win. You can be a catalyst for change and are unafraid of facing competition. Uniting different people and viewpoints requires a particular skill and you have it in abundance. Strategy and tactics are your forte. Your independence and self-motivation allows you to tap the reservoirs of strength in others. You know when to pick the time to act and this usually leads to success.

No. 8
CO-OPERATION

BI 比

You are inherently a social person and cannot function without others. If you become isolated, you can become disillusioned and drift aimlessly. You possess an innate reconciliatory nature and see yourself in context as part of a whole. You will intervene to help others if the need arises, but you can have a tendency to hesitate and this usually backfires. You always retain a sense of responsibility and, if you are given the opportunity, can accomplish great things. If you do not achieve elevated status, you could become renowned for being late and lagging behind. You are not good at muddling through: you like to be organized and bring like-minded people with you in a common purpose. If a team of people need someone to bind them together towards a shared objective, then you're the one to do it.

No. 9
PROCEEDING WITH CAUTION

 XIAOCHU

Your character possesses a smouldering, undiscovered potential which is expressed through small and seemingly insignificant achievements. You possess an inbuilt restraining impulse which disguises your hidden, untapped potential. You tend to exercise restraint when expressing your opinions and beliefs, and grand schemes will often come to nothing. This is because you are inclined to be over-cautious at times. Make the best of the qualities which show your good side and use this to persuade others of your merits. Patience is your greatest virtue and artistic and creative endeavours the most likely career choices. Steady improvement is your natural attribute rather than roaring success. Good things come to you in small doses.

No. 10
DOING THE RIGHT THING

 LU

Retaining a sense of dignity and composure is a must for your character in order for you to develop as a person. Occasionally you can be opinionated and sometimes indiscriminate with your viewpoint. This can often produce the wrong choices in career, friendships and close personal relationships, and this eccentricity can result in turmoil from which it takes time for you to recover. Only a developed sense of perspective, which comes with experience, will enable you to detect the warning signals that will bring order and equilibrium into your life. Your capacity for detailed analysis and peculiar sensitivity to others' needs will lead your career choices. Through self-analysis, moderating your conduct and caring for others, you will find focus on what's important, and this will enable you to avoid the stress of unwanted responsibility.

No. 11
MUTUAL UNDERSTANDING

TAI

Your character possesses a harmonious and co-operative nature which encourages growth and development in everyone it touches. Interaction with others is especially fruitful, and your character is designed to prepare the ground for others to achieve their ambitions. Wise decisions come easily to you, and you are equipped to work in service organizations which facilitate the nurturing and growth of great potential in those around you. The ancient Chinese believed your character reflected springtime, when the seeds of life are sown, giving the potential for remarkable outcomes. You will achieve positions of great responsibility, since giving, listening and talking are your innate skills. Peacemaking and successful innovation are most likely, as your keen communication skills allow you to express dramatic insight which all around you will enjoy.

No. 12
RESOLVING ISSUES

PI

There always seems to be something stopping your character developing harmonious relationships with lasting fulfilment, and you occassionally appear uncommunicative as a result. You can find it difficult to achieve something productive, as a sense of stagnation frequently develops. Your physical strength is not always balanced by an inner contentment, yet you possess tremendous determination to succeed and will achieve a position of authority and great influence. You are an independent spirit, which results from coping with everything life has thrown at you. It's given you a rock-solid resilience but you can be over-fearful of the unexpected. To achieve fulfilment you must develop a capacity to sit back and observe, rather than follow your natural tendency to jump in, both feet first. A dark power lies at the centre of your character and a volatile outcome always appears to be just around the corner. Sometimes you need to bite your lip and restrain yourself to let things pass and resolve themselves.

No. 13
WORKING TOGETHER

TONGREN

You have a deeply ingrained sense of duty to those around you. Caring for others is paramount for your character, which is selfless and sincere. But you usually expect others to be equally generous and to possess an understanding nature, and as a result you often become disappointed with their conduct and lack of commitment and reciprocation. This can make you disapproving and resentful. A strong moral fibre runs at the core of your character and you possess a great capacity to get things done rather than sit at home and watch the world pass you by. The ancient Chinese regarded your character as capable of gathering an army to conquer all before you. You therefore revel in collective pursuits, are a great organizer and dislike lonely occupations. On certain days you can move mountains, if only others can tune into your wavelength.

No. 14
GREAT PROSPECTS

DAYOU

You have unlimited potential. The ancient Chinese described your character as 'full of heaven's grace'. Good fortune follows you around and great success comes naturally. You are under the spotlight on a regular basis, but you must keep your ego in check as the path is not always smooth. Historically, the word 'sovereignty' was attributed to your character as possessing kingly or queen-like characteristics. You like things to be in their proper place and, when acting unselfishly and with kindness, your personal and professional relationships blossom. Only when things get out of proportion, and self-control is lost, will you experience misfortune and humiliation. Otherwise, great wealth is often in prospect for you – either in monetary form or in terms of a tremendously fulfilling personal life and career.

No. 15
SELF-RESTRAINT

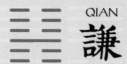

QIAN

A sense of moderation and deference is the key to your character achieving fulfilment and balance in your life. Carrying your principles over into matters of career and public duties is fundamental to your success. If you keep your personal sense of perspective and measure your words and conduct carefully, you can become very successful indeed. But if you lose this capacity for self-restraint, then the consequences could be very unfortunate and downright embarrassing. People everywhere respect those who are modest and contain their pride. Admiration for what you do achieve and how you've achieved it is built upon such self-effacing modesty. You strive hard – and sometimes in vain – to contain these aspects of your character because you are often placed under public scrutiny. If you can contain a natural tendency to boastfulness, then great things can be achieved.

No. 16
READY FOR ACTION

YU

Like a river finding the course of least resistance to its destination, your character finds harmony and balance more easily than others. This capacity to reconcile others and bring clear messages out in the open to all who will listen is your single greatest skill. You possess an inbuilt enthusiasm and are a natural decision-maker, completely free from hesitation and uncertainty. Simply put, you're always ready for action. In ancient times your character was compared to an elephant, prominent in China 3,500 years ago, representing power and the capacity to move mountains. The Chinese also likened it to music: it can adapt and change and go with the flow. You have the chance to influence great numbers of people around you and bring them to a common purpose. Only personal neglect can bring you failure, as your focus on achieving things at all costs can have unforeseen personal consequences.

No. 17
FOLLOWING THE RIGHT COURSE

SUI 隨

Like all life forms, which adapt to the changing seasons, your character knows inherently when to act, when to rest, when to talk and how to lie silent in the face of dramatic changes. Your power lies in your perceptiveness. You have an inbuilt intuition which is triggered by others' problems. You know when to pursue a matter and when to just leave it alone. You are a natural counsellor and may find a career related to giving advice and supporting others. This is because you know how to navigate through life's intricacies to find solutions. Fortunately, you are free from prejudice and don't waste time in fruitless struggles against the odds. You are one of nature's great survivors and provide constant reassurance and comfort to those who need you the most.

No. 18
VALUABLE INSIGHT

GU 蠱

Your character naturally detects the weak point in everything. This is not because you are always negative, but because you have a careful eye for detail which exposes flaws quickly to you. You are a great analyst and a very hard worker who cannot resist putting things right; indeed, yoahowever, then you can make spectacular mistakes with dramatic consequences, so don't let yourself be rushed. You prefer reflection and a period of introspection before taking action. You will resist corruption and repair damage; you're a great sidekick in risky ventures and will stir things up if necessary to achieve a desired outcome. Someone like you leads a challenging life, and you may even have been born into adversity, being forced to cope with tricky responsibilities at a young age. This prepares you well for things to come later in life.

No. 19
TRANSFORMING POWER

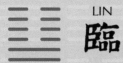 LIN

The ancient Chinese defined your character as symbolizing the end of winter and the beginning of new life; dramatic change was imminent. Your character represents renewal, and you will be rewarded for initiating and embracing change. You are adaptable and you need to be, as life will be subjected to many twists and turns. You learn how to handle closure and start all over again. You don't harbour regrets or grudges because you come to understand that this can cloud your judgement. You are blessed with charisma and a persuasive nature and use these attributes in teaching others to bring a calm authority to difficult situations. You're better at understanding complex issues than anyone else and recognize when to time important decisions. This brings you wide recognition and sometimes adulation.

No. 20
CONTEMPLATION

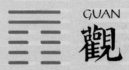 GUAN

Your character reflects the regularity of nature. The seasons and solar system have built-in mechanisms which vary within themselves but never in relation to each other. You embody the same steadfastness and steely determination. You possess the gift of miraculous insight and this can be used to exert power and influence over others. You have the capacity to distance yourself from difficult situations and reflect on their causes and consequences. This is a rare skill and reveals an unruffled nature. The ancient Chinese interpreted your character as someone who washes their hands and takes their time before making a sacrifice, thinking of the significance of what's to come next. Your character is active, judicious, courageous and ambitious, and people like you are usually found in professional careers requiring excellent judgement, often becoming politicians. Profound judgement is your single most important skill.

No. 21
CLEAR VISION

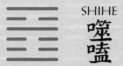

SHIHE

噬嗑

The need for reform, justice and transformation is deeply embedded in your character. Eliminating obstacles is the key to your purpose. Misunderstandings and confusion can abound in your life unless you develop a clear and penetrating focus. Radical changes occur regularly throughout your life, since no compromise is allowed and you simply don't have the patience to wait for things to sort themselves out. A dramatic coming-together of elemental forces produces thunder and lightning; such cataclysms are not infrequently experienced by you. Confronting problems and dealing with them is your greatest attribute; framing laws and judicial careers are to the foremost. You're a great troubleshooter and unafraid to bite the bullet.

No. 22
FACILITATOR

BI

賁

An inherent grace and beauty are the principal features of your character. Grace can be described as a state of balance and tranquillity where all things find harmony. The ancient Chinese odes related your character to the happy occasion of a wedding celebration. You enjoy unusual insight, but can sometimes lack an eye for detail and mistake obvious signals because you tend to focus on the big picture. Nevertheless, you possess an inner capacity to shed light on situations, crystallizing difficult issues and opening doors for others to become creative. Material and physical success often follows your character. Advertising, marketing and public relations are characteristic careers, with a tendency towards ostentation. After experiencing occasional disillusionment, you usually achieve an inner tranquillity.

No. 23
RELYING ON OTHERS

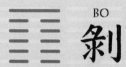

BO

You need to go through dramatic reconstruction to become fulfilled. There's simply no other way. The original Chinese interpretation refers to the flaying of a yew, implying an experience of the full cycle of life; of complete destruction and rebirth as peculiar to your character. You will need the support and co-operation of others to get through. You will be criticized. You're rarely in control of events and must dodge and weave in order to cope with what life throws at you. This makes you astute and quick-witted. You may occasionally be confronted with disappointment and sometimes poor health, and develop an ability to sit tight and do nothing when the occasion arises, as you observe dramatic events unfolding around you, stripping issues to the core. This makes you a solid, reliable friend and colleague as a result.

No. 24
STRENGTH BY RENEWAL

FU

You will need to start over again many times during your life. The ancient Chinese omens likened your character to returning successfully from battle. A recurring pattern of activity in the events in your life becomes recognizable, and eventually leads you to fulfilment. You could become neurotic due to repeated disappointment, as if fate has dealt you a difficult hand. But your luck changes regularly after these setbacks, and returns to transform and improve your prospects time and again. This applies both to recovering health and mending relationships. Care is, however, always required, as new opportunities need to be nurtured in order to become fruitful, and the important role of others close to you needs to be recognized and respected. You are a great innovator and become entrepreneurial as you take advantage of your inbuilt resistance.

No. 25
EYES WIDE OPEN

WUWANG
无妄

There's innocence in your character which can lead to naivety in decision-making. The ancient Chinese scripts likened your character to being startled by the unexpected. However, you are spontaneous and ready to take new paths and seek challenges. This makes you exciting and interesting to others, because they don't know what you will do next. Often unexpected events transform your life and this forces you to develop a refreshing open-minded attitude. You believe in natural authority, a strong society and loving families and wish to preserve these at all costs. You have an inner conviction which makes you a good communicator. This is your single greatest career influence.

No. 26
EXPLOSIVE ENERGY

DACHU
大畜

A great store of potential energy is trapped in your character. Timing is the key to success. As with hexagram 14, yours is one of the very few characters to be described in the ancient Chinese odes as blessed by heaven and full of grace. You quickly develop a great wealth of information and insight. The original Chinese also talked of 'hidden treasures' and 'the taming power of the great'. You have enormous potential and are the kind of person friends want beside them when the going gets tough. You're naturally courageous and wise and possess solid judgement. Morality is important to you, and you take solace from looking back in time to learn from others' mistakes. Artistic endeavours often come to the fore in your chosen career.

No. 27
SUPPORTING OTHERS

 YE
頤

All of life is sustained by a self-perpetuating interdependent system. Your character acts as a critical link in this system and provides nourishment for others to flourish and grow. You normally prefer to play supportive roles rather than leading the way or taking risks; you are persistent but will occasionally be out of your depth, with your limitations exposed. The ancient Chinese oracles described your character as a set of teeth exposing someone's health or illness. You frequently require clarity before taking action and don't enjoy confusion or disorder. You therefore excel at diagnosis and can display extraordinary vision on occasion. You need to be very selective in whom to trust and can become disappointed if friends and colleagues won't listen to your advice. But you are a catalyst for clarity of vision and this generally produces career success.

No. 28
CRITICAL MASS

 DAGUO
大過

Your character is blessed with an intense determination to succeed. You will frequently find yourself at the centre of extraordinary events and play an important part in a complex chain reaction. In times of crisis you tend to withdraw and collect your thoughts, acting only when all things have been fully considered. The ancient Chinese odes compared your character to the growth of a tree to give support to a structure – but if it grows too far, the whole structure could collapse. Your steely determination enables you to identify when critical mass is achieved in order to increase the chances of success in career matters, but your decisions could backfire if this pent-up energy is allowed to flourish in the wrong direction, leading to over-indulgence and extreme behaviour.

No. 29
TRICKY SITUATIONS

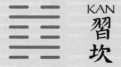

KAN

習
坎

Your character is constantly put to the test and, like flowing water, always finds a way around things. Confronting the abyss before you is your strength. You tend to be immovable and can sometimes be difficult; the closer you are to someone, the more difficult you may become. You meet the challenges of life head-on – and there will be many in store for you. Time and again you overcome danger only to be confronted with it once more. This tendency is turned into a virtue, and you develop a principled, unflinching attitude which helps guide you through tricky times, providing you don't allow the challenges to make you become stubborn and awkward. You're a great comfort to those who do not possess your capacity to withstand pressure.

No. 30
POWERFUL LIGHT

LI

離

Your character has the capacity to exert an extraordinary influence over the lives of others. You create a synergy between partners or participants and are a great team leader. You can transform the world like a bright light and bring clarity of purpose in what you do. This intensity renders you an expert in very specialized areas, but you could become narrow-minded if left to become isolated. Your character tends towards extremism, but can be gifted in your chosen pursuits. You can also be revolutionary, and are often to be found at the forefront of great changes. The ancient Chinese texts likened your character to a bright yellow bird, signalling radical times and sometimes a harbinger of cataclysmic events. When your tendency to go overboard is contained, you can act as a tremendous force for good. But if the light shines in the wrong direction, watch out!

No. 31
MAGNETIC ATTRACTION

XIAN

From the atom to the solar system and personal relationships, the attraction of opposites is one of the essential building blocks in nature. Your character possesses this in abundance. Embracing this virtue can bring you true contentment and a balance in everything you do, from career prospects to loving partnerships. The ancient Chinese odes refer to your disposition as 'If you fidget and can't keep still, then a friend is following your thoughts.' It is, therefore, crucial that you provide others with the opportunity to display their own feelings for a mutual attraction to reveal itself. A spontaneous mutual influence is what causes upheaval and change in everything; you act like a catalyst for change in other people's lives, particularly those with dynamic energy. In social and political matters you're the type of person who, if you maintain your integrity, is capable of becoming a great leader.

No. 32
PERSEVERANCE

HENG

The secret of eternity is said to be reflected in nature's cycle of birth and rebirth. Your character has this feature of consistency and endurance. The ancient Chinese oracles regarded your character as possessing the virtue of constancy or fixing things permanently. This is why you never give up and refuse to be deflected or distracted from a true or ethical course. Enduring values are important to you; you know inherently what's right and wrong and have an inbuilt and unshakable morality. You prove time and again to be a steadfast friend. Sometimes you may become disorientated by life's trials and tribulations and this can lead to confusion. You can occasionally be deflected along completely the wrong path. However, your natural durability and perseverance enables you to come through whatever life has to throw at you, but it requires faith in those proven principles and a tireless determination.

No. 33

STEPPING BACK

DUN 遯

Your character usually retreats to analyse any situation – you never rush head first into confronting life's issues. In nature, there is a time when plant life and the seasons close down for a period in order to replenish themselves and be reborn with full vigour. This is the wonder of nature, and the closure process is fundamental to it. This is the role played by your character in other people's lives. You're equipped to deal with recurring difficulties and hostilities in a benign way, but you must at all costs avoid being dragged into situations fraught with outright conflict and into making quick decisions. That's just not your style. You avoid discord like the plague and will do almost anything for an easy life. Ultimately, you are a realist and bring wisdom and considered decision-making as your permanent strength.

No. 34

POWER AND INFLUENCE

DAZHUANG 大壯

The ancient Chinese interpretation of your character is 'The little man uses his strength, the prince uses his wits.' With great power comes the true test of your character. You possess the power to influence everyone who comes into contact with you. This may bring great enlightenment and progress or, if unrestrained, total chaos. You could become a superstar in a particular field and exert magnetic attraction over others. But power is a means and not an end in itself. Power unrestrained by wisdom and caution can lead to disaster – and stubbornness could follow if your character is left to operate freely and without question. You naturally attract adulation and unconditional love from an army of admirers. Though this appears a wonderfully fortunate trait, it brings with it immense responsibility, as others may see you as intimidating.

No. 35
RAPID PROGRESS

 CHIN

Your character doesn't like to hang around and is always advancing. You are inventive and your ideas are generally taken on board by others. Your communication skills are strong; you're capable of binding people together in a common purpose and are usually found at the front barking instructions rather than following others meekly. Your character is often likened to a shining light emitting wisdom and confidence but sometimes provoking jealousy. You tend to be richly rewarded for your efforts and capture the wind of change with ease. You tend to be lucky when taking risks, such as starting new ventures. If you succumb to temptation or mix with the wrong sort of people, then all you've achieved can collapse. Maintaining a clarity of purpose and retaining a moral perspective is vitally important.

No. 36
POWER THROUGH CAUTION

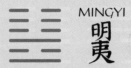 MINGYI

You will find your convictions being tested time and again. The original Chinese readings described your character as 'the darkening of the light', which means that you tend to conceal your true feelings and take a back seat when all around you is challenging and confrontational. You use your intelligence to best advantage by hiding it from view. If you're forced into revealing your true intentions, then you can be exposed to dangerous risks. You achieve power and gather momentum by preserving your inner strengths. When things go wrong you're the best person to go to for help. You allow things to take their course: problems wash over you until issues come to a head and the fog of confusion lifts. Then, and only then, do you act decisively – and you usually succeed. Yours is a strong character full of moral conviction.

No. 37

FAMILY RELATIONSHIPS

JIAREN

家人

You are a strong believer in cementing rela-tionships, especially in family matters but also in wider society. Everyone must adhere to their proper roles and functions. A sense of order and custom pervades everything you do. Responsibility is hard-wired into your psyche and you take no notice of opposing views. You could spend a great proportion of your life ensuring others comply with their given roles, and maintaining your sense of order. Leadership skills are paramount and virtues of faithfulness, loyalty and obedi-ence are your strong traits. You often raise family issues above all others and like to see a settled position all the time. By avoiding disorder at all costs, however, you can create conflict. Your character is often forced to adopt many roles and to sacrifice itself for the good of others, but will not be walked over. When you are careful with your words, and choose them selectively, you will become a pillar of society.

No. 38

CONTRADICTIONS

KUI

睽

Just as fire and water don't mix, so your character frequently displays contradictory behaviour which reflects an inner duality. The ancient Chinese scripts describe you as react-ing to many chance meetings. You therefore adapt to any situation. By your nature you are helpful but tend to over-enjoy the limelight. Artists often possess this characteristic, and you will regularly challenge others' conven-tional views. You need to pace yourself and achieve small victories to make progress in your chosen career and close relationships, since others will require real evidence of commitment before cementing a long-term relationship with you. Misunderstandings frequently arise within the family unit and you can sometimes act as a dampener on the enthusiasm of others. Taking small steps and focusing on resisting the tendency to be contradictory will lead to contentment.

No. 39
WITHOUT FEAR

 JIAN

Your character will face many obstacles to progress in life but can overcome them all. The ancient Chinese scripts describe your character as 'stumbling', which is still regarded as a good omen today. You gather strength and get your act together slowly, often seeking the support of friends in the process. They always help you. You know your limitations and often find cunning ways around problems rather than confronting them head-on. You are a team player and frequently find yourself at the forefront of decision-making to judge others and frame rules. You also enjoy heights, as this gives you the perspective you desire. You rarely act in haste, but prepare the ground carefully before taking action. You are solid as a rock when confronted by adversity. If left unfocused, you could have a tendency to go over the edge and fall into the abyss; this is where friendships are needed, to refocus your attention on self-discovery.

No. 40
BECOMING FREE

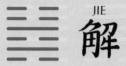 JIE

Just as a thunderstorm releases tensions in the climate, so you frequently face anxiousness and conflict when taking positive action for good. You deal with life's struggles by confronting them head-on and resolving them fully before moving on. The ancient Chinese texts referred to your character as follows: 'Relax your thumb on the bow-spring, a friend not an enemy is coming.' This liberates you from tension and gives you the balance and harmony you strive for. You're a brave person who knows when to forgive others their weaknesses and then act decisively. This is how you achieve fulfilment, and this happens time and time again in matters of family, career and health. You work best in issues of public interest, as both your decisiveness and forgiving nature give you the qualities required to cope in positions of leadership. You can occasionally go about things too laboriously and be overly fastidious, and your friends and family will recognize this – but it's not always obvious to you.

No. 41
STRONG OPINIONS

SUN

You hold strong opinions and need to restrain your natural inclinations. You could become fixed in your ways or display a certain stubbornness. This is not always the fault it appears to be, as you know when not to throw in the towel and usually get your own way, helping others to stay the course too. You need to keep your life simple, as complex arrangements only serve to obscure your true capabilities. When your life becomes over-complicated, or you're buried under pressure, you become angry and irrtable. You need to compose yourself to achieve the best outcomes, and taking your time is your preferred choice when dealing with sudden challenges. Financial loss is not uncommon to you and you may have a tendency to live in the past, occasionally needing a strong wake-up call to refresh your attitude and bring you back on track. But you usually get it right in the end, though the path is rarely smooth.

No. 42
ENRICHMENT

YI

Your character is strong enough to cross continents and achieve success. You are blessed with boundless energy employed in pursuit of your goals and frequently enrich the lives of those around you. In positions of leadership you know how to bestow benefits upon those who rely on you for motivation; this often requires some kind of personal sacrifice. You prefer the carrot to the stick. This enhances your social standing and you're often invited to occupy positions of social prominence. Clearing the air and nourishing others is the role of thunder and rain in nature, and your character possesses this feature in abundance – to the benefit of both career and community. You are a great mixer at social gatherings and are wise and energetic. You achieve impressive status early on in your life, but need to work hard to retain a position of trust and leadership.

No. 43

GETTING YOUR ACT TOGETHER

JUE

Resolving issues is your character's greatest need. The ancient Chinese texts likened your character to an emperor sacrificing prisoners and being attacked while distracted. You don't like loose ends and let other people know it. This requires tact and diplomacy, as confrontation is not your best route to achieving balance in your life. Calmness, a cheerful outlook and a confident authority are features of your personality. You can, however, be ruthlessly uncompromising and determinedly resolute in standing your ground for what you believe is right. This makes you a great communicator with children. You believe in self-improvement, but should never be deflected by a major setback – it's just part of the deal. It's the small steps forward which lead to your eventual success. You're destined to work hard for what you get. Nothing comes easy.

No. 44

MEETING CHALLENGES

GOU

The ancient Chinese oracles depicted your character as two goats locking horns. You develop to your full potential through a series of clashes or accidental meetings. Sometimes you find it difficult to resist temptation and this can lead you down the wrong track. On the other hand, you are able to retain a capacity to stand firm and wait, take a deep breath and observe events; then you can exercise your natural ability to use any situation to your best advantage. Investigating matters in great detail is fundamental to making progress in personal and career decisions. Allowing minor issues to distract you can be a weakness and counterproductive. You must learn to control any tendency to try to enjoy too many simultaneous relationships or occupations at the expense of achieving true fulfilment.

No. 45
GATHERING AND LEADING

 CUI

Your character acts like a catalyst in gathering and assembling people to create dramatic outcomes. Originally described in Chinese antiquity as a favourable character associated with great men, this was intended to imply great leadership skills. You display the capacity to tune into others' belief systems and find elements to attract them to a common purpose. Eliminating problems and confronting disruption is your most significant feature, and removing impediments to progress is your greatest claim. You should resist over-celebrating, but if you do make mistakes you are readily forgiven, for others are usually sympathetic to your ambitions and admire your focus and energy. You are rarely discouraged and an ideal sidekick in tricky family or business situations.

No. 46
FIRM PROGRESS

 SHENG

You were born with unrestrained ambition. People like you have often experienced humble circumstances and this triggers an intense determination to succeed. The ancient Chinese oracles described your character as travelling upwards from a firm base. Power and influence fall naturally in your path and you quickly identify and use the levers of influence to make an impression and get your way. If you retain a sense of humility and modesty, then success is guaranteed. If you don't, then being deflected into the wrong direction is entirely possible. You're not intimidated by authority, and both assertiveness and confidence come naturally. But you always need to build credibility with others to ensure your success is not short-lived.

No. 47
CONSERVING ENERGY

 KUN

You are blessed with bountiful energy and are ambitious, always striving for improvement. This brings you occasionally to the brink of disaster, which renders you weary and can sap all your energy. The analogy used by the ancient sages was one of wood striving to grow from the earth but meeting obstruction at every turn. This was described in the ancient Chinese texts as hampered and thwarted, and sometimes 'befuddled by drink'. But your character develops an intense strength as a result of some difficult experiences. Steadfastness and perseverance, plus knowing when to stop, become your strengths. Choosing your time to act can ensure success in everything you do, providing you know when to step back and resist being overcome by life's pressures. Frequent changes of career and location may result.

No. 48
INNER DEPTHS

 JING

In ancient Chinese, 'Jing' referred to a well. This is where people replenished their energy and lifted their spirits – and this is what you are capable of. The ancient Chinese oracles noted that the well is the font of all nourishment but requires constant tending. Helping others to renew their determination and lifting the spirits of those around you is your key strength. Selling yourself and teaching others are your natural occupations. The well is an inexhaustible supplier of refreshing water and also a meeting place for discussion. You act like a catalyst for change and enable those close to you in family or business to achieve their ideals. But you must remain focused. Just as the water in a neglected well can become stagnant and poisonous, your actions could have similar consequences if you don't maintain your stance of fairness and objectivity.

No. 49

TRANSFORMATION

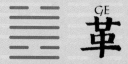

GE

Revolutionizing and abolishing old-fashioned ideas is fundamental to your character. Confucius commented that 'The time and meaning of abolishing the old is truly great!' and this applies to you. Conflict is a feature of your life, as it's always necessary to confront tradition when initiating radical changes. But your character is never subdued by adversity and confrontation. You rarely have regrets, even when you get your timing wrong, which is not uncommon. Ancient Chinese texts refer to stripping tigers and leopards of their fur – then they have the same appearance as goats and dogs. You question everything, but without disposing of the old and adopting transforming ideas progress in your personal and business life could not take place. However, there will be risks along the way, and timing is always the key to getting things right.

No. 50

NOURISHING LIGHT

DING

Your character reflects the ancient Chinese use of the sacrificial vessel (a tripod), which was usually made of strong material such as clay or bronze and highly decorated. You possess a unique capacity to provide sustenance and nourishment to those around you. This creates strong family ties, and you are often called upon to display strong leadership and – because of your unshakable integrity – to intercede in disputes. Nine highly decorated bronze vessels (now lost), representing each Chinese state, were used as the permanent source of authority for thousands of years, and there is an inner divine spiritual authority which also drives you. This enables you to provide mental strength to others, and you will often be called upon to provide vision and purpose in reorganizing others' lives.

No. 51
SHOCK AND AWE

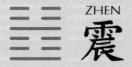 ZHEN
震

Traditionally your character has been associated with the sound of thunder, when nature is aroused and dramatic action is under way; when anything can happen. The ancient Chinese sages used thunder as a metaphor for fertility. Taking action is your birthright, and blinding activity and dramatic outcomes are in store for you. You are associated with an awakening in everything around you and the initiation of a new era. You are always at the front, taking charge of major projects and a wide range of events. But your capacity for shock and awe needs careful control. As an agent for change you are beyond compare, but you can upset people. Remaining calm and restraining your comments are your greatest challenges. If you maintain such personal control, success is bound to be yours.

No. 52
STILLNESS

 GEN
艮

Your character is traditionally associated with a mountain. It sits, brooding and still, unmoved by everything that happens. Restfulness and an unbounded capacity for calm reflection are your principal virtues. Many people need to practise techniques such as yoga or meditation to achieve the stillness and capacity for self-analysis which comes naturally to you. You also possess the ability to cut right to the bone; taking stock, meticulous planning and getting through the skin to the core of all issues are natural aptitudes. You don't enjoy clutter and can be irritated by confusion, but you are selfless and charitable. Sometimes this is regarded as an old-fashioned virtue, but it reflects your capacity to get in touch with your spirituality by sweeping away what's not necessary to achieve balance in your life.

No. 53
TAKING YOUR TIME

 JIAN 漸

In ancient times your character was likened to a river whose source lay in the mountains of central China. It gathered pace and grew in stature to become a vast wall of water which flowed east to the ocean. This metaphor reflects your given character traits. You possess patience and make inexorable progress in all you do. Everything you achieve is long-lasting but is accomplished by a gradual, step-by-step attitude. You will not be hurried and do not believe in the quick fix, because it has no depth and is bound to be temporary. The ancient Chinese odes referred to you taking action 'only when the wild geese take flight', which is a good omen for making positive progress. You are prepared to work tirelessly. Your character is also sometimes likened to a swan, steadfast and tactful, but sometimes quick to anger. Self-reliance and education are paramount to you.

No. 54
LOYALTY

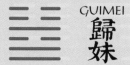 GUIMEI 歸妹

A capacity for harmony and a steady hand are your principal attributes. This requires an understanding of personal relationships and the intricate mechanics of how they work. In ancient Chinese literature a marriage partnership was used as an analogy to describe the relationship between a king and his first minister. You will become the prime mover in a long-term partnership. You achieve your ambitions through the exercise of patience and judgement, often prepared to take a back seat to collect your thoughts and develop your strategy. You will be tested. Thrusting yourself into the limelight seldom works and can have unfortunate consequences, especially in career matters. You should never rush to judge, as your first impressions can be wrong. You can sometimes feel restricted and sometimes ignored, but that's because your enthusiasm could get the better of you. Don't let it.

No. 55
SUCCESS WITH CAUTION

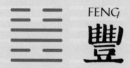 FENG

Your character enjoys a fantastic combination of the power to both nurture and grow, which can lead to an overflowing of success. You reflect the zenith of the full moon, the equinox and the pinnacle of self-esteem. The outcome is not always good, however, and if left uncontrolled can lead you astray. Your mood can change like the waxing and waning of the moon and there always seems to be a barrier to your carefree enjoyment. You need to retain a bright and positive outlook, and this will sustain and enlighten anyone who comes into contact with you. You tend to be active and energetic and need always to share the benefits of your success. You usually act swiftly to take advantage of great opportunities, as they can have a tendency to evaporate quickly.

No. 56
TRAVELLING

 LU

Your opinions carry weight and influence. They benefit from the wisdom of a traveller who has seen it all and can act patiently under pressure. Travelling strangers were common in ancient China, as so many people were displaced by seemingly constant warfare. Just like a travelling stranger, you need to be selective regarding your chosen companions. Your character can be moulded by many experiences, but rooted in none of them. Once established, the strands of love and friendship in your life are rarely broken. Both diversity and stability are embedded in your character; these are your most endearing traits. You are loyal to the end. Exploring new worlds and ideas is what keeps you entertained. But you must beware of becoming too wilful and boastful when confronted with others less blessed than yourself. Your ability to sit and meditate for long periods helps you make the correct decisions.

No. 57

GENTLE PERSUASION

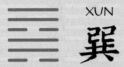

XUN

You make progress at your own pace and will under no circumstances be dictated to by others. Your character's equivalent in nature is the wind – the primary driver of change, sculpting mountains and shaping trees. But it moves at its own pace. The ancient Chinese texts referred to your character as bowing down reverently with calm fortitude while observing events unfolding. You are generally successful in all you attempt, and attain startling results in a quiet way. A firm and clear purpose is what you want; indecisiveness and muddle-headed thinking are given short shrift. You gain the trust of others by being humble and adaptable. But no one should confuse your humility and gentleness with weakness. You bring harmony because you understand the importance of equilibrium and balance in all things and use this deep-seated knowledge to achieve success.

No. 58

INNER CONTENTEDNESS

DUI

Happiness and joyfulness through interaction with others are your principal assets. You are unshakably truthful but very firm in your views. Harmony with others is developed through open dialogue, but caution should be exercised so that your steadfast intentions do not translate into high-handedness and being dismissive of others' opinions. Otherwise, the periods of joy can become short-term and superficial. You tend to be solid as a rock inside with a soft exterior, and provide boundless encouragement to others. This equips you to lead discussion and procure education in many different ways. People like you are talented leaders and enjoy success, with the occasional lapse into over-indulgence of worldly pleasures which brings your downfall every now and again. You recognize when to find your own level and achieve satisfaction this way.

No. 59
RECONCILING

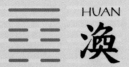 HUAN
涣

You are able to act to deflect problems by bringing a calm decisiveness to everything you do. The ancient Chinese odes likened your character to gelding a horse – beneficial but risky. Like the wind moving over water, you can bring gentle change to any situation, but you were not born a natural leader and need the benefit of training and practice. You possess a strong mental capacity and employ this faculty to reconcile others and resolve issues. Overcoming and restraining disorder is your natural habitat, like a legislator or counsellor, and you use modern devices to promote harmony and disperse conflict and discord. This skill is fundamental in uniting others and getting them to work together – it's a revolutionary trait. Your talents enable you to take the lead in social events, through music and social ceremony, but training is essential to allowing this innate strength to be realized. You are usually the person who is determined to reunite family and friends.

No. 60
AVOIDING EXTREMES

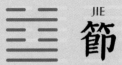 JIE
節

You inherently know your limits and stay within them, much like nature's calendar is expressed in the changing seasons within the year. Your tendency for keeping things within a prescribed area extends to people, possessions and your own activities. You are no risk-taker. Like a lake or river which needs to be managed so as not to overflow or become stagnant, your character contains and manages its excess behaviour and frowns upon such weakness in others. In your daily life you strive to strike a balance between excess and insufficiency, and you can be very valuable to others when involved in planning, forecasting and general management. You are ideally suited to local politics and benefit from an innate wisdom. But others you deal with in life need to know what to expect from you, or discord could develop. Imposing limits upon others in a clumsy way will always backfire; this is due to your inherent thriftiness, but not everyone shares your gift for moderation.

No. 61

INNER TRUTH

ZHONGFU

中孚

Your character exerts a tremendous influence over the lives of others by possessing powerful insight. In ancient texts your traits were described as trust and truthfulness. Your power stems from an inner sincerity originating from trustworthiness. This is the source of all virtue and the root of getting along with others. You are open-minded and adaptable, free from prejudice, and pride truth above all else. You may sometimes use your comprehensive understanding of situations to exert leverage over others. If you push your luck in a very public way, you could come to regret it. For this reason a quiet but firm influence is your chosen mode of operation. Developing an open dialogue with others is critical to your success, and your influence extends not only to close family and friends but overseas as well.

No. 62

HOLDING BACK

XIAOGUO

小過

You possess intense self-belief and a capacity to focus on detail. This makes you an ideal candidate for serious duties, but you need to play second fiddle to others or you could get into trouble. The ancient Chinese texts likened your character to a bird giving an omen. If it's high in the sky, it means bad news. Like this bird, you should not fly too high. You can have a tendency to stray into excess and, in overdoing things, upset others. Flamboyance on your part always leads to disaster. Personal humility should be retained, and this breeds success through a series of small, favourable and significant achievements. If you keep within your sphere of ability, you will be successful in both career and in personal relationships. But sometimes you may not be able to contain yourself.

No. 63
SAFE HARBOUR

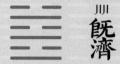

JIJI
既濟

You like to see things settled. You dislike intensely things being left undone and are prepared to engage fully and take risks if necessary to get your way. You are a great planner. Your Chinese sign is rare, in that it reveals perfect equilibrium: all the lines in your hexagram are balanced. This means you are born level-headed and sensible. But nothing lasts for ever, and your state of perfect equilibrium needs to be maintained through modesty, hard work and dedication to a cause. The ancient Chinese texts described you as 'already arrived' and therefore safe and secure. But this apparent success can leave you becalmed, as everything must change. You can be distracted, lose focus and lack drive because you may feel you've achieved enough. Avoid this at all costs, as it means success has gone to your head. Staying focused on minor matters and things that really count, like your family and friends, usually brings you to your senses.

No. 64
ALMOST THERE

WEIJI
未濟

Nothing comes easy to you. The ancient Chinese scripts likened your character to a fox crossing a river – slowly and carefully – and if its tail gets wet, then this could mean disaster. Yet you will achieve your goals in life. It's just that you will tend towards a recurring feeling of being unfulfilled. There is always a new challenge around the corner; your life rarely remains static for long. And you face these challenges in a resigned and absolute manner, half-expecting some new problem to turn up. But this is usually the dark before the dawn. You always cope, because this is your character's greatest strength. Confucius commented on your sign that you 'discriminate carefully the nature of all things and keep each of them in their proper perspective'. You use this insight on a daily basis to help keep a balanced view of the world and make sensible decisions.

I keep six honest serving men,
(They taught me all I knew),
Their names are What, Why and When,
And How, Where and Who.

RUDYARD KIPLING

CHAPTER FOUR
Your Daily Oracle Reading

Six is all you need. Now that you have created your Digital-DNA and discovered your Hon-Shō character profile, you are ready to move on to the next step: accessing your daily oracle reading.

As we learned earlier, the ancient Chinese diviners believed events unfolded not as a result of cause and effect, but as a result of a resonance which can be detected in all living organisms as they take their place in the natural order of the universe. According to some, ancient numerology (and magic) was concerned with similarity and contagion, and this caused correlation in events which can sometimes appear surprising:

Things influence one another not by mechanical cause but by a kind of induction effect.

> *Tao of Chaos: DNA and the I Ching* K. WALTER

Others have sought to express a more scientific explanation:

Within the pattern, things move and react upon one another not so much by mechanical causation (like one billiard ball guided by a cue hitting another) or by chance collision (like bumping into someone on the street) but by a kind of mysterious resonance. Things which belong to the same category give energy to each other ... it works by intuition rather than by analytical reasoning.

> *The Philosopher's Stone* PETER MARSHALL

Musical notes which correspond with each other will vibrate in harmony, and water which falls on the land will always find its way to other water, because such things are said to know their place in the universe and will always tend towards it. We accept this without question and normally think nothing further of it.

This philosophy underpins the Hon-Shō divination system. It tunes into a natural order and pattern expressed through our personal label and detects how our lives interact with chance every day. Reading the oracle daily enables us to paint a picture of our choices by allowing the shape of a moment to reveal itself to us through synchronicity.

The daily scores

As we saw in Chapter Two, the Hon-Shō system reveals our Life Numbers from our Digital-DNA. Now Hon-Shō uses this data – along with the date and your age on the day of the reading – to consult the oracle. It does this by producing a daily hexagram. Here's a brief summary of the stages involved. We will then go through it, step by step.

The Hon-Shō box records all your information on any given day. Reading downwards, it contains the day's date, month and your age, followed by each of your Life Numbers in turn. These are inserted in the first column, under the asterisk (*) – see panel **A**, opposite. Next, by performing a search within a set of random numbers (known as a Random Number box), you then count the number of times each set of digits in your Hon-Sho data appears. This gives you your daily scores, and your daily scores are then combined with your personal data to access your oracle reading.

Your daily scores are specific to you that day and are an incorruptible measure of coincidence. They direct you to a Yang or Yin hexagram reading, according to the number of odd and even numbers present in your score. Your reading is likely to be accompanied by one or more messages relating to specific lines in the hexagram. Messages are especially important, as they offer specific guidance to consider regarding a particular course of action. Consulting the oracle will enable you to consider your actions carefully, and will help shed light on the decisions you make that affect your life, either reinforcing them or giving you cause to think again. You could receive up to six messages on any day, or none at all, but most people receive between one and three. The more messages you receive, the more changes there must be taking place in your life at that particular moment in time.

The chances of anyone else receiving the same reading and messages as you on any given day is one in tens of thousands – which, according to the ancient oracle readers, is the number of different things that could possibly happen to any one person in their lifetime. So it's extremely unlikely that the person sitting opposite you on the train, for example, will receive an identical oracle reading – and this is what distinguishes Hon-Shō from a daily horoscope. The readings are specific to *you*.

Working out your daily scores

Once again, let's take Samantha Smith as our example. As we saw in Chapter Two, her Digital-DNA revealed her three Life Numbers to be 60, 77 and 69. These are now inserted in the Hon-Shō

A

Samantha's daily scores:	Hon-Shō box				Random Number box							
			*		8	2	8	3	4	2	4	4
	Today's Date	01	4		6	4	0	4	0	3	0	6
	The Month	03	13		8	2	3	3	1	9	8	0
	Your Age	40	10		7	1	9	7	0	6	3	7
	Life Number 1	60	4		9	7	6	1	9	3	4	0
	Life Number 2	77	2		6	7	3	4	9	5	3	4
	Life Number 3	69	7		8	5	1	0	6	2	1	9
					4	1	7	4	9	4	6	3

DAILY SCORES

box in the column under the asterisk, along with that day's date (1st March, expressed as 01 and 03) and her age (40) – see panel **A**, above.

To calculate her daily scores, Samantha then selects a Random Number box from the sheet included in the pocket at the back of this book, and counts the number of times each set of digits appears together in the Random Number box. The digits must touch each other vertically, horizontally or diagonally. Each Random Number box contains sixty-four random numbers, maintaining a symmetry and balance with the number of hexagrams in the Book of Changes.

Taking Samantha's first Life Number, 60, as an example, we can see that there are **four** instances where the numbers 6 and 0 are adjacent to one

another in the Random Number box. If two numbers share a partner (see upper-right corner, above), then that scores twice. So, a score of 4 is entered alongside 60 in the Hon-Shō box. Each score is calculated in the same way: for example, the month, 03, scores 13, while Samantha's second Life Number, 77, scores 2.

The scores in the Hon-Shō box are unique to Samantha *on that day*. Remember: the random numbers are generated by 'chance', and if you miss the moment – that unique combination of a specific day's Hon-Shō data together with the chance numbers in the Random Number box – then it's gone for ever. The oracle cannot be read retrospectively (though you can, of course, keep a record of your readings for future reference).

Now it's your turn. This time you will be filling in Template 2 (see pocket at the front of the book), so take a photocopy of it before you begin, if you haven't done so already.

Completing your Hon-Shō box
Start by turning to stage **1** on the template. Fill in the Hon-Shō box with your personal data, using Samantha Smith's example as a guide. Put today's date and month in the left-hand column, under the asterisk, and then fill in your age along with the three Life Numbers you calculated in Chapter Two.

Once the left column is complete, choose a Random Number box from the sheet tucked into the back pocket of the book, and do a number search to identify the scores. This bit is fun, but do take care over it, too: remember to look for the numbers next to each other in any direction – above or below, to either side, or diagonally. They must be touching each other to produce the coincidence. If you can't find adjacent digits for any of your sets of numbers, then score zero. Fill in your scores in the right-hand column in the Hon-Shō box. You have now completed the first step to retrieving your daily oracle reading.

Note: If you have a three-digit Life Number, don't worry – you can still calculate your daily scores. You simply need to find all three numbers adjacent to one another, in the correct sequence, to score. So Rosemary – our three-digit example

from Chapter Two, with a Life Number of 114 – would need to search for the three numbers 1, 1 and 4 all next to each other in order to score. Again, if no adjacent numbers are found, she scores zero.

When you use Hon-Shō to obtain your daily oracle reading, don't forget to write down your personal question for the day on a slip of paper, or in the space provided on the template. It should be serious, simple and relevant to your life. If you need guidance on framing your question, refer back to Chapter One (*see page 29*). If you wait for a day, then your scores expire as the world turns another revolution; the date changes and a new set of random numbers is produced, allowing you to access the oracle afresh. Each day is unique, and you are faced with a different set of circumstances to frame your choices.

Working out your Oracle Numbers
Once the Hon-Shō box is complete, the Hon-Shō system is ready to access your oracle reading by using your pattern of numbers to create a unique code which lasts for that day and that day only. Using an ancient Chinese system from the Book of Changes, the method recognizes which digits in the completed Hon-Shō box are odd and which are even (or zero), then allocates particular numbers to create a code. We call these the Oracle Numbers. These are then used to access your oracle reading.

Using Samantha as an example once more, let's look at how her Hon-Shō data is easily converted into her Oracle Numbers. First, the numbers in her Hon-Shō box are split into three columns: the asterisked numbers are split into two digits, while the daily scores are written into the third column (see panel **B**, below). Again, if you have a three-digit Life Number, split it into two just as you did when setting your Life Numbers out vertically in Chapter Two. So, Rosemary's Life Number of 114 is split into 11 and 4, for example. Next, each individual number is then converted into either a 2 or a 3 – 2 if it's an odd number, and 3 if it's even (or zero). These converted numbers (in the white boxes) are then added together across each horizontal line to produce the Oracle Numbers.

So now it's your turn. Go to stage **2** on the template and simply transfer the numbers from your completed Hon-Shō box to the Oracle Number grid, using Samantha's example for guidance. Then fill in the 2s and 3s according to the odd/even rule, to convert your data into your Oracle

B

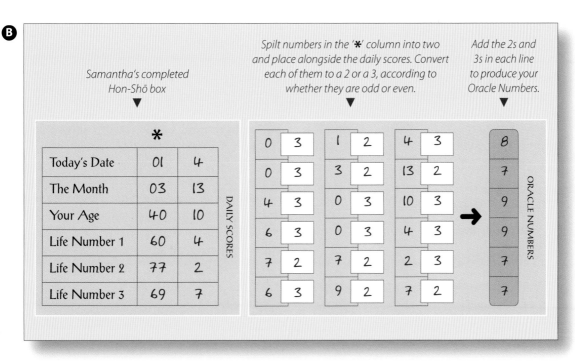

Spilt numbers in the '✳' column into two and place alongside the daily scores. Convert each of them to a 2 or a 3, according to whether they are odd or even.

Add the 2s and 3s in each line to produce your Oracle Numbers.

Samantha's completed Hon-Shō box

	✳	
Today's Date	01	4
The Month	03	13
Your Age	40	10
Life Number 1	60	4
Life Number 2	77	2
Life Number 3	69	7

DAILY SCORES

0	3	1	2	4	3	8
0	3	3	2	13	2	7
4	3	0	3	10	3	9
6	3	0	3	4	3	9
7	2	7	2	2	3	7
6	3	9	2	7	2	7

ORACLE NUMBERS

Numbers. When you've done it a few times, you'll never forget how to do it, making it quick and easy to obtain your oracle reading on a daily basis.

The final step is then to convert these Oracle Numbers into a hexagram for that day. This allows you to identify the appropriate reading and any associated messages from the oracle. So how do you go about this?

The Chinese Code

The answer lies embedded in ancient Chinese folklore, set out in The Yellow River Map (the story of which is described in Chapter Six; a copy is also displayed in the Appendix, on page 250). This map is said to link nature to the lives of all mankind. It is a counting map connecting us all to the compass and to the universe. Quite simply, it illustrates that our lives are driven by coincidence, which can be expressed at any time through a set of oracle numbers obtained by divination.

The map shows that the number 6 always produces a broken line with a message attached (▬ ▬ *), 7 gives a solid line with no message (▬▬▬▬), 8 produces a broken line with no message (▬ ▬), while 9 produces a solid line with a message attached (▬▬▬ *). These four variants – which form the Chinese Code – are the only possible outcomes (see panel **C**, below left). This enables us to identify which hexagram, with its associated messages, describes our situation each day. Whether or not the hexagram carries messages will depend on whether or not there are any 6s or 9s in your Oracle Numbers on any given day.

So far we've followed a formula which reveals our personal daily scores. These scores arose by measuring coincidence in a set of sixty-four random numbers. This is a measure of things happening around us and interacting with our character. We've used the scores to complete the Hon-Shō box, and then converted this data into six Oracle Numbers in a vertical line. Due to the method by which the Oracle Numbers are calculated (by adding a combination of 2s and/or 3s), each number *must* be either a 6, 7, 8 or 9; there can be no other numbers. The Book of Changes engineers this situation because it adheres to The Yellow River Map. This is why 6, 7, 8 and 9 are known as Oracle Numbers. They link the universal laws to our behaviour and are driven by the lunar calendar.

C

6	▬▬ ▬▬ *
7	▬▬▬▬▬
8	▬▬ ▬▬
9	▬▬▬▬▬ *

* = message

The Chinese Code
Use this code for easy reference to identify your hexagram and which reading and messages are for you on any day. The Oracle Numbers will always be 6, 7, 8 or 9.

Creating your daily hexagram

Let's continue by obtaining Samantha Smith's reading. Samantha has calculated her Oracle Numbers (shown in panel **B** on page 81), and now applies the Chinese Code to create her daily hexagram (see panel **D**, below).

To find her oracle reading for that day we simply go to the table in Chapter Five and locate her hexagram (*see page 87*), then turn to the relevant page in that chapter to discover the hexagram reading and the specific guidance relating to the messages she received. The table reveals that the hexagram is number 43, and we know she has messages in lines 3 and 4. But before she can consult her hexagram, she needs to find out whether to refer to the Yang reading or the Yin reading, for each carries a slightly different interpretation. For this, she needs to check back to her daily scores in the Hon-Shō box. If the daily scores contain more odd numbers than even (or an equal number of both), this signifies the Yang reading, while four or more even numbers indicates Yin. Samantha has four even numbers, so she turns to the Yin reading for hexagram 43 (page 173), and also reads the advice given in messages 3 and 4, which both apply to her on that day.

Note: According to Chinese practice, hexagram lines are counted from the bottom rather than from the top – so message 2, for example, would be indicated by an asterisk on the second line from the bottom, and so on. It's important to remember this to ensure you are referring to the correct messages!

Now return to the template and complete stages **3** and **4**, to discover your own daily oracle reading. A step-by step summary of the full procedure is given overleaf as a reminder, using Samantha's data as a guide. The method will soon become familiar, once you've completed your first few daily oracle readings.

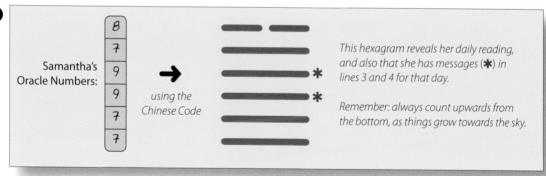

D

Samantha's Oracle Numbers:

| 8 |
| 7 |
| 9 |
| 9 |
| 7 |
| 7 |

→ *using the Chinese Code*

This hexagram reveals her daily reading, and also that she has messages (✱) in lines 3 and 4 for that day.

Remember: always count upwards from the bottom, as things grow towards the sky.

Step-by-step summary

There are six distinct steps in the complete process, which splits into two stages as follows.

In Stage 1, there are four steps:

1 Insert your personal details and the day's date into the first column of the Hon-Shō box. Select a Random Number box from the sheet included with this book and do a number search to reveal your daily scores. Write the daily scores in the second column of the Hon-Shō box. The Hon-Shō box now contains twelve distinct numbers.

2 These twelve numbers are now turned into eighteen numbers by splitting those contained in the first column into single digits (or, in the case of a three-digit number, into two separate numbers).

3 Each of the eighteen numbers is then converted to a 2 or a 3, according to whether it's odd or even/zero. Each converted line is then added together to create the six Oracle Numbers.

4 The Oracle Numbers then produce your hexagram for the day, with solid or broken lines (with or without messages) being assigned according to the Chinese Code.

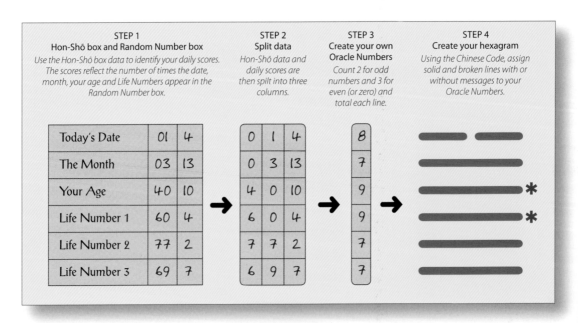

	STEP 1		STEP 2		STEP 3	STEP 4
	Hon-Shō box and Random Number box		Split data		Create your own Oracle Numbers	Create your hexagram
	Use the Hon-Shō box data to identify your daily scores. The scores reflect the number of times the date, month, your age and Life Numbers appear in the Random Number box.		*Hon-Shō data and daily scores are then spilt into three columns.*		*Count 2 for odd numbers and 3 for even (or zero) and total each line.*	*Using the Chinese Code, assign solid and broken lines with or without messages to your Oracle Numbers.*

Today's Date	01	4	0	1	4	8	
The Month	03	13	0	3	13	7	
Your Age	40	10	4	0	10	9	
Life Number 1	60	4	6	0	4	9	
Life Number 2	77	2	7	7	2	7	
Life Number 3	69	7	6	9	7	7	

Then, in Stage 2, there are two final steps:

5 Check back to your daily scores in the Hon-Shō box. If there are more odd numbers (or an equal number of odd and even), take the Yang route, and if there are more even numbers, take the Yin route.

6 Look up your hexagram in the table on page 87, and then turn to the relevant page in Chapter Five to discover your reading and any messages that are set out for you that day.

And that's it! You've got your oracle reading.

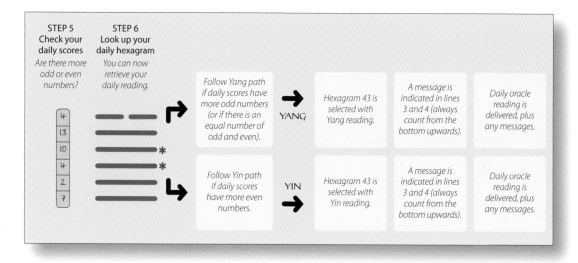

STEP 5
Check your
daily scores
*Are there more
odd or even
numbers?*

STEP 6
Look up your
daily hexagram
*You can now
retrieve your
daily reading.*

*Follow Yang path
if daily scores have
more odd numbers
(or if there is an
equal number of
odd and even).*

YANG

*Hexagram 43 is
selected with
Yang reading.*

*A message is
indicated in lines
3 and 4 (always
count from the
bottom upwards).*

*Daily oracle
reading is
delivered, plus
any messages.*

*Follow Yin path
if daily scores
have more even
numbers.*

YIN

*Hexagram 43 is
selected with
Yin reading.*

*A message is
indicated in lines
3 and 4 (always
count from the
bottom upwards).*

*Daily oracle
reading is
delivered, plus
any messages.*

But the major problem is the origin of the genetic code and it's translation mechanism. Indeed, instead of a problem it ought rather to be called a riddle.

JACQUES MONOD

CHAPTER FIVE
Daily Readings and Messages

Having folllowed the instructions in Chapter Four to calculate your daily Oracle Numbers and find the resulting hexagram, you can now locate your daily reading from the table opposite. In Samantha's case, it's number 43. Now check your daily scores in the Hon-Shō box to determine whether to follow the Yang or Yin route. Simply turn to the relevant page in this chapter to discover your daily oracle reading and any messages the oracle has for you that day (don't forget to count the lines from the bottom upwards for your messages).

UPPER TRIGRAM

	☰	☳	☵	☶	☷	☴	☲	☱
☰	1	34	5	26	11	9	14	43
☱	25	51	3	27	24	42	21	17
☶	6	40	29	4	7	59	64	47
☳	33	62	39	52	15	53	56	31
☷	12	16	8	23	2	20	35	45
☴	44	32	48	18	46	57	50	28
☲	13	55	63	22	36	37	30	49
☵	10	54	60	41	19	61	38	58

LOWER TRIGRAM

No. 1

YANG • CREATIVE ENERGY

QIAN

乾

Nothing can get in your way if you persevere. The time is exceptional for inspiration and energy, as your creative capacity is at its peak. But you must be true to yourself; don't be distracted by fame or material things. Work with those close to you and your personal ambitions will be reached – don't just rely on your own formidable inner strength. Cast off your old baggage and don't squander this opportunity. Be ready to make decisions without hesitation. Colleagues and close friends will find happiness with your help, and you'll become the centre of attention in personal relationships.

Messages

1 Your creativity and use of knowledge cannot be realized yet. Things are happening in the background over which you can have no control. Be patient and the situation will improve.

2 You need an outlet to achieve your goal and become noticed. Consult those close to you and you will benefit immediately. Someone new on the scene could provide inspiration.

3 Soon you will be motivated. Take a chance when you can and you'll be amazed at the outcome. Be cautious and avoid making mistakes, but don't let others deflect your energy from achieving your goals.

4 Go with the flow and don't make commitments, otherwise you may become the centre of attention and you won't enjoy it. You're facing a dilemma, but don't be rushed by those you don't trust.

5 At last you're free to choose. Be creative and consult someone you believe in; you can only benefit, since your creative energy is now at its peak. Your influence on others is now paramount.

6 Don't be misled by your own capabilities or lose touch with reality. You have a tendency to enjoy adulation a little too much. Bragging will work against you and you'll live to regret it. Despite this, a friendship blossoms.

No. 1
YIN • TAKING CONTROL

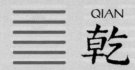

QIAN

乾

Your energy and decisiveness is at its peak. But you must not pause now in pursuing your goals; you're at the fulcrum of great changes taking place. This positions you at the centre of a natural cycle and you will be called upon to support others in taking decisions and moving on. Persistence is now needed, but it won't be easy and may be interpreted by some as stubbornness. You need to stay focused, as there are those who may try to distract you and shift you in a different direction. Don't let them. You may well have to go back to basics and start again, but you won't regret it. Others rely on you remaining strong in your current situation and you cannot let them down.

Messages

1 Timing is everything. You're fully equipped and ready, but in your situation it would be as much a mistake to start too early as it would arrive too late. Bide your time and don't provoke anyone.

2 Align yourself with an ally who has experience. You've got great skills and the personality to carry responsibility. But you have to know when to allow others to fill their roles; this way, yours becomes more critical, as you're at the centre pulling the strings.

3 Creativity and vision are to the fore. You can achieve anything you want today if you keep to your moral compass and recognize the contribution of others. This will sharpen your organizing skills and amplify the reward that's coming to you.

4 Success brings choices with it: whether to quietly enjoy the trappings of success, or to use victory as a springboard towards public recognition. Think about it carefully and ask whether you're really ready to meet the challenge. You're certainly good enough.

5 It's as if the clouds have lifted. A clear vision has descended and your judgement is at its sharpest. Creativity and design come to the fore. You can shape the future of others now; you will be in company of other high achievers.

6 Don't push things too far, despite your recent exceptional achievements. Make sure you've considered all the issues and covered the exits before progressing any further. Your visibility could work against you if you are not well prepared, as your motives will be questioned.

No. 2

YANG • PATIENTLY POWERFUL

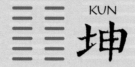

KUN

坤

You can achieve great things if you just take your time and concentrate on what matters. The earthly traits of strength and endurance come to the fore and allow you to play the role as catalyst for others. You enable those close to you to be creative. Don't dismiss opportunities but, equally, don't rush too quickly into things that are not clear. Give them time to develop and an obvious path to success will present itself. Be sure to focus your attention, however; if you allow yourself to be distracted, you'll get into trouble. Resist the temptation to give up – you're being tested. This is a successful time for you, with a cataclysmic event on the horizon. This will bring great change and the potential of significant fortune.

Messages

1 Don't bury your head in the sand. Let matters become clear, because things are deteriorating. Batten down the hatches and prepare yourself for imminent changes in your career and personal life. Don't let others distract you.

2 Don't force the issue. You have a tendency to be intolerant and not listen to others. Let those close have their say and everything will sort itself out. There's an improvement or promotion on its way; just let it happen.

3 Keep your plans to yourself and don't listen to others. They have their own ambitions and these could conflict with yours. Keeping a low profile is the best thing to do.

4 Difficulties are building around you and confrontations could lead to great antagonism. Follow your own instincts and don't let friends distract you. Concentrate on detail, as this is where your problems could arise. Invent some kind of delay if you have to.

5 Accept what's happened, be modest and keep a low profile. You won't see it at first, but things will come good in a big way – way beyond your imagination.

6 Don't fight battles you can't win; concede something now, and immediate benefits will follow. If you don't, both you and those around you will suffer badly. You may be forced out of your comfortable position; if you fight it, you'll lose out, so let things blow over and contain your energy for a better time.

No. 2
YIN • GO IT ALONE

KUN

坤

You may have to be prepared to accept a subordinate role and devote yourself to supporting others in a common goal, but sometimes you'll find it difficult to stand by and not get involved. Be receptive to new ideas. Although you may play second fiddle, it's time to take responsibility and force an issue into the open. A solution is about to reveal itself and you will be the one who will get the message and take the initiative. You cannot wait any longer, as your patience is exhausted. You need space from someone close. Go straight to the heart of the matter and confront the issues. This will crystallize the really important matters you need to address. Don't be distracted by others' opinions; they're not important any more.

Messages

1 Something at the core is beginning to deteriorate. Investigate carefully and take action to address an issue. You could be skating on thin ice and you need to know where you stand.

2 Don't forget how nature functions. The world revolves and everything is reshaped and reconfigured. This is when you need to keep things in balance. A wind of change is coming and you're right in the middle. Keep your perspective and sense of duty, and this will help you cope.

3 It's time to hide your light under a bushel. Let someone else enjoy the limelight and they will become the target for ridicule. This will allow your own true contribution to be revealed and you'll be rewarded by a promotion above them.

4 It may be best to draw stumps and take control of the situation. A period of introspection is called for. This will give you the chance to reassess the matter and your role in it. Once things become clear, you can make progress with confidence.

5 Modesty and discretion are the name of the game. Restrain your natural inclination to be demonstrative; contain your emotions and use the energy to focus on what's needed. A solution will then reveal itself and you can entrust someone with what they need to do.

6 This is not a time to hang around. A real test is about to arrive and it could be difficult for all parties concerned. Let things ride, as no one can win this tussle. Walk away and think again, then come back stronger.

No. 3

YANG • OVERCOMING EARLY OBSTACLES

ZHUN

屯

There is a decisive step before you, but you're entering the realm of the unknown. This can apply to your personal relationships or career and there could be serious obstacles to overcome early on. Prepare carefully, and your bad start can be reversed, but you need to wait longer, as you don't have enough control over your destiny just yet. If you're entering a new phase in a relationship or career, then you could face an uphill struggle at first. Confusion and indecision reign, but there's little you can do about it. You may need to speak to another person to crystallize the issues – don't be too proud to ask others for help. Knowing your limitations allows you to review your position with honesty and you can reshape your strategy with confidence.

Messages

1 You're uncertain what to do, as something is blocking your path. Be determined but contrite, as this will convince others of your sincerity. Keep calm and consult those close to you. You're due to make progress on all fronts.

2 It appears impossible to make a decision. You need things to return to normal. Hold your breath and take no action. Once things become clear, press ahead with confidence.

3 You feel you are in an awkward spot, and you could still fail if you act too quickly. Change your plans or they won't work. You may need to adapt your expectations or else you're certain to be disappointed.

4 You need help at this stage in your career or personal life. Actions speak louder than words, and something has happened very recently which heartens you. You will have a chance to work with others. Take it.

5 You're pretty good at leading others along the right path when it comes to making everyday decisions. Bigger decisions, however, don't look good at the moment, and it might be best to delay if you can. You can have what you want but will enjoy it more if you learn that it's not important.

6 Things don't look good right now, and a setback is troubling you. You must give up something; let it go and you will be surprised at how you don't miss it. Start over again.

No. 3
YIN • KEEPING CALM

ZHUN

屯

You may need to keep your patience at the moment, as things are changing fast. It's like being on the edge of a cliff and danger presenting itself. Everything seems to have come to a head suddenly. With hindsight, you probably should have seen it coming. The signs were there. So, step back and take stock, disentangle all the knotty relationships and repair the damage from a recent dispute. Don't fall into the trap which might be set by others. Look after those who really depend on you and this will bring into focus what's important. This will distract you and enable you to look at things in a different light. You may need to reverse a decision you just made as part of the process of dismantling things before rebuilding again.

Messages

1. It seems you may have been getting ready to start and something's come up – so you need to consider what you're doing all over again. It could be irritating, but a fresh start won't do you any harm, as you'll see things in a different light.

2. A period of confusion has developed. Someone needs to take a deep breath and reorganize. A seed has been planted and it will bear fruit eventually, but hard work and dedication will be required during the maturing process.

3. You had already detected that something wasn't quite right. Your sense of order was tested and it's not clear how you should deal with it. A wiser person would give up the chase and change their tactics. Perhaps you should try it.

4. Maybe you just have to admit you're not up to the challenge. This would relieve your conscience and allow someone to give you the advice you need. Take it on board, then pick up the benefits without a second thought. There's nothing wrong with admitting your limitations.

5. You're getting your act together with respect to a number of minor jobs that needed doing. But this doesn't automatically qualify you to attempt bigger projects which require entirely different skills. Don't push your luck, or everything could fall apart.

6. You've tried your best and it's not worked out. There are times when you just have to accept defeat and move on to another project or relationship. There's no point in persisting any more; sadly, it's time to back off.

No. 4

YANG • WINDING PATH TO SUCCESS

MENG

蒙

You're experiencing uncertainty and it hurts, because you normally manage to cope with everything. You're trying to learn as you go along but, unless you take counsel from others who know better, it will prove to be a painful process. Going with the flow is all you can do, as there are simply too many things to learn and the issues confronting you now lie outside your usual sphere of experience. No matter how much you ask, things still aren't clear, so you just have to accept that you don't know the answers. Experiment and you will learn; it's the only way. Trial and error teaches you valuable lessons, as it exposes the blind spots in your life. This is not a good time to take big risks.

Messages

1 Although the atmosphere is not conducive to problem-solving at the moment, you must begin to sort things out now or they will only get worse. You need to back down and jettison your natural tendency to contest decisions.

2 Don't bottle things up. Be honest, and others will appreciate it. Your leadership skills come to the fore, and others will find you both inspired and knowledgeable.

3 Don't make friends for the wrong reasons. This can apply to career or personal relationships. Things are not quite what they seem. The expected benefits won't materialize, and you will get absolutely nowhere.

4 You're deceiving yourself and have been fantasizing for a while. This is beginning to consume you, and you could end up humiliated. Get real; you will regret it if you don't stop. Don't engage in new ventures.

5 You may have just had a close shave. Don't make the same mistake again and just accept your position as it is. Take advice from others in your career and personal life, and dramatic changes for the better will take place.

6 You must be very careful and watchful. Technical or legal problems have come to the fore and won't go away. One false move and you'll regret it, as you'll be punished for the mistake.

No 4
YIN • SAYING NO

MENG

蒙

You may have gone too far recently in trying to unravel the truth without allowing yourself to fail, which is only natural when you're learning. There are different layers of uncertainty around at present and, if you're not careful, you could overlook an important piece of information. You may imagine it would have been better to let things lie, but sometimes you need to experience disappointment in order to strengthen your resolve. Now you may have bitten off more than you can chew by taking on too much. You cannot reverse a natural process and you need to come to accept that you are not in control. Let things progress at their own pace and learn by experience, rather than just winging it. If you push too far without doing so, then you won't succeed.

Messages

1 Sometimes plants need assistance in order to reach their full potential; a support, for instance, may help them to avoid weeds and to grow. This is what you need now. Find someone to help you remove the shackles that hold you back. Somebody close by can help.

2 It's possible that another person needs you just as much as you need them. Reveal your weaknesses to them and give them chance to reciprocate. You will both be strengthened by the experience, and will benefit.

3 You can see the goal vividly but the path is fraught with difficulties. Don't jump in with both feet before you've tested the water, otherwise you'll find yourself up to your neck in problems. Check your facts before you speak out.

4 Don't allow your dreams to lead your decision-making – use your brain instead. If you don't, you may become embarrassed by something that's happening over which you have no control. The experience may teach you a valuable lesson but it won't be enjoyable. Brace yourself.

5 You could just have got away with something. You decided to wing it and do half the job, and hope that no one notices. You'll escape unscathed this time but you won't get away with it twice. Try to be more thorough from now on.

6 Someone may need a stiff reminder of their duties. Everyone makes mistakes, but action is required and sometimes penalties must be imposed to keep others on their toes. Unfortunately it's your responsibility to invoke discipline – you can't avoid it. Everyone needs to know their limits.

No. 5

YANG • WATCHING AND WAITING

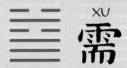

XU

You are waiting in anticipation for something which will have dramatic consequences. It's always darkest before the dawn, so don't rush things. Trust yourself and be patient. Life is generating a complex flux of changes, producing opportunities for new associations and relationships – so don't waste time on things you don't need to do and live for the moment. A great change is about to take place, and circumstances beyond your control will dictate its momentum. Take time out to analyse the situation and prepare for this transformation. An outward display of calm will assist you, and you'll be better prepared for what's coming.

Messages

1 Problems may be on the horizon, but don't get agitated. Tread water for now – you'll need your energy for what's coming. There's still a great deal of uncertainty around.

2 There will be consequences resulting from what you are trying to do. Don't be deflated; remain confident, despite the disagreements and ensuing aggravation. You will sort out the major issues from the minor ones.

3 You've gone too far, but it's not too late to retrace your steps. Be very careful in order to avoid disaster, and prepare meticulously if you intend travelling in the near future.

4 You're at the centre of a number of radical changes and it becomes stressful. You could be in dangerous company and need help from people you trust. Extract yourself from a situation; there's danger around, so adopt a low profile.

5 After a period of turbulence the climate is calming down. You're strong enough now to make progress. There could be a financial windfall in prospect or a property deal. Go for it.

6 A number of complex issues have come to a head and recent bad fortune or a period of ill health is about to resolve itself. Only people with real influence and expertise can help you. Don't hesitate to consult them and accept their advice.

No. 5
YIN • BIDING TIME

XU
霂

Your current situation is like waiting to cross a great river. There will be risks, but at some point you will need to make a decision. You are about to embark on a new enterprise and you may be afraid of the challenges ahead. But you have to reap a harvest when it is ready, not when you think you are ready. Let nature take its course and don't try to interfere until the time is ripe. Allow yourself to go with the flow and talk to those with more experience; this will prepare you better for what's coming. There's an unceasing and inevitable momentum which has you in its grip. Something will flick a switch and your waiting will be over.

Messages

1 There's a real challenge on its way and you're going to have to deal with it, but there's no point in worrying about something that hasn't happened yet. Get ready for action. You may need to wait longer than you wanted, but when it's needed drive a hard bargain.

2 You're about to embark on something which will test you to the full. Play safety first and don't be led by others' half-baked ideas. This will only serve to confuse the objectives. Stay focused despite the distractions.

3 You could get stuck in the mud now because you acted prematurely. Someone or something just wasn't ready. You won't be able to recover your composure until some time has passed and an issue has been put to bed. Be cautious from now on.

4 You could find yourself at the centre of an upheaval and everyone is pointing the finger at you. You were not to blame but just wanted to make a contribution. Try to extricate yourself from this situation. It can only get worse.

5 An issue you've had to grapple with may now be moving on and the wait is over. Things have clicked into position. Use this opportunity to divert your attention to something else. A delivery is overdue and perhaps now is the time to chase it up.

6 An uninvited guest may turn up. You might feel concerned at first, but they can help if you give it a chance. Accept an offer with gratitude, whether you asked for it or not. You can only benefit and then they will leave.

No. 6

YANG ● STRENGTH THROUGH CONFLICT

SONG

There seems no way out for you at the moment. You're up against it and it appears impossible to resolve disputes. You could have been more careful at the outset when weighing up the options. Mutual accusations abound and no compromise is on the horizon. Stay away from confrontations, since you're looking at things from your own point of view. People of varying ages or different attitudes or characters within families often find themselves in positions of conflict. This is a natural part of life. Confrontation won't work. There's no point in being stubborn, as it only makes things worse. You may be best to consult someone you trust whose independence and objectivity is clear.

Messages

1 Stop what you are doing or try to do something else to distract you, so you can revisit the issue later. Backbiting and wrangling are the order of the day. You may feel victimized, but it will come good if you back off.

2 You may as well give in, as there's no point in winning any more; otherwise, it's just more grief for everyone, including yourself. It's time to stop the conflict, regain your equilibrium and come to a reconciliation.

3 Keep a low profile at the moment because the atmosphere is just too hostile. Be happy with what you've got and get issues out of the way quickly before you become exhausted.

4 You don't need to prove you're right – you already know it – so give up struggling and be confident in your own position. You will recover any losses if you pull back and resist a confrontation.

5 Don't push too far; you've got what you want, so meet the other person halfway. You'll benefit them as well as yourself. Trust another person's opinion, and this will allow you to enhance your career prospects.

6 There's both good and bad news around, and you're not in a position to predict which will arrive first. If you push it, you won't be happy with the result and your victory will quickly disappear. A hollow success is not worth the effort.

No. 6
YIN ● RESOLVING CONFRONTATION

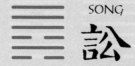

SONG

訟

Disputes abound. They may remain personal, but could also become legal. This has caused you to worry and could impair your health if you don't keep things in perspective. There are more important things in life, so concentrate on the needs of family and friends, especially those who need your care and attention. You cannot resolve the issues, as they have become intractable. You could offer to meet someone halfway, but the other side just refuses to see things from your point of view. You may need to step back and review how you reached an impasse. Revisit your assumptions and encourage others to do the same. The next stage will be painful, but this is a necessary phase in order to reach a settlement or reconciliation which will ultimately prove beneficial to both parties.

Messages

1 It's not the time to remain engaged in a joint endeavour. Try to bring things to a head quickly and withdraw. If you don't, then a decision made will backfire. While you'll be disappointed, you'll get over it quickly and switch your attention elsewhere.

2 You don't really have enough firepower to overcome a tricky situation. Try not to be drawn into the open or you could become exposed. This would not only cause you problems but could also have unfortunate consequences for those around you.

3 Keep your head down. There's a bust-up coming and you need to be ready to escape a situation. Save your energy and try not to tire yourself. Prepare another strategy for recovery when things settle down.

4 Blaming someone in a weaker position than you won't rescue the situation you're in – it will just delay the repercussions for a while. Stick to your long-held beliefs and you will ultimately be proven right. Then you can apologize for what you did.

5 It could be that someone independent and with authority is needed to arbitrate in a dispute. A compromise may be required but the current conflict won't allow it to reveal itself. Find someone else who won't take no for an answer to resolve the matter. Both sides will listen.

6 You could win the battle today but not the war. Forcing something through just to get your own way can leave someone bitter and have lasting consequences. You may need their co-operation in the future, so concede something now and bring them into line.

No. 7

YANG ● WINNING OVER OTHERS

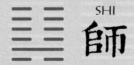

SHI

師

It will take great leadership skills for you to win over others. The more friends and acquaintances you have, the greater the challenge. You are currently up to the task and possess the necessary attributes to be successful in your chosen career and in a variety of social situations. You're showing great restraint and determination now and others will follow you, but you must become more disciplined and organized. You need to work together to cement personal relationships. You must adopt the right tactics and convince others of your arguments; if you don't, you won't succeed.

Messages

1 Watch your back. Don't make the decision unless you've sounded out those close to you. Personal discipline is the key to convincing others to see your point of view and get your own way.

2 Take the initiative; no one else is equipped to make progress like you. Your communication skills are at their peak and you will be rewarded publicly for an achievement which is richly deserved.

3 You're going to get into serious trouble unless you focus your mind now. Someone is jeopardizing your position and threatening your future. There's a conflict between you and those in authority, and this could become disruptive.

4 Take a break and then come back with renewed energy and have another go. You're facing an insurmountable obstacle and need to adopt a different strategy. Unwind what you've done or you will make things worse.

5 Take time out to prepare your agenda, but don't act yet. Get help if you need it – you need guidance at this point. Once you've planned your strategy and found a way to build teamwork, then things will go smoothly.

6 There's a great chance now to assert yourself and enhance your position, but be careful not to take on too much. Don't allow others less qualified than you to dictate events. It's time to celebrate and rejoice in resolving a particular problem and achieving great success.

No. 7

YIN • LEADING BY EXAMPLE

SHI

師

You have earned the respect of others through your actions. This will enable you to take more responsibility and engage directly in teaching and leading friends and colleagues. This latent ability has always been there; it's just lain dormant for a while, waiting for the appropriate time to reveal itself. Through your example others will follow, and you will act as a spur to renew their efforts. Someone's got to do it and this is your time to take the initiative and bear the responsibility. Remain flexible and give way on something in order to bring someone closer to you. Leading a powerful team will allow you to reap enormous benefits.

Messages

1 Keep your discipline and gather intelligence. Remember: knowledge without wisdom can lead to mistakes. Don't go half-baked into a confrontation or competition; you'll fail if you do.

2 Take the initiative and gather others around you to strengthen your case. You could be asked to repeat yourself or do something over again in order to reinforce some key messages. You'll learn from this; it will enhance your reputation and strengthen your hand.

3 Look around you and ask yourself where guidance is coming from. Someone needs a new leader as head of their team. Unless this can be addressed the ship will remain rudderless and go round and round in circles, heading nowhere.

4 It may be time for a breather. You've assessed what's before you and the way forward is not obvious. Take some time out; exit stage left and watch from the sidelines before rejoining the battle.

5 Maybe someone who is trusted by all is needed to take a lead. The situation demands someone with authority that stems from experience and belief in a common cause. If a novice is allowed to take over, this would be a grave mistake. Don't let it happen if you can help it.

6 You're getting there, but it's been hard work and tiring. However, more responsibility is about to be heaped on your shoulders. This is what you wanted, but you need to ensure that proper roles are allotted. Experience counts for a lot, so make sure you use it.

No. 8
YANG ● CO-OPERATION

BI

比

It hasn't always been the case, but your current situation requires greater harmony with both friends and family in order to make progress. You need to encourage a unity of purpose to get the best out of the situation. You often make decisions without consultation, but you now need to work with others to succeed. There could be an opportunity for you to become a leader at this time, but it brings an onerous and sometimes frightening responsibility – so don't act alone. It would be ideal for you to merge or create a joint venture with someone else. You are needed by others but you also will not succeed without them. Don't hesitate to bring them into the loop, or you'll jeopardize the future.

Messages

1 Don't hide anything from your friends. If you are open with them, they will be honest with you. An unexpected opportunity will then present itself and you can take full advantage of it.

2 Don't become self-absorbed or use people, or you will lose your dignity. Only firm foundations create lasting relationships. You'll get help from an unexpected source and time is on your side, so don't rush things.

3 If you don't see eye to eye with someone, then it's better to break up than try to change them. You're probably mixing with the wrong crowd, so create some space. It could cost you seriously if you don't.

4 Make sure those you are close to get their deserved respect and appreciation. You will achieve much more by working together, but don't give your support too cheaply. This is a great time for you to make progress.

5 Don't make others do what you want to do unless they are willing partners. There's a mutual attraction developing and there's a great prospect in the offing. You could receive an accolade beyond your wildest dreams – and one you're not sure you deserve.

6 If you are determined to go it alone, then there is little help for you. Sometimes personal space is important, but if it persists this will be a mistake and you'll be lost. Be careful to protect your health, as this is a tricky period for you.

No. 8
YIN • BRINGING FOCUS

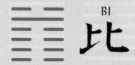

BI

It's time to analyse the situation and focus on its core elements in order to identify a common purpose that you can use to bind people together. Everyone needs to feel they are a genuine part of a project for it to work out. What caused you to get to this point? Only by getting to the heart of the matter will the solution to a knotty problem reveal itself. There are limits to everything, and you need to find the boundaries of your behaviour and restrict yourself. You can sometimes try to do too much too quickly, and this could work against you if it provokes others to question your motivation. You'll meet this challenge now and, although it will be a trial, you will succeed, but only if you convince someone else to co-operate.

Messages

1 There's a piece of good fortune coming your way; you just need to be open and honest about the details behind a scheme or arrangement. Revealing the details results in someone transforming their attitude, but you must get your oar in first so everyone knows where you stand.

2 Hold on to your strongest convictions. This will attract the attention of someone and bring them closer, forming the foundation for an enduring friendship that will last for the rest of your life, if managed carefully.

3 It could be that you are involved with those whose motives are not quite sincere. They may even break the rules or law. You won't be immune from the consequences, even if you don't participate fully. Stay clear and protect your reputation; it's more important than weak friendships.

4 A coming-together with someone in a position of authority and at the centre of things is imminent. Find some common ground. Use it to your best advantage and express your solidarity with them, otherwise you could be moving on quicker than you think.

5 An opportunity is running away from another person you respect and admire. You can help by watching closely and not alarming anyone. Let things progress at their own pace and point out the solution to them in your own time and in a cautious tone. They will be grateful.

6 Something's not quite right. You had a funny feeling about it all along but couldn't put your finger on it. Keep your distance, as things are about to backfire. Exit the scene quickly or you'll catch the flak.

No. 9
YANG • PROCEEDING WITH CAUTION

XIAOCHU

小畜

Every so often, it takes someone sensitive like you to show others the way. You may be required to play this role in other people's lives. There's a fog of uncertainty surrounding current events and it won't shift, so you need to show considerable restraint, particularly in personal relationships where you're not in control of events. Aggression is not your style and would be counterproductive; be calm, and you will overcome everything in your way. Rest and prepare for what's coming. It could be fleeting when the time comes, but don't hesitate to act, as your persuasiveness is at a peak.

Messages

1 You can be confident in your own actions, since you have carefully weighed up your current situation and know your options. A return to peace and harmony is the order of the day. You can't fail if you follow your instincts.

2 Don't discount listening to others who know better than you. If you do, you could make mistakes. Retreat and let those who have the necessary experience lead the way. A promotion or positive change in direction is on the cards.

3 Sort yourself out first before dealing with others. The circumstances you face could cause embarrassment and annoyance. You may need to resolve a situation by spending time alone.

4 There's a real threat coming and this is making you anxious. Keep your head, and things will work out; act prematurely, and this could lead to disaster. You have friends in unlikely places who will support you, so don't ignore them.

5 Don't just think about yourself – think of others, and the outcome will be better than you ever imagined. Spend time networking, as your career prospects are on the up.

6 Know when to stop. You've achieved a great deal already, but you must recognize when to hold back, as there's a trap set and waiting around the corner. If you push things too far you could lose everything.

No. 9

YIN • STOPPING TO THINK

XIAOCHU

小畜

A variety of unrelated and unpredictable events have combined to create confusion. This could leave you exhausted if you're not careful. It's not the time for quick decisions. You need to gather some composure after a recent test and try to replenish your energy; just like the winter season, it's a time for rest and consideration of where you're going. Save yourself and don't follow others when you're just not sure yet. Sometimes you have to go with the flow and carry on learning from your mistakes, as you're not yet qualified to make momentous decisions. This is what you're experiencing now. Listen to everyone's opinion before reacting and offering your own; only then will you know what's right. A new-found wisdom will then guide you in making the correct decision.

Messages

1 Don't push things as the timing is just not right. It's time for self-restraint and for re-examining the arguments on both sides. You won't make a mistake if you stick to what you know and avoid what you don't. The right decision will then appear from nowhere.

2 A climb-down or retreat is favoured. Watch what others have done and learn from their failures. They thought they had the answers, but they were wrong. This will show you how things should be done and the right path to follow.

3 There doesn't appear to be anything in the way and you are making sound progress. Don't be fooled. Something surprising is around the corner and about to appear from nowhere. The wheels could fall off if you don't keep your wits about you. Be careful.

4 There's a kernel of truth in what someone did, though it may have made you feel quite uncomfortable. This could make you anxious and may even be painful. After this period of uncertainty, truth and calm will appear and you'll feel it was worthwhile – but you won't enjoy the process.

5 The strength of a close relationship has never been more important. You need this to steer you through the uncertainty and discomfort you might currently feel. Co-operate and keep loyal to your shared beliefs; this will allow an association to strengthen and guide you through a tricky patch.

6 You're getting there. The rain has stopped and it's time to smell the flowers, delight in new relationships and build bridges. Enjoy the freedom that you now have, but always be aware that a run of good luck may be short-lived. Remain diligent.

No. 10
YANG • DOING THE RIGHT THING

LU

The current time presents great opportunity and inspiration, but an issue could overwhelm you if you're not careful. Keep your head down and assess the risks while considering your options; don't take those risks without doing so, or you'll come to regret it. Personal relationships could become particularly strained, and it's not the best time to make great changes. You need to recognize that everyone is built differently, and that people often see things in a different light. The right choice may be to do nothing and allow another perspective to become exposed. Confronting issues head-on is not always the best course of action, so keep your own counsel and maintain your composure at all costs.

Messages

1 Be realistic about your limitations and try not to become too dependent on others. Don't fight battles you can't win, and you'll learn a useful lesson. You should, however, continue to press ahead, as your immediate prospects are good.

2 Keep your head down and play to your strengths, and you'll make progress. Keep your own ambitions private and don't let others dictate your life. It's time to be cautious, and the best advice is to sit things out for a while.

3 Stop tweaking someone else's tail or you'll regret it. Know when to stop provoking people. This could be a very tricky time, and conflicts could arise if you are not very careful.

4 You're on a knife edge and everything appears to be going against you, but your confidence is high and you can take risks at this point. You must keep your own counsel or you'll end up making the wrong decisions. Follow your intuition.

5 Past mistakes keep coming back to haunt you. You must sort them out before you can progress, as your hard work is not being recognized as it should. Although what you intend to do could be dangerous, it's worth the risk, and recognition that you were right will come.

6 A piece of good news could arrive. It's time to re-examine what you really want out of life; think about the past before looking to the future, then you'll have nothing to fear, but don't make the same mistakes again.

No. 10
YIN • DELICATE NEGOTIATIONS

LU
履

Resist the temptation to snap at people who contradict you. This is a fractious time and your current situation can be compared to treading on a tiger's tail. You could get more reaction than you bargained for. But that doesn't mean you can avoid risks in the current situation; it just means you need to assess where the pressure-points arise and avoid those tasks which lie beyond your skill-set. You're in a strong and dominant position, and other people are following your lead. They will lose their way without you. Delegate to others or feign ignorance to distract attention from your weaknesses. Once the really tricky issues have resolved themselves, you will be able to cope alone. In the meantime, there will be a few real tests for you to face.

Messages

1 Stop struggling against an inevitable wave of counter-influences or you'll be overwhelmed. You're not in a strong negotiating position, so it's time to recognize this. Be careful and minimize your mistakes – and thus minimize the damage.

2 It would be easy to just adopt the dreams of someone you're close to and follow their lead. This should be avoided. Keep focused on what it is that you alone want. Follow your own, independent course; it's time for your leadership skills to come to the fore.

3 You don't have the equipment to do what you would like. Try not to provoke a reaction from someone, otherwise it really is like stepping on the tiger's tail and you'll get more than you bargained for. Retain your awareness at all times and don't take any risks.

4 If you remain considered and cautious, you will make great strides today. Your luck is changing, although what you will be asked to do is daunting and could be risky. You are up to it – just be careful.

5 The task before you is not only tricky but could be dangerous. Make sure you look at all the angles and follow the correct procedures. Remember that safety comes first. You've done it before and just need to keep your discipline.

6 Are you happy with how you've conducted yourself so far? If you are, then carry on; but if you have any misgivings, then you need to address them now. Examine the detail before taking the next step. It's never too late to stop and just say no.

No. 11

YANG • MUTUAL UNDERSTANDING

TAI

泰

The perfect balance is being achieved, and the really important things in life are being revealed to you. Harmony with someone close brings you peace, understanding and great success. The atmosphere is like springtime, where all of life is renewed. It's time to progress your plans and you will prosper. You must learn to listen to others, as they do to you. Don't force the pace, and be even-handed to get the best from your relationships. You'll feel an inner strength developing, which will benefit you physically and personally. You're getting closer to realizing your personal ambitions.

Messages

1 Don't be fooled by face value; get to the truth, however difficult it may be. You can now benefit from getting closer to others in both career and personal relationships. Those in authority, or with whom you have a particularly close relationship, are inclined to support you at the moment.

2 It's time to step back and reconsider your tactics. Everything has two sides. Don't be afraid to express your view forcibly – then confront narrow-mindedness, and avoid being led by those you don't respect.

3 Everything has an upside and a downside. If you forget this, you will lose out; sometimes you have to sacrifice some upside to reach agreement. Don't worry – everything is going to work out.

4 Go it alone if you have to – don't depend on others who may have a different agenda. Your determination will gather momentum and bring success – just be more selective and cautious when starting new ventures.

5 Grant others the benefit of your given talents freely. If you keep them to yourself, they will remain hidden for ever – but try to act with humility and modesty. This is a very successful time in career and academic pursuits.

6 This could be a down period for you. There's gossip around, and this could lead to hostility. Don't be afraid of constructive criticism – use it to appear receptive and considerate. If you're too sensitive, this will contribute to your downfall.

No. 11
YIN ● RAPID RECOVERY

TAI

泰

Something really significant in your personal relationship is on the cards. After a period of friction, things are coming together, and you've made the correct decisions. There's a sudden end to feuding and peace prevails. What you imagined were small and insignificant actions to help others have had the effect of changing someone's views about you. Matters which were out of sync have now become better balanced, and both your spirit and your health can now improve. It's as though the clouds have lifted, allowing a piercing light to envelop everything and evaporate all the uncertainty and conflict. You don't need to try very hard to make progress any more – a natural and welcome harmony and momentum has developed. Enjoy the peace that's now descending.

Messages

1 You're about to become the catalyst by which the understanding of others is transformed. Through your words you will spark inspiration and create connections between your ideas and objectives. A calm will descend on those you touch. This brings you to centre stage.

2 Take a longer-term view of recent events. Someone needs to adopt a wider perspective – and it's you. You are in touch with natural laws today, and this gives you the edge to take on a challenge and help guide others to success. Look up and view the horizon; it will change your attitude.

3 You may be asked to grapple with a major decision. It could go either way, but you must choose. Look for the obvious signs – they are there for you to see. Take notice of what others say, and you'll then head in the right direction.

4 Keep your concentration and focus on communication. You can't afford to let others stray off-message, as they may disappear in the wrong direction. If you are indecisive, then you'll lose the initiative, and responsibility will be taken from you. Take the initiative today.

5 An objective attitude is called for. You can see both sides of an issue but you must allow the arguments to surface for the benefit of others. Share your talents with others and encourage them, and this will clarify their vision. You will gain from this too.

6 A turning point has been reached. The pendulum is about to swing back again, and bring with it a change of strategy. Go with the flow. Adapt to the changes, and don't become defensive or it will backfire. A natural impetus is dictating the pace, and there's nothing you can do about it.

No. 12
YANG • RESOLVING ISSUES

PI
否

Today you need to let go of the past or it will bury you. A cloud of uncertainty surrounds events at the moment, and a stalemate has arisen. The foundations of what you've achieved could be under threat. Poor communication will only make this worse, and the whole atmosphere is one of apathy and rejection. The wrong person is making the wrong decisions, but there's nothing you can do about it right now. Certain relationships are simply out of sync; you weren't the cause, so don't blame yourself. Don't withdraw yourself completely, even though relationships may become strained. You are needed now by those close to you, so wait patiently, then act decisively.

Messages

1 Stop what you are doing and take a step back. If you don't, matters could spiral out of control. Your character and your principles are being tested, and certain people may interfere if you let them.

2 Don't criticize others without good reason. Listen to them but be positive in your own stance, and this will produce success. But it's not yet time to act, so be patient.

3 Don't set off in one direction now or you'll regret it. Hold off from taking action until you're absolutely sure. It's difficult to resist, but the time is just not right.

4 The tide will soon turn and your luck will change. You've been waiting for some good news and it's just around the corner. Be ready for it, as it will sweep you along and everyone else with it.

5 You're getting close to success now, but be careful. You could lose everything if you act without thinking, but a sweeping change for the better is imminent. Bad luck retreats and interference from others recedes.

6 Today's problems will become tomorrow's opportunities. Let go of the past and stop pitying yourself; only you can decide what's going to happen, so you may as well get on with it. A rapid recovery in health, career and personal relationships is on the cards.

No. 12
YIN • TIMELY WITHDRAWAL

PI

Things are not quite right at the moment. It's a difficult time to make progress, as a deadline has set in, just like in early autumn when the year has passed its zenith. Obstructions to your progress are being presented, and it was other people who brought this about. You've tried to unite others and it may have backfired; now any further attempt at communication could make things worse. It's time to sit on your hands and watch what's happening rather than getting too involved. The way forward is uncertain, so it's not the time to make risky decisions. Withdraw from the front line and don't be tempted by lucrative proposals. Bite your lip and cross your fingers, as matters are now out of your hands.

Messages

1 If you can't change things around, then find an escape route. You can still get out clean and no one will blame you, because you had no choice. There's really no alternative if you want to end the frustration. Take the disappointment on the chin.

2 Things will only continue to stagnate if you carry on in the same way. Voicing criticism can only work if others are prepared to listen. There are none so blind as those who will not see. Accept your differences but try to remain on good terms.

3 You may have employed certain tactics you're not proud of. It couldn't be helped, as you really had no alternative. An announcement's about to be made, and this will deflect attention from you. You should then get away with it, after all.

4 You'll receive a call which you were awaiting more in hope than expectation. Accept the news calmly and act surprised. Take the challenge on board and look out for a good omen which will encourage you further. You'll get a result you want.

5 A sweeping change is imminent. Don't let the opportunity escape; things are changing quickly and you'll need to be fast on your feet. Define the parameters at the outset to avoid any misunderstanding and prevent things from going off at a tangent, and then you'll get through it.

6 After a period of calm and no movement, the breakthrough has arrived. It's like a sudden thunderclap striking, and everything around is shaking in response. It won't be a smooth ride, but if you persist and forget recent history you'll be glad you can now move forward.

No. 13
YANG • WORKING TOGETHER

TONGREN
同人

Today you cannot make any progress unless you work in union with others. A sense of community pervades everything at the moment and you are part of it. This will shed light on common problems and reveal the best course of action. Remember: two heads are better than one. The time is right for you to make changes and begin to move in the right direction, but you can't do it alone. It's a favourable time for achieving your social aims but you may have to take a back seat to realize your ambitions. This will not interfere with your goals, but will bring clarity and strength to a new endeavour.

Messages

1   You haven't lost the chance to make progress, but you can't do it on your own. There's a great opportunity on the horizon and this could be the beginning of a strong fellowship. Things will work out, so long as this teamwork holds together.

2   A disagreement may arise with someone close. Don't be distracted by your own feelings or allow your ego to take charge. Settle for something less, and a much bigger prize is on offer.

3   There's some friction in the air. Don't let it distract you. Others are only after what they can get, whereas you know what you actually need. It will only last for three days, then disappear.

4   Dismantle the barriers you've built to keep others away, which may have made you lonely – you'll be surprised how you will benefit from renewing friendships. A property deal could bring new responsibilities.

5   You may have become downhearted recently as obstacles presented themselves. Don't hesitate to say what's on your mind. Revealing differences of opinion can be constructive, and you'll become recognized for your leadership skills.

6   Keep your head and don't make any dramatic changes in your life. There's a new relationship coming into view; at first it appears superficial, but it can become much more than that.

No. 13
YIN • BUILDING WITH CONFIDENCE

TONGREN
同人

Constructing things with other people has taken centre stage. It's a time for fellowship and close co-operation, but this will require everyone to adopt a set of universal principles and relegate personal ambition to the background. There's a team spirit developing, which will enable you to conquer all before you. Be grateful for the opportunities you're being given, and offer a gift if you get the chance. There's a positive spin on everything you're doing, and other people have now got the message and are willing to accept your lead and guidance. You will be asked to dismantle something and identify a solution before moving forward. But you will achieve success if you work with others towards a common goal.

Messages

1 A strong fellowship and a communal meeting of minds is developing, and you will be part of it. You may need to reconcile differences of opinion; if you're all singing from the same hymn sheet, the sound will be amplified and you'll achieve more than you would on your own.

2 People who work together in a co-operative enterprise expose each other's limitations to closer inspection. This is how you find out who is best for which role. You can't avoid this process if you want to succeed.

3 The roads are diverging and someone's gone off on their own. Sometimes you have to climb to higher ground to get a better perspective. You need to do this to discover where you stand. Find out what's on their mind, review the situation and bring them back on board.

4 Because you are quite accomplished at something, you may have come to expect too much of another. This may have disheartened them. We each have our own contribution to make, so lower your guard and admit a weakness. This will encourage others and bring harmony.

5 Resolve your differences fast, as there's a much greater challenge on the way and you don't want to be preoccupied when it arrives. You need to muster all the support you can get to meet it. If you don't, you will be steamrollered out of the way and there'll be no way back.

6 It may be necessary to form new relationships, as you still don't have the firepower to crack an issue if you stay as you are. Make sure others are as committed as you. You — and they — can't afford to be half-hearted, or things will disintegrate.

No. 14
YANG • GREAT PROSPECTS

DAYOU

Today reveals you restraining your natural impulses to direct your energy in a positive – and possibly alternative – direction. Seldom will you get the kind of opportunity to succeed that is presenting itself now. You are blessed with inspiration and can see the bigger picture, which brings great success and potential wealth. You are now in a position to reap the benefits of recent hard work. Others will be surprised by your capacity for creativity and problem-solving, even those in positions of authority. This enables you to manage a process in a balanced way to produce a fantastic result, way beyond your wildest dreams. Be modest in enjoying this success, and the harvest you reap will multiply.

Messages

1 After recent difficulty, things are beginning to settle down. Keep your self-control, even now things are clearly going your way. The process has not yet finished and you could bite off more than you can chew.

2 You've got everything you need to succeed and can afford to take some risks. But don't be distracted or you'll get sidetracked. Keep going.

3 You need absolute and total focus to get there. Forget everything else; ignore others, but allow someone in a position of authority the chance to change things around. Success is just around the corner.

4 If you can restrain your natural impatience and not let others distract you, then you will reap remarkable success today. The news could be great, and it's certainly very welcome.

5 Some people are attracted to you because you are so sincere. Just give something up, and you'll be surprised how you will achieve what you want a thousand times over. It's time for charity.

6 There is great potential on the horizon, so just be patient today. Bite your lip and trust everything to chance – success will fall in your lap. Things couldn't get any better for your career, health and personal relationships.

No. 14

YIN • CLEARING YOUR HEAD

DAYOU
大有

You've come to recognize how to apply your skills most effectively, and the results will now become apparent. After a period of time focusing your energy on negative arguments, a change in climate has brought you to your senses, but may have caused some regret about your previous actions. You may have to give in to others in order to bring them on board, but your capacity to restore faith in a common purpose and unite others behind you is at its peak. This will release you to achieve your ambitions and assume a degree of responsibility you once thought was beyond you. You are about to become a catalyst for great changes with dramatic personal benefits. Keep your feet firmly on the ground.

Messages

1 You could feel that you've got to where you are without really being tested. You've achieved a great deal, but it will all count for nothing if you lose your sense of discipline. You don't need to change direction; your talent has not yet been fully exploited and there's much further to go than you think.

2 You're now fully resourced and have the assets at your disposal to support your programme. Your opinions carry a lot of weight and you have plenty of firepower at your disposal. Nothing can deflect you, and a clear victory stands before you.

3 A leadership opportunity presents itself. You've become recognized as someone with special skills by those who make the most important decisions. Make sacrifices for others, but don't prevaricate or compromise. Your time has come.

4 You don't need to try to compete any more. After some courageous decisions, everyone now recognizes your talent, and it's time to exploit this to the full. Maximize your advantage by pushing hard, but keep your head clear and employ self-restraint.

5 Don't get too close to the team you are leading. The exercising of authority and responsibility carries a degree of risk that over-familiarity could jeopardize. Sacrifice your personal needs and keep your distance. They will respect you all the more.

6 All you need now is to keep your patience. Nothing can stop you getting the result you want if you balance your personal ambition with the needs of others. Enjoy the moment.

No. 15

YANG • SELF-RESTRAINT

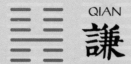

QIAN

謙

You need to be self-effacing today in order to cope with the problems you have experienced. There's a call to exercise moderation in everything you do, but be unflinching in your determination to do what's right. Contain your tendency to speak first and think later; observe events as though watching a movie, but don't interrupt them, as your part has not yet been revealed. It won't be clear at first what's best to do, but when the mist disappears it will become perfectly obvious, and this will allow you to bring a better balance into your personal and working relationships. This may involve travel or a change in location or even occupation.

Messages

1 You're not always naturally modest, but your outspokenness could reveal your plans to those you want to keep in the dark. You need to restrain yourself today, or you'll get nowhere. Make a positive decision but do it quietly.

2 If you contain yourself and don't show off too much, you will make others respect you more, and, with co-operation, you'll get what you want. Play down the great benefits you are about to reap and you'll enjoy it more.

3 You may not think you're too good for others – but that's how you can come across sometimes. You'll learn more if you fall in with the crowd today, and this will allow you to complete a job more successfully. It will work out well.

4 You've got rid of the biggest issues now, so slow down and take your time before dealing with the next one. A more considered and moderate approach to life is now called for, so don't make any commitments until another time.

5 You can't afford to let others take the lead. You can do it on your own, and this will improve the situation dramatically – but do it quietly or you'll lose the initiative.

6 You can be proud of what you've achieved. Hold no regrets about the actions you have taken, because they were made for the right reasons. Take responsibility on board, as you are now strong enough. Sort out what's fair and what is not and follow your intuition.

No. 15

YIN • BECOMING HUMBLE

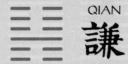

QIAN

謙

When some people become successful in their chosen career, pride and arrogance consume them and tip their behaviour over the edge. This could happen to you if you're not careful. Your life is settled and recent achievements have exceeded your own expectations, but you can have a tendency to enjoy the limelight too much. If left unrestrained this could lead to vanity and greed. These emotions can swamp a person's character and intentions, and change them beyond recognition. It's time to recognize that nature functions to bring those who are arrogant right down to earth and elevate to greatness those with humility. Modesty and self-restraint are required today. You need to become content with yourself before you can form lasting relationships with others. Step back and think of this when the applause dies down.

Messages

1 A visit from someone in authority is on the way. Don't overdo things; keep your modesty intact and understate your skills. They will recognize this as confidence in your abilities and a justified reward will arrive.

2 It's not always easy to keep your head when being complimented by everyone. This is a test of your ability to keep your achievements in perspective and give proper recognition to those who deserve it. Don't let them down.

3 You're gaining the support and trust of someone important by your example. Hard work and modesty is what drove you to this point, and you deserve the success that's coming. Don't lose your concentration or you will jeopardize all you've gained.

4 Keeping a balanced attitude is important today. You'll need to remain sober and assess the consequences, so that you see both sides of an issue before deciding what to do. Take your time and don't be rushed – operate at your own pace and your judgement will stay sound.

5 You're about to undergo a real test. Be patient and listen to what someone has to say – and then you need to be forceful, and not hesitate. It's not the time to delegate to others – you now need to go it alone. It will work out fine.

6 Maintain your composure in the face of the test that's coming. You'll be surprised at the opportunity this represents. It's a favourable time to embark on a major new project. The environment will become the focus of your attention, and everyone – even those who don't agree – will benefit.

No. 16
YANG ● READY FOR ACTION

YU

豫

A new era appears on the horizon for you, and it's time to start new ventures or change direction. After a period of harmony in all things surrounding you, a great prospect appears and you are ready for the challenge. Following this relatively dormant period, your life is about to change drastically. Be confident and forceful and enlist the support of others close to you. Fresh ideas, inventions and innovations abound, and this inspires you to become more creative, and even musical. It's time to act; cast off your inhibitions and go for it. There will never be a better time to prepare and implement a new project or change direction.

Messages

1 You may need to curb your enthusiasm, as you can see the big picture yet others can't. Keep it to yourself but use your powers of persuasion to bring others with you. Recognition is coming at last.

2 Deal with each matter one at a time and look for the early warning signs. But don't look too far ahead, or you'll miss something really important. Proceed with caution in your decision and take it slowly.

3 The time for self-restraint is gone and you've waited long enough for someone else to take the lead. Go for it now – forget the past and let the future unfold. Sometimes you have to give to receive.

4 Be positive in order to achieve the success that you deserve. The timing is just right for self-development – for a new team or relationship to form and then go forward together. Financing opportunities are on the cards.

5 There are always issues to be resolved, but these are merely short-term. It's only natural, and it doesn't matter in the long run, as they will all be dismissed, so don't let minor problems ruin your personal and working relationships.

6 You've gone up the wrong alley. It could even look to others like you've been dishonest. It's not too late to do something about it. Alter your course now or you'll come to regret it.

No. 16
YIN • BEING PREPARED

YU

豫

Every day the world turns and reveals a new spectrum of possibilities. After a stable period in your life, things are about to change. You need to prepare now, as you won't get the chance later. A renewed enthusiasm is on the cards, and it will find a unique form of expression in you. This could be a musical or other creative accomplishment. There will be an unexpected signal that something needs rebuilding. Look closer and examine it fully. It's a signal for you to get ready for action, and you'll find a solution which works. Know your limitations and this will prepare you to absorb the shock of discovering what was wrong. Take note of someone else's advice when it's offered. You will need their help.

Messages

1 Although the mood around you seems harmonious, there's an awkward situation developing. Maintain a low profile and especially keep your opinions to yourself, or you'll invite problems. Wait for things to move on before rejoining a group.

2 Polish your antennae and pick up the subtle messages. Don't be fooled by the noise and reactions of others; be guided by your own views on the matters arising, and don't let yourself be swayed by another's selfish arguments. You know what you want, so stick to it.

3 A degree of caution has developed. Normally this would be good news, but you need to take the initiative and push hard now; waiting around for others to take the lead won't work. Go it alone, if you have to – you've nothing to lose.

4 You're adjusting to a new set of circumstances and everything will now come together nicely. It's like completing a jigsaw. Others will see the advantage of co-operating with you and will assist in finding the final pieces. Take a risk, make an investment and it will pay off.

5 Although you're getting there, you need to ensure that those advising you know what they're about. Assess their skills carefully, so they don't scupper what you've already achieved. Then you will survive the scare which is heading your way.

6 You can't survive for ever on past achievements. A note of disharmony is about to be sounded; listen out for it, and be alert. Feel the change in wind direction and alter your course. This will limit the damage, and you may escape completely unharmed.

No. 17
YANG • FOLLOWING THE RIGHT COURSE

SUI

隨

You've recently been around someone with a greater understanding of what's important and a shared sense of purpose. Think about what drives them and some of it will rub off on you. Just as a river takes its course from nature and winds around the obstacles placed in its way, adaptability is the key to success – in both the natural and physical world. And this is the attribute you most need to develop in order to succeed. Get a grip on what's really important in your life and leave others to their own devices, as they will only fail while you succeed. Your inner doubts and prejudices need to be addressed, but you can't do this on your own. Rest and recuperation are called for; this will give you the freedom to think things through, and your leadership skills will then come to the fore.

Messages

1 You've just got to let go of certain long-held beliefs, because they haven't worked for you. Things could change quickly in your career, and you need guidance from someone better qualified. On the other hand, your social life couldn't be better, but you must try to slow down.

2 You run the risk of completely losing your grip on what's important and what isn't. You can't blame anyone else if you become self-obsessed, so jettison the unimportant things in your life and focus on those you love. The anguish should then evaporate.

3 At last, the important things in life are coming into sharper focus. Let go of your old preoccupations and your life will change for the better. This may include reviewing your friendships.

4 Don't become hooked on one thing or let someone flatter you in order to get their own way. Chance dictates events, not your own preferences, so just let things happen. You can then choose the best route once your options have crystallized.

5 It's time to become more focused. You've been distracted, and this has distorted the future opportunities available to you. Choose only one thing, concentrate on it and do it well. Aim high, because the prospects are good.

6 You just have to admit that trying to help others has backfired, although you are still expected to lead the way in many instances, despite the blow to your reputation. Take some time out to focus on your own needs and leave others to their own fate.

No. 17

YIN • FINDING SOLUTIONS

SUI

You are a link in a chain reaction at the moment. You can't be expected to compensate for others' inabilities to see what they need to do, so just leave it alone. Focus on your own contribution exclusively; then the others will fall in line. In nature, the rivers which find the path of least resistance and work around obstacles also mould the earth through their action. This is how you need to conduct yourself, and others will respond. An outward display of calmness will be the right course of action, and this will give someone close a chance to see what's really important. They have become distracted and need your help to redirect them onto the right path. Keep faith in your principles, don't give up and others will follow your example.

Messages

1 Changes are taking place which will require you to adjust your sight and possibly the location. It's like a building has collapsed and you lived in it. Start over again if you need to, but rescue important lessons from the debris. Then you can rebuild.

2 Are you sure you are heading where you really want to be? You might be following others rather than deciding for yourself. Don't blame someone else if things turn sour, since you didn't take the initiative when you could have. Maybe you should do this now.

3 You might need to jettison old relationships in response to the changes now taking place. This will allow you to form new ones with people better placed to help you. You need to relax and go with the flow. It could mean moving to a new location, but you'll benefit from it.

4 You're not getting the support you deserve. Maybe you're just speaking to the wrong people. Change direction and go it alone, but be wary of entering into an agreement too hastily. You need to assess things carefully first.

5 It's time to strive for the best, since it's there before you. Focus exclusively on one major objective and your other goals will fall into place. You'll capture everything you ask for at the moment, so aim high.

6 You've skirted around an issue lately but the focus of attention is now falling upon you. Take the responsibility on board. Others need your guidance and advice more than you think. Help protect them, and they will thank you for ever.

No. 18

YANG ● VALUABLE INSIGHT

GU

Corruption arises when something becomes infectious or when resistance to change allows something rotten to develop. Some form of emotional disease appears to be spreading, and it's leading to decay. Something in the air just doesn't smell right for you at the moment. A weak point has developed in a situation or relationship and needs repairing. Be prepared and on your guard, or you'll be overwhelmed by forces beyond your control. Deal with what's unhealthy, corrupt or false – both in your professional and personal relationships – in a constructive and positive way. Cut it out before it spreads. This is not a time to act in haste, but you will need to persevere to get out of the current situation.

Messages

1 No matter how close to you someone is now, you should come to recognize their misdeeds and distance yourself – but keep it quiet for the time being. You may need help from a member of your family.

2 You need to become a reconciler of other people's opinions today. You may regret things you've done in the past, which could hurt those close to you. Don't take sides and try to stay in everyone's good books, and this should help you to repair the damage.

3 Stop finding fault in everything. Your rush to condemn can appear heartless, when deep down you are really caring. Just because something's wrong doesn't mean you can't still learn from it.

4 You appear to have allowed issues to stagnate for some time now, and things could get worse before they get better. If you confront everything that's wrong head-on, you'll achieve the opposite of what you intended, so take your time and things will change for the better along with the season.

5 To convince someone that what they're doing is wrong you must be prepared to compliment them. Let them begin to see their errors through their own experience; criticism won't work. They will then support you and you will feel no regrets.

6 Don't accuse others unless you are squeaky clean yourself. Setting an example is far more effective than shouting – so try not to adopt a cynical attitude. Be patient, and this will allow you to bring better knowledge and more skill to the current situation.

No. 18

YIN • PATIENCE NEEDED

GU

蠱

Something has to die back before the process of rebirth can begin. Decay has set in, and it appears that nothing can be done. Let things run their course, and within three days a change of direction will occur. This will shake things up and could imply a removal or enforced reorganization. This may affect your position or location.

Sometimes we need to stir things up a little to get a reaction going. Only then can our energy create real momentum to resolve matters and enable progress to be made. Persistence is going to be the key, so you may need to reconsider your attitude and become more flexible; the alternative could be very uncomfortable indeed.

Messages

1 Sometimes the same routine seems comfortable, whereas all you're doing is treading water and going nowhere. You should push out of this comfort zone, as it's not healthy. A relationship between father and son could become destructive. This needs addressing and putting in perspective.

2 Your history could come back to haunt you. Think about what you did and how things – and you – have changed. Look objectively, and be sensitive. Don't take female advice today – it won't help.

3 You may already be trying too hard to remedy something that happened years ago. It's in the past, and there's no lingering issue – it's all in your mind. Your perspective needs reviewing – then it will simply fade from memory.

4 A state of disharmony may have been allowed to fester longer than it should. This will only cause further distress if you let it continue. Try to renew a relationship, to start to repair the damage. It may be uncomfortable at first but it will get easier.

5 A reforming process has begun and you're at the centre of it. Rebuild the bridges and reinforce the basis of a mutual understanding. Turning negative messages into positive lessons is your challenge. It's a useful technique to learn at this point.

6 Sometimes a lingering problem drives us into submission and we give up. This would be very unwise. You need to set an example to others never to give up while there's hope. Persistence and perseverance are the name of the game. Your reward is coming; you won't have to wait long.

No. 19
YANG • TRANSFORMING POWER

LIN

臨

You're getting closer today to what you desire. It's as if a winter of discontent is ending, and promotion or a new start is in the air. This momentum is unstoppable, but you can only make progress by reconciling yourself with others. You will need to be flexible and adaptable to others' views; show some kindness and an understanding of their position. People can change – so allow them to, and all misunderstandings will evaporate from your life, creating lasting relationships. It's like springtime: you have arrived at the point of renewal in all things, and you should become more optimistic regarding the future.

Messages

1 Open your mind and don't respond too quickly to questions. You'll be amazed what doors will open up for you today. Someone in a position of authority could be more than helpful.

2 Take your time; just hold off for a while and something will happen to confirm you are already on the right path. You're due to get support from an unexpected direction and you can celebrate afterwards.

3 Something entirely unexpected is about to fall into your lap. You'll be subjected to great temptations today but you must resist them and look for something else to occupy your attention. Anticipate the downside and you won't make the wrong decisions.

4 The web of confusion is unravelling fast. You're on the right path and this will soon become evident, so stick with it. The other choices will then fall away and leave a clear course of action for you.

5 The best choice will be made if you consult someone with the experience you don't yet possess. If possible, let them take over the responsibility while you look on. This will smooth the process considerably.

6 Don't give up on your natural ability to be flexible and see others' points of view. Make a bigger commitment to your objectives and throw yourself into new ventures. You'll achieve what you want this way, and the benefits could be staggering.

No. 19
YIN ● GETTING CLOSER

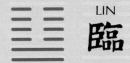

LIN
臨

Something's heading in your direction. You always hoped you might get there, but were never really convinced. Well, now it's happening, but matters will develop at their own natural pace – you cannot dictate the speed with which others reach their decisions. A new dawn is arriving. Just as the approach of spring in nature's cycle was always a source of hope to ancient cultures, giving them encourage-ment at winter's low point when their very survival was in question, so you should not try to hurry things. They will take their own time. Tolerance and patience are required, and this could leave you feeling uncomfortable – but it will be worth it. Those who know less than you have to discover the limits of their own capabilities; then, you can all enjoy the result when it comes.

Messages

1 There are others who support your opinions enthusiastically. This should give you the confidence to press ahead. When asked to make a decision, take your time and don't be rushed. Weigh the evidence carefully.

2 You have a renewed sense of purpose at the moment, and it's been helped by your more sober approach to everything. Stick with it; you're getting closer to climbing that ladder. Then, you can see better where you're going.

3 Everything you touch turns out right today, but don't get over-confident. Everyone's entitled to a run of good fortune, and this one's for you – but keep things in perspective. It's just your turn, that's all.

4 You'll slot into a new position and level of responsibility with ease. In fact, you will wonder what you were so concerned about. You may need to get out of an arrangement you made, because you don't need it any more. Someone will understand.

5 Assuming authority and responsibility is one thing; learning to delegate and relinquish a little power is quite another. Unless you learn to trust others to complete a job, you'll become over-stretched and stressed out. Your ambition will then be limited, and this will hold you back.

6 A momentous promotion or deal is on the way. You've surpassed even your own expectations, and others in a strong position have come to recognize your contribution. Enjoy the moment and ensure you get your fair reward.

No. 20

YANG ● CONTEMPLATION

GUAN

觀

You're full of confidence at the moment. This gives you unusual insight, and you have the capacity to observe situations from a different perspective to others. This grants you a clarity of vision which you can use to influence people. Your convictions are now deeply embedded. You need to come to recognize what's fundamentally important in your life and how certain natural laws govern all events. If you focus on what's really of value, other matters will fall into place. The outcome is that your opinion will be taken seriously in your career activities, and this will also be reflected in your personal relationships. All of those relationships will move to a higher level as a result.

Messages

1 You're not going to get what you want and things don't look good. Are you sure you're not just dealing with the symptoms rather than the cause? Address the real personal issues; you won't make progress until you focus on this.

2 You need to develop a wider view of the world and your place in it. Don't be fooled by flattery, as it will only reinforce your prejudices and distract you from the really important matters you need to address.

3 You can't see the wood for the trees. There's too much going on for you to decide which way to go, so step back and think for a while. You need to see where you fit into the world as a whole, and not be totally absorbed by personal issues.

4 After a setback, you're about to extend your social network and become an important cog in a much larger wheel. This could involve travelling a great distance. Take advantage of this opportunity; the time is right now.

5 Your insight enables you to see others' positions in a clear light and how you interact with them. They recognize you for this, and your personal standing can be improved dramatically. You'll recover now from a recent setback and make rapid progress.

6 No one will blame you if you lead the way. Your detachment from a situation gives you the strength to act without restraint, so don't have any second thoughts and get on with it. The risks are more apparent than they appear.

No. 20

YIN • COLLECTING YOUR THOUGHTS

GUAN

觀

At the moment it feels like you're watching life from a distance, like a movie with you at centre stage. A golden period in your life could be nearing its conclusion. In nature, when the weather is settled and the wind changes, this usually indicates a dramatic shift. This is happening in your current circumstances, but it's taking time and all you can do is watch and wait.

Collect your thoughts before making a move. You need to become contemplative and explore what you really want to achieve. This will clear your head and clarify your vision. Reflect on where you stand on the issues now being revealed to you, and your judgement will improve. You need to start something completely new now. Take your time and you'll get it right.

Messages

1 Put your thinking cap on. There are connections you've missed, but you've been distracted by other jobs you were given. Look closer at the detail. If you still can't spot the core problems, forget it and carry on; they'll resolve themselves eventually.

2 You're going to have to decide whether to stick to what you know or push the boundaries of your ambition. Nothing ventured, nothing gained. Take a quick look at the wider picture and decide whether you're really ready for more responsibility. You may need to get some lessons quickly.

3 At the moment it's how you fit into the world that will dictate what you achieve, not your dreams. Be prepared to take new ideas on board; this will shift your direction, but you need to think through the consequences a bit more before deciding which to choose. You'll learn from this process.

4 Get involved with a wider social issue. Don't restrict yourself to the mundane and parochial – you're much better than that. You're about to assume a wider responsibility which will affect many people. Enjoy it.

5 Your judgements will have far-reaching consequences. Make sure you've assessed all the connections between the different parties who will be affected. You won't then be blamed for any side effects, but you will get a lot of credit for the benefits.

6 You can afford to be an independent observer at the moment. You have restrained your ego and demonstrated a keen eye for quality. You'll be asked to make an assessment for someone in authority. Take it on – they're depending on you.

No. 21
YANG • CLEAR VISION

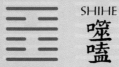

SHIHE

噬嗑

A breakthrough is imminent – and it's about time, too! The deadwood and excuses are being cleared away, and it's time to get rid of your personal excess baggage and rearrange things. You cannot compromise or you'll be suffocated by the past. Be frank and honest with yourself and others. The current situation could interfere with personal relationships if you aren't reasonable and learn to reciprocate. The problems you face are tangible and real and won't go away on their own, so don't bury your head in the sand any longer. It's precisely because you did this in the past that misunderstandings have arisen, and this has led to confusion. Be firm and detached in your decisions and they will work out.

Messages

1 You should have taken more time over something and it's all gone horribly wrong. You could receive a rebuke for something you've done, but you don't get it wrong very often. Just take it on the chin and move on.

2 Those who continue to ignore mistakes will be destined to repeat them – but you cannot revisit the past. Take time off if you can. Don't try too hard, and things will turn around.

3 While you think what you're doing is right, there will be painful setbacks and others could put obstacles in your way. Remember your old friends and get support from them. Be strengthened by this and forge ahead anyway.

4 You appear to be overwhelmed by what confronts you. The breakthrough has arrived. Work around any problems rather than confronting them head-on, and you'll identify their weak spots and then make progress.

5 Don't be indecisive. What you have lost can now be found again; choose a path and stick to it, even if it exposes your weaknesses. Sometimes we're just being tested. Honesty will prevail.

6 If you don't recognize your own limitations very quickly, disaster could ensue. Stop what you're doing, overcome your insecurity, step back, consult others, then try again.

No. 21

YIN • RECOVERING COMPOSURE

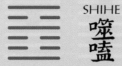

SHIHE

噬嗑

Something's been eating away at you for some time now. This has weakened your willpower and sapped your energy. You will need all your powers of recovery to get through the obstacles that have been put in your way. Once you've discovered the truth, this will give you the authority to compel others to resolve a situation. It could be the resolution of a legal dispute or clearing away a major obstacle to progress. This will create a sudden clarity through your own efforts, which will act like a bolt of lightning and enable everyone to see things clearly. There may be penalties imposed for infringements. A way forward will, however, become clear to everyone – thanks to you. And then you can decide what you want to do next.

Messages

1 You're about to be taught a lesson you shouldn't forget. There's a stalemate on the horizon, and you can't do anything to stop it. This will have the consequence of restricting your options and you might feel cornered. Just wait and things will change for the better, but this could take some time.

2 Your first big loss is where you learn the greatest lesson. You probably pushed things too far and tried to screw everything out of a situation. If you come away unscathed, then think yourself lucky. Lick your wounds and move on.

3 You need to get through to the other side. It won't be easy and will require a certain amount of discomfort, or even distaste, as you may be forced to deal with something beneath your dignity. Put up with it; it's just a minor irritation.

4 You're going to discover something unexpected and, although you will be shocked, it will turn out to be a challenge you can deal with. Stand firm and learn from the experience – it will strengthen your resolve and make you more determined. A tricky situation will then be settled.

5 You're aware of the options available to you but you can't bring yourself to make that decision. Go for it anyway, and take a wild guess if you need to. It will release you from the pain of uncertainty and you will find you were right all along.

6 It's not that some people cannot see; it's just that they won't. Others can't see where you're coming from – so you need to take their views on board before convincing them. If you don't listen to them, then you'll suffer the consequences.

No. 22
YANG • FACILITATOR

BI
貴

Clarity and tranquillity are on offer for you at the moment, but it's not the best time for making important decisions. Creative and artistic endeavours are at the forefront now. You need to enjoy this and grasp the moment, as it won't last for ever. Suddenly a light has been switched on, and this will bring clarity to all your ventures. Showing off will work against you, so be restrained and your qualities will shine through to others even stronger. Don't ask for anything and you'll get more than you ever expected. Take your time and allow close associates to be working quietly for your benefit. This is a time of grace and enrichment of the soul, so make the most of it and be contented.

Messages

1 You'll be valued for yourself, not for your deeds. Don't take any shortcuts, but also don't be afraid to take chances. It's a time to make preparation, as a new era is coming into your life.

2 Don't be fooled by appearances. Examine what's behind a particular development before acting; you may be missing something, and it might be just too good to be true.

3 You're having an interesting and fulfilling experience, but don't forget to learn from it. You desire more than mere material success and you can achieve it if you approach matters cautiously. A recent setback will clear if you give it a chance.

4 A development in the media is in prospect, and indicates a period of good fortune. You can either become a celebrity, and evaporate into the night like a shooting star, or you can settle for inner contentment and be happy with yourself. But you can't have both.

5 You want to get closer to someone but you're not sure you're good enough. Follow your heart and you'll be delighted with the outcome. Things should go more smoothly afterwards.

6 Keep it simple and open your eyes to the opportunities which are about to present themselves. It's a blessing in disguise. You don't need to advertize your capabilities any more; they're there for all to see, and are being recognized by others.

No. 22
YIN • REWARDING INITIATIVE

BI

贲

You can afford to enjoy yourself now, as this should be a time to celebrate. You came through a tricky patch and, though it's taken time, it's been worth the wait. A dispute has also been resolved after a vicious difference of opinion. It won't be enough today to just contemplate something and resolve it only in your head; take the courage to initiate overdue changes and bear full responsibility. When you've done this, it's time to take advantage of the opportunity you now have to harvest what's yours. You deserve it, after bringing matters to a head and convincing others you could do the job. Enjoy the applause and accolades that will now come your way. Relax and take pleasure in the moment, but don't forget to thank those who helped you get where you are – you'll need them again in future.

Messages

1 A testing period has now passed and you're entering a time of balance and a state of harmony with others. You're in control of your own destiny. Keep a clear head and avoid over-indulgence, as you could be dragged back again if you're not careful.

2 It's not how things look but what they really mean to you that matters. Don't let someone paper over the cracks – see through the mirage and get to the bottom of things. You need to discover some uncomfortable truths.

3 Even though things are going well, you're not there yet. Don't confuse material gain with your own contentedness. How you got to where you are matters more than the material possessions you've accumulated; that's why it's said to be better to travel than to arrive.

4 You're faced with two choices: one is complex and risky with enormous potential, and the other is more simple and restrained. You're about to discover which is the most important to you. Don't be deceived by appearances, or you may bite off more than you can chew.

5 It's time to get closer to someone, but you may be wondering whether you're good enough. What matters is that your intentions are honest and sincere. Despite a setback which occurs at first, the outcome will bring you both happiness.

6 Keep it simple and you won't make mistakes. There are core codes of conduct that are very important to you, and you may need to reveal those feelings to another. Stick to your priniciples and you can't fail.

No. 23
YANG ● RELYING ON OTHERS

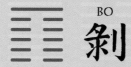

BO

剝

Things could deteriorate rapidly if you're not careful. Be on your guard, especially in affairs of finance and social events. If you want people to be glad to meet you, you must be glad to meet them – and show it. If you get the chance to avoid attending something, then it's best to grab it. Your health could also suffer, so take precautions. Spend time in the fresh air and try to stabilize matters; don't attempt anything dramatically different. Keep a low profile and this will help you avoid misunderstandings. You may need the assistance of someone outside your circle of friends to help turn things around.

Messages

1 This is an uncomfortable time and you shouldn't try to resolve the irreconcilable. You are being undermined by others you currently think of as unimportant. Limit the damage, because you can't do anything about it.

2 Your allies have vanished. Don't pretend you can do without them completely or you'll get hurt. It's not going to be an easy ride. Be patient.

3 You may need to work with those you consider of a lesser standing than yourself in order to escape from the current predicament, because the others are going to be of no help at all. Be cautious, and this will enable you to avoid dreadful errors.

4 Something dangerous is approaching and cannot be reversed. Be careful, or you'll suffer a heavy defeat or loss. You need insurance or protection – quickly.

5 Best to put some distance between you and close colleagues for now. They'll come round to your point of view and you will benefit materially. Things will change for the better in due course.

6 Be patient, and a fraught period will come to an end. If you are currently in a legal wrangle, it may now turn in your favour. Those who pursued their own agendas against you are doomed to failure, and you will win through. Enjoy the feeling of success.

No. 23

YIN • RETHINKING THINGS

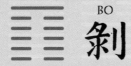

BO

剝

All you've achieved recently could be put at risk if you don't watch out. Things you were not aware of are revealing themselves, and differences of opinion have been exposed. You've devoted all your efforts to resolving matters you thought were settled. Think again and be on your guard, as it's still not over. Misunderstandings may yet arise and legal redress may be required. It isn't cowardice but wisdom to be brave enough to submit to doing nothing. You can't dictate the pace with which certain events must now unfold. Be careful what you say at social events, as it could backfire. Sometimes you may be too close to matters to see all the issues clearly; consult others who are qualified to provide an independent view.

Messages

1 There's an opposition gathering momentum and you could be right in the way. Your position is weakening, and you need to start taking action to rally support and build a framework to protect yourself. Start today.

2 A cautious approach is required, since negative arguments have been creeping up on you, and this is testing your resolve. Address the reasons why your position is under threat, because you won't get the opportunity again; it will be too late, and the cycle will have moved on.

3 Avoiding being outflanked should be your immediate priority. Distance yourself from those working against you – they've had their say and it's not relevant any more. Now you need to repair the damage in your own way, and then the tide will turn in your favour.

4 You're on the brink of a defeat. Maybe your tactics were wrong, as you chose the wrong arguments at the wrong time. Never mind; you're now strong enough to cope. Take it on the chin, lick your wounds and move on. There will be another chance.

5 Co-operation will resolve the issues and allow you to recover from a recent setback. This may require putting a distance between you and someone you thought was an ally. A material gain will then arrive as if by chance, and you can then celebrate with those who depend on you.

6 The deterioration cycle is turning full circle in your favour. Negative attitudes are being reversed, and you can now sort out the problems without delay. You've been waiting for this for ages. Get on with it.

No. 24

YANG • STRENGTH BY RENEWAL

FU

Things are turning to your advantage, after what's been a difficult and prolonged period of uncertainty, giving you the opportunity to start over again. It's not unusual to reach rock bottom before things begin to turn around. Matters may now be drawing to a close. Repair and recovery are in store, and it's like spring has come early. New career opportunities and relationships are heading your way. You may well be recovering from a particular setback or illness, but the cycle of life will present new energy and put a spring in your step. Take care, however, to look before you leap, in order to reap the greatest benefit. Don't push things too far too soon – give them time to develop naturally.

Messages

1 Something unusual presents itself – something you wouldn't normally do. You may need to swallow your pride and give it a go now – you can't lose. You will profit from it.

2 It's easier to do the right things if others go the same way. Follow your friends' advice; you're in good company at the moment, and the change in direction will be more painless.

3 Don't be indecisive – it just annoys others – and forget the past. Things are going to improve, so make the best of your current situation. The pace of development could be frustratingly slow, however, and you will need to restrain your impatience.

4 An opportunity presents itself and you may need to go it alone, but keep a clear head or you'll go the wrong way. Don't be distracted by the decision of others; just ignore them.

5 You are aware that a real opportunity is becoming available. To get the best from the opportunity, you must avoid misunderstandings. Be clear what you mean and repeat it if necessary.

6 You've missed a great opportunity because you were too slow to respond to others' needs. Your competitive instincts may have disturbed your clarity of vision. Just wait, for now, before attempting to make progress; the opportunity will come round again.

No. 24
YIN • A FRESH START

FU

An opportunity to start all over again is presenting itself. Nature's action behaves like clockwork; it's like the winter solstice is over and the days are getting lighter. The process takes its natural course and returns to the beginning to start afresh once more. This is what's happening to you today. You may be forced to go back to the beginning of something, and this could be frustrating, as you thought you'd done enough. A renewed partnership or commercial arrangement may need to be put in place to enable you to reach your goal. This requires careful preparation. If you don't settle the outstanding issues, they will come back to bite you. Travelling will be involved in the near term, but this is just part of starting something new.

Messages

1 You could be presented with an opportunity that violates what you believe in. It could be a renewed friendship or rediscovered information. Despite your caution, it's worth taking up an offer which will enable you to change direction.

2 There's a short journey coming along. Don't hesitate to take advantage of what's on offer and use it as a learning exercise. You'll come back stronger and can only benefit from the experience.

3 It's not the time to be indecisive. There is no optimal, risk-free route, so don't dither when considering the options, or this may irritate someone. Choose your course, take responsibility for what happens and plough on regardless. Be brave and accept the consequences.

4 It could be that the grass is greener somewhere else, but not everyone is convinced. Once the momentum gathers pace, you may find that friends and colleagues fall by the wayside and you're on your own. Be prepared – you may need to get some help.

5 It's time to ring the changes and accept a new challenge. Avoid any misunderstandings about your motives by stating your position clearly to those around you. Then, there will be no trouble when you take on more responsibility.

6 An opportunity to embark on a new venture could escape your grasp if you don't act quickly. Don't let it. If you miss it, then it could be a long time before the chance arises again. Grab it while it's there.

No. 25
YANG • EYES WIDE OPEN

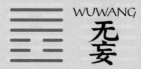

WUWANG
无妄

Your tendency to plan ahead and try to anticipate events should be set aside for the moment. The natural order of things to which you have become accustomed may be challenged. You need to open your eyes and look in completely the opposite direction. Be prepared for a surprise – but you still won't see it coming. Spontaneity and discovery are the name of the game, rather than your usual search for certainty and security. It requires an altogether different mindset. This will generate intrigue and heighten the pleasure derived from close personal relationships, and also provide solutions to sticky problems.

Messages

1 If you let the gods guide you in your decision-making, it will produce success. It's not the time for rational and scientific assessment; the role of chance is too overwhelming. Trust your instincts and don't try to be too organized.

2 There's a spectacular outcome on its way. Don't prevaricate or you'll lose the opportunity. It's only when you've done the hard work that you can reap a harvest. Attention to detail is still called for.

3 Something unsettling and unfortunate is on its way, and it may take time for you to recover – but it will soon pass. Don't build up your expectations. Be realistic.

4 Don't follow others blindly or you could become the big loser; they have their own agendas. Follow your instincts – they are far more trustworthy.

5 What happens to you next appears unexpected, but it's your own fault. You could have seen it coming, in fact. Look at yourself and your motives, and don't waste your energy on useless projects.

6 Don't try to make any progress or even try to be helpful; it would be a grave error, because you just don't have the skill-set to sort things out. Lie low – or, better yet, hide if you can.

No. 25
YIN • RETREAT QUIETLY

WUWANG
无妄

You arrived at your current predicament by getting involved in something you might not have fully understood. This was out of innocence rather than gullibility. Sometimes it's best to extricate yourself from a situation and allow matters to take their course, and then just see where you can fit it. You can be inclined to be impatient and this makes you reckless, as you want to stir things up. This would be an error at the moment. You won't be able to resolve another's issues; they have to do this for themselves, in order to become stronger and more independent, and able to make their own correct choices. You can't do it for them. It's because you may have done so in the past that they haven't learned the lessons. Keep your eyes wide open and allow others to learn from their own experience.

Messages

1 You don't need to worry about what you're doing – it's the right thing. Nothing can deflect you now and, while others may have needed some convincing, they now understand your point of view and the doubts have evaporated. Carry on.

2 Keep your concentration. You have been lucky recently without making much of an effort, and everything's come off. This is all about to change. Prepare yourself and organize your belongings and finances; you may need to go somewhere quickly.

3 A setback is about to arise and you may have been a little gullible. You sometimes accept the views of others without any evidence – and this trusting nature may come to haunt you today. Just take it on the chin – it will soon pass – but expect some financial damage.

4 Make instinctive decisions today, as your perception is keen. After an unforeseen health setback, you'll recover and be stronger. A renewed confidence will accelerate your progress, and you'll be back in full swing.

5 Something inside your head has unexpectedly become a problem. External remedies won't work, as this just papers over the cracks; you need to look inside yourself for the solution. Take time to explore your inner world and the solution will reveal itself to you.

6 You're stuck in a rut and not sure which way to turn. There's nothing you can do to help matters; step back and don't get involved. Don't try to travel distances, either, as this can't help – and may even make things worse.

No. 26
YANG • EXPLOSIVE ENERGY

DACHU

大畜

Powerful forces have given you an excess supply of energy which, if you time it right, will convert into far-reaching success way beyond your imagination. Matters of public service and leadership of certain groups of people allows you to extend your circle of influence tremendously. Creative endeavours are paramount, and you're blessed with an unusual maturity in all aspects of your life. Don't be afraid to look fear in the face. This is an exciting time and you should take courage in this knowledge. Personal relationships could literally blossom overnight, fostering a maturity you never knew you possessed.

Messages

1 Restrain your natural inclination to act quickly and spontaneously; the time is not right, so take no action. Stop the process and bide your time – you'll know when to make your move.

2 Stay where you are and don't look for conflict, or you'll regret it. You need to rebuild relationships before moving ahead, as your health may come under pressure and you'll require the help of others.

3 A surprising opportunity is in the offing, and you may be joined by someone unexpected. Don't rush into anything, however, as caution is the key to success. Your creative power is at its peak.

4 Something's been holding you back and it's made you stronger. This stored energy is about to be released to your advantage, and the upside potential is enormous.

5 It's the root of a problem which needs sorting out, not the branches. Get down to basics and avoid pointless arguments, and you'll be amazed how much progress you make. You could even end up in a position of surprising authority.

6 Even if you do nothing, everything is about to fall into your lap and all your innermost desires could be achieved. There's nothing to hold back your dreams any more. Choose your time and enjoy unparalleled success.

No. 26

YIN • REACHING THE PEAK

DACHU

You've worked hard to accumulate the knowledge and experience you possess, and will now achieve more than you could have expected or imagined. It's time to profit from your investment, and embarking on a major new enterprise is on the cards. It's difficult at this point for you to comprehend what you are going to accomplish. You will move mountains and be at the centre of dramatic changes. Recording or memorizing what you're doing will become critical to moving forward. Take one issue at a time and prioritize them, so you don't become distracted by the agendas of others. This will concentrate your attention on the matter in hand and help you accelerate your progress.

Messages

1 Things seem OK at the moment, but there's danger around the corner. You won't see it coming, and there will be no advance warning. It's not a good time to try something new or travel a great distance; just hang around and it will soon pass.

2 Although you might want to press ahead, it will be difficult to make any genuine progress. Things are a little fraught and others need to settle down and return to first base. Only then can the necessary repairs be made.

3 Problems are resolving themselves and a clear solution will now present itself. You just need to take your time. When you get the signal to move, think before you speak or travel. You won't regret it.

4 Instead of wasting your time on fruitless learning and pursuits, you now have the energy to take advantage of a great opportunity coming your way. Grab it – the time is right.

5 When you're presented with a problem you must attack the source, not the outcome. What you see is the result of decay and bad practice, so you need to ensure others get back to basics.

6 A contentedness will wrap itself around you today. Everything is within your grasp – just choose your timing and take a risk. The gods are with you and you won't fail.

No. 27

YANG ● SUPPORTING OTHERS

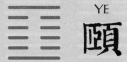

YE

颐

At this time you can contribute significantly to the career and personal lives of friends and colleagues – but you must be guarded in what you say. You're acting out a typical scene in the cycle of life, and providing the nourishment for others to grow and accomplish their dreams. This takes courage – the greatest virtue – and there is a risk that you may end up extending yourself too far. But creativity, however, knows no bounds. Cultivate your natural capacity to adapt. Resist going over the top, but don't prevaricate, because your judgement is your strength today.

Messages

1 You're becoming aware how much better off others are compared to you, but you mustn't allow this knowledge to create resentment and cause trouble. If you're not careful, this could become an obsession and very destructive.

2 Don't extend an argument or debate too far. It will only have the opposite effect to the one you want, and cause resentment in others. You cannot succeed in your present course of action, so it's time to change tack.

3 You're looking in the wrong place for solutions to your problems and it's influencing your behaviour, which has deteriorated. Examine your motives carefully or you'll lose out.

4 You could become extraordinarily helpful to others, so let them express their needs. You might, however, require some help, or you'll be out of your depth. Keep searching for it.

5 Don't go it alone – you haven't got the necessary ammunition. Be patient and help will arrive. Travelling does not bode well at the moment.

6 Your sense of duty is at its peak, but don't let the past dictate how you behave. It's time for a new beginning, and you should now take advantage of the many improvements taking place all around you by bringing others into the equation.

No. 27
YIN • JOINT DECISIONS

YE

We sometimes need the support of others to fulfil our ambitions; we can't do everything on our own. Just as flowers and plants cling to each other to grow towards the sky, so you need to pay close attention to what someone says to you today. You will use this advice – and you must be open to receiving it.

Only by expressing what you actually feel will this let others know how to support you. Just choose your words carefully. So, open up, disclose your feelings and the feedback will encourage you. Listen to it. This will enable you to reach a better decision, and it will be the correct one.

Messages

1 It's best to ignore the benefits others have enjoyed; everyone seeks contentedness in different ways. The only certainty is that material possessions create the illusion of happiness. Don't be distracted by what others have – find your own route to success.

2 There are correct procedures and incorrect ones. If you choose a shortcut today, it will backfire badly. Stick to the well-trodden path and use the wisdom of those who've been there before.

3 You may consult the wrong person in connection with an issue that needs resolving. Look elsewhere, as their motives are different to yours. You'll then get the help that you need, rather than the advice you've been offered.

4 Offer advice to those who need it today. Even though they may be in a position of authority, you're in a strong position and it will be welcomed. Others may be clever, but you offer them wisdom; the two are not the same.

5 Although you think you have the solution to another's problem, it's not your position to resolve it. Choose your words carefully, and offer an opinion only when asked. You can't solve it for them – they must arrive at the answer after a careful nudge from you.

6 It's a great time for you to grasp the nettle of responsibility and take a lead. Jettison any doubts and forget past mistakes. You cannot fail, so there's no point in waiting.

No. 28

YANG • CRITICAL MASS

DAGUO

大過

Matters are coming to a head and things could go either way. It's like a nuclear reactor overheating; there's a lot going on and you are not in control of events. Your reputation will be measured not by your strength but how you choose to use it. If you lose your nerve the whole edifice could collapse around you, so hold steady and prepare an escape route. Stand your ground and focus your natural energy. If necessary, let something go that's had its day or it will poison your future. This is a decisive time, and whether you shoot off in one direction or another depends on your composure, considered judgement and self-restraint.

Messages

1 Before you start something, assess it in great detail. Something dramatic is in the air, and you cannot be too careful at this point. Take your time and don't be rushed into a decision.

2 There are others looking to you for guidance. They need you to offer your views and show them the way. You can revitalize a situation, but if you keep it a secret it could backfire.

3 You're pushing ahead with something regardless of the advice you've received, and you could crack under the pressure. It will all end in tears if you're not very careful. Distract yourself, and put some space between you and another.

4 Only after a period of rest will you be rejuvenated. You know you have the talent and vision to progress rapidly – so don't rely on others, because you just don't need them at the moment. You could build a solid foundation on your own from scratch.

5 You're at a critical point in matters of career and personal relationships. Someone older than you has caused a few problems. You'll need to encourage those close to you in their efforts and accept their support, otherwise you'll get nowhere.

6 Enormous opportunities and the prospect of great wealth are appearing before you, but it's daunting. Keep on course and hold your nerve, because unexpected misfortune is hiding on the horizon.

No. 28

YIN • KNOWING YOUR LIMITS

DAGUO

大過

You've become too engrossed in one thing recently, and you've taken your eye off the ball. Without you noticing it, the matters you put at the back of your mind could come back to haunt you. There's a delicate balancing act going on and things could tip over the edge. Withdraw a little and sit on the sidelines – don't become preoccupied by thoughts of what you might miss out on. Successful investors rarely sell out at the top; they know when they've made enough. This applies to you in every sense, and your close relationships will benefit if you redirect your energy, your gains and your attention upon them. If you get greedy and try to over-indulge, you may well come to regret it. If it's obvious that things are about to collapse, then you need to act very quickly.

Messages

1 A major event is in prospect. This brings great opportunity but also some risk. It's important to make a good start. In order to do this you need to be well prepared: look at the detail and be very cautious.

2 You're not the only one of a group that's new to something. Share your early experiences with others. A complete reorganization and restructuring is in view.

3 If you keep pushing and don't listen to advice, then nothing will prosper. Control your inclination to forge ahead without any help, or it will end in disaster.

4 You're going to have to do things yourself – advice from others won't help the current situation. You have enough talent now to see the way to proceed. Just get on with it – but you will have to negotiate one tricky item.

5 Your ideals are going to be tested now. You may need to face up to reality – the world doesn't necessarily function as you would like. You thought you had established a firm foundation. Think again; it could all give way.

6 Something just isn't worth the price you're being asked to pay. Weigh up the pros and cons again, and ask a third party for their view. There are other alternatives – you just need to look for them.

No. 29

YANG • TRICKY SITUATIONS

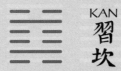

KAN
習
坎

This is not a good time to hang around. The tide has turned and a wall of water is heading in your direction. You're going to be challenged and tested, and it's not going to be easy. There are threats on the cards, each coming from different directions. Be decisive and hold your nerve – only perseverance and steadfastness will see you through. Any coward can fight a battle when they're sure of winning; true courage comes from those who strive when the odds are stacked against them. Brushes with danger can strengthen you, because they breed fortitude and make you thankful for small things and the friendship of others. Don't give up and bite the bullet – the danger will have passed very soon.

Messages

1 You've let certain problems or a dependence on something man-made dictate the pace simply by getting used to them. The solution may require you to review your resolve and this dependence, and it could mean changing jobs, avoiding friends or moving location and starting over again. However, timing is critical.

2 You're in a tricky position and need to focus on small, mundane tasks, as anything more complicated could sink you. Don't stick your head above the parapet; resist the lure of instant changes, as it will backfire.

3 Confusion reigns in your personal and working life. You can't really get to grips with the issues, and the more you push, the more you'll fail – so don't bother, and let the time pass. Hold firm, and the problems will resolve themselves.

4 Try to crystallize one issue at a time and deal with it. This will allow you to tick one box and move on to the next problem. Such an orderly process will help focus your attention.

5 Don't struggle against the whole world – there's no point, since you can't change it. The turmoil has begun to subside. The worst is over. Try to settle for what you've got for now; be thankful for it, and things will turn around.

6 You could feel you're stuck in a rut. If you continue to struggle in this manner, you'll become completely hemmed in and will be overwhelmed by a deluge of problems. Forget about them, then go and do something else. Consult a higher authority if you need comfort.

No. 29

YIN • FACING THE MUSIC

KAN

習
坎

You're caught between a rock and a hard place. The situation requires taking a risk in order to get out of your current predicament. There's no other way out. Sometimes in a dream we feel we're falling helplessly, and there's nothing to cling to – then we come to our senses with a sudden jolt. This is your situation today. You need to get hold of an issue and learn how to cope with it. Only by doing so will you confront a problem head-on and deal with it. You may have to teach those around you what to do, otherwise they will hold you back. Your occupation may need to change dramatically – concentrate on legal issues and systems and procedures. When you're taking a risk, you need to be properly prepared.

Messages

1 Sometimes it's difficult to extricate ourselves from bad habits. This could just be down to the pernicious influence of others whom were trusted. Wake up to the coming reality and get real, before it's too late. Then you can start all over again.

2 Staying afloat while those around you thrash around in the water is your current occupation. You've been put in a difficult predicament. Take small steps and leave the big issues until last, and then it will work out fine.

3 You may feel bound by restrictions and lost in the dark. Since the way out is not obvious, there's no point in grasping at straws. Wait for the dawn to come and then begin anew.

4 You can confront a coming threat with confidence. You know what the solution is – you just have to convince someone else. Get to the point quickly and this will avoid confusion.

5 Don't do more than the minimum you were asked to do. If you push it, you don't know what the consequences might be. Revise down your expectations and you'll be safe from harm.

6 You've tried your best and failed to resolve the problem. Your scope to continue is limited and there's little point in opening up old wounds. Shut yourself off from the world and wait until later.

No. 30

YANG • POWERFUL LIGHT

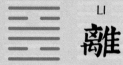

LI

離

You're blessed with special vision at the moment, and a real opportunity is knocking at your door. There's a mutual dependence between you and others, and this combination can achieve remarkable things, way beyond your individual contributions. This should make you fearless. You can transform others' lives by using your special power, and this creates a synergy and energy beyond belief. Your artistic and intellectual creativity and vision is at its peak, allowing you to realize new goals for yourself and assist others to do the same. A quiet confidence will bring your assertiveness to everyone's benefit and shed a bright light on many issues, bringing them more clearly into focus.

Messages

1 New experiences will test your mettle, as the signs are ambiguous and you could burn yourself out. Stay focused, and stick to what you're good at. Don't be distracted from the central objective.

2 This is not the time for extreme measures or being stubborn. New light has been shed on an old problem; timing is critical, however, so give it a lot more thought before you make that decision.

3 Don't waste time pondering what's inevitable. A process needs to reach its own conclusion, at its own pace. You can't do anything about it, and it will bring you bad luck if you keep pushing too hard.

4 You could fall into the trap of over-celebrating a victory or success. Don't let your potential volatility get the better of you; no good will come of this, so you'd better change your attitude.

5 There are dramatic changes taking place over which you have no influence, and your plans could come to grief. Just take such disappointments on the chin. This signifies a turning point in your life, with wonderful opportunities ahead for all concerned.

6 The responsibility is all yours. Others have taken the wrong path, and it's your duty now to win them over, despite getting what you thought you wanted. You may have to change some bad habits or restrain your natural instincts in order to do so.

No. 30

YIN • INSPIRING OTHERS

LI

離

You will draw people to you today through your clarity of vision and your communication skills. Public speaking and performance come to centre stage; you will light up the imagination of others and receive merited and welcome applause. In nature, it's the sun's powerful light that enables life to flourish, by wrapping everything in its perfect glow. Everything then works in synchrony. Similarly, radiating confidence will help you supervise a group, and the number four features in all you do today. This gives everything the correct balance. You're going to make rapid progress from now on, but you've not yet reached your final goal – so don't count your chickens until they hatch.

Messages

1   First impressions can be deceptive. You need to shine a light on something and look a lot closer. This may expose your lack of experience in handling the issues at hand. It's all part of your learning process.

2   Step back and take a deep breath. The right moment to move is on the horizon, but it's not here yet. There's a gathering momentum taking place and synergies are being created. Very soon a blinding clarity will appear, and you'll know what to do.

3   You can't do anything about what's occurring, so just resign yourself to letting things happen. The signs are not good. Keep your head down, as things could go pear-shaped.

4   There's little point in putting in too much effort and energy, as this might just exhaust you. Don't try to get instant results or you'll burn yourself out. Take a back seat today and occupy yourself with mundane tasks – you need to be distracted in order to take a break.

5   What might seem like failure is about to turn to your advantage. The swings and roundabouts which once looked grim are going to change things around dramatically and, at last, you'll get there. Hang on in there.

6   Others are now going to turn to you to get to the core of a particular matter and sort it out. Their muddled thinking caused this situation, and bad habits and practices developed. Act decisively, and on impulse, and jettison the garbage. Everyone will benefit.

No. 31

YANG • MAGNETIC ATTRACTION

XIAN

咸

Opposites often attract, and currently it is mutual attraction which is paramount. Mutual attraction is required for personal relationships to settle and develop – and for materials to bond and create secure foundations. In nature, the attraction of opposites is fundamental to any creative process, and it is hard-wired into our genes through our DNA. It brings all things together in our careers and our personal relationships – and this is what is emphasized for you at the moment. The time is right for displaying affection, because it won't be misconstrued. Family ties will be strengthened, and you can allow others in your personal relationships to decide your direction without inhibition. This will be truly fulfilling and open new doors, providing unexpected career opportunities.

Messages

1 A recent conflict is about to subside. This will create an opportunity for a new career or relationship. Observe what's happening carefully and make sure you don't jump to the wrong conclusions. But change won't happen all by itself – you have to work at it.

2 You feel you need to do something, but in fact you're not qualified or properly prepared for it. You're sleepwalking into problem areas and it's best to do nothing. Don't even go there, or you'll regret it.

3 Take a firm grip on your emotions and don't let them boil over. Only by being self-disciplined can you cope with the situation. There's no upside in what's happening currently, so don't push things.

4 It appears you really want to exert influence over someone or something, but you may have been forced into a position of making a choice. Don't try to be manipulative or calculating – just say what you mean and it will happen.

5 You have a profound gut feeling about a certain matter. This opinion is not necessarily shared by others. Allow your views to develop and take root, and this will help you through the situation.

6 It's not always clear that you're sure what you're doing. Don't be tempted to grasp at straws by listening to others' hastily contrived conclusions. Confusion reigns but actions speak louder than words, so just get on with it and see what happens.

No. 31

YIN • GETTING TOGETHER

XIAN

咸

Two heads are better than one. It's time to forego your independence and learn to become part of a team. This applies both to the workplace and your personal life. It's time to grasp the nettle and get together with someone. Accept their position and submit to their superior knowledge in some situations; it's the person who can both accept their own mistakes and endure the pain of forgiveness who is the stronger. If necessary, make an effort at reconciliation. Forgiving someone their weaknesses can be difficult to come to terms with, but once you do it releases you from being a prisoner to bitterness and turns the relationship into true friendship. You'll wonder why you didn't do this earlier.

Messages

1 It might be just the beginning, but something or someone clicks into place today. This could be the start of something big. Don't be too cautious; show your hand and you'll find out whether the other party means it or not.

2 You can't sleepwalk into making a commitment. Wake up to what's going on and ask more questions, or you may come to regret it. You may need to recognize that you need to work with someone else, even though you might prefer not to.

3 Control your emotions in order to ensure an encounter of significance is real. Taking a little time now will give you the opportunity to become more convinced. If you're still sure, then grab your chance, but try not to travel too far, as this could be risky.

4 Things are now turning in your favour. It's a time to cement relationships, but try not to influence others' views; they must make their own judgement. A mutual trust will then develop.

5 Only by forming relationships with strong roots will they last. Shallowness is easily uncovered. Even a separation or parting can withstand the test, if you remain sincere in your beliefs.

6 It's time to be realistic. What people say comes easy; it's what people do with their limited time available that really counts. The time for talking is over. Either get involved or forget it.

No. 32

YANG • PERSEVERANCE

HENG

恆

The secret of eternity is reflected in nature's process of rebirth and renewal, which manifests itself from plants and animals to all human activity. You are confronted with a stark reality, which you must meet with all the fortitude you can muster. You will need to be courageous and endure many pitfalls and setbacks; this is temporary, as you gather all your strength and radically change your life. You will need to remain steadfast to face the issues confronting you, and at times it could feel very lonely indeed. Decide what you really want from life, because it's available to you now, if you continue to strive for it. Just don't allow others to distract you or deflect you from your chosen course.

Messages

1 Take your time adjusting to the new challenges that will present themselves. There are no short-cuts to resolving them. Your lifestyle is about to be transformed but it won't happen overnight.

2 Don't be pushed into taking extreme action. On the other hand, don't stand by and do nothing. Deal with matters as they come into focus and the rest will fall into place. You're about to successfully resolve a long-standing issue.

3 You're going to be subjected to rapid and unpredictable mood changes, and this could unintentionally upset someone. This will lead to embarrassment unless you learn to control yourself and stabilize your behaviour. It's not too late.

4 If you daydream and search for unrealistic goals, you run the risk of failing completely. This could have been unforeseen financial consequences as you become overstretched. Come at issues from a completely different angle and you'll be surprised what you find.

5 If you follow others blindly, you'll run into a brick wall. Detach yourself and review your position, otherwise you'll get nowhere. Sometimes you need to clear your head; step apart from friends and colleagues to see things in a different light.

6 You could allow anxiety to pile up, and this will exhaust you. Take a break from colleagues or a partner, spend time alone and come back refreshed, or you'll hit problems – both physical and psychological.

No. 32
YIN • PERSISTENCE NOT RESISTANCE

HENG
恆

You are persistent and durable today. Let things ride and allow those problems to slide away and resolve themselves. This will test both your strength of character and your determination to succeed. Contain your inclination to doubt others' abilities. We all have our strengths and weaknesses, but it's the gift of knowing your own that will work in your favour and give you the strength to persevere. You will need to be on your toes. You will receive mixed signals from someone, and this will cause confusion. But your perseverance will see you through, as you currently enjoy a clarity of vision that others don't possess. Some may see your stance as stubbornness, but you have the benefit of knowing you are right this time. So, remain firm in your resolve and the outcome you want will materialize.

Messages

1 It is not time to change your lifestyle or view of the world – just revisit what you really want to achieve. There's no shortcut solution available, so there is no point in a quick fix.

2 Today you need to employ sensitive management skills. Stay focused on the objectives and don't let anyone deviate from the chosen strategy, and you can make genuine progress. If you push someone too hard, they could go over the edge.

3 Mood swings and confusion are the order of the day. Try to get some consistency, or you will fail in your objective. Practice makes perfect. Centre yourself and develop a calm, considered approach.

4 You should re-evaluate your short-term objectives – they may now be unrealistic. It's like pursuing something that doesn't exist. Revise your goals and try again.

5 You get out only as much as you put in. You must decide how important an issue really is to you, and try to see it with another's perspective. You need to choose between two alternatives, but you cannot have both.

6 Getting agitated about things will just eat away at you, and could affect your health and well-being. Don't let it happen. Take a deep breath and compose yourself. Don't do something reluctantly, or it will fail. Either go for it or leave it alone.

No. 33

YANG • STEPPING BACK

DUN

You're due to make a timely withdrawal from a difficult state of affairs, but you must neither act too hastily nor react too slowly. When left unattended, gardens can become overgrown and unwieldy – and so can your personal life. Things have just gone too far, and it's time to cut back to the roots to allow regrowth to take place. You shouldn't become too emotionally involved with what is now a futile position. A hostile environment could develop in career matters; detach yourself or you'll suffer badly. Personal relationships may become strained, so regard this as a phase and give it time to heal or the stress will get to you. It's not a time for new ventures; it's a time for repair and renewal.

Messages

1 You may be too close to someone who is in trouble. Don't try to distance yourself immediately or it will arouse suspicion; just sit tight and wait things out. You can't win, so try not to get embroiled in a situation.

2 Get ready to escape from a tricky situation and, when the chance arises, jump to it and retreat quickly. The situation could try to provoke you into a reaction, and that's the last thing you should do.

3 You could become the focus of a very difficult situation not of your own making. You'll need the support of family and friends to resolve it, as getting out of it without consequences will prove very tricky.

4 You will know when the time is right to extricate yourself from something, but you must do it willingly. If you get worked up, this will only make things worse. You may have to accept that you have lost this particular battle, but try to regain your strength for the next.

5 Don't be talked out of your retreat from others' problems and don't regret decisions you made earlier – there's no point. The tide is beginning to turn in your favour; let it develop and grow at its own pace.

6 You've now placed enough distance between you and a particular situation to withdraw without blame. No one will be angry with you and you'll instead reap significant benefits – so enjoy the freedom this will now give you.

No. 33

YIN • TIME TO DETACH

DUN

A period of detachment is called for. Take time out from everything that's been going on; you will benefit from walking away, because getting involved will get you nowhere. Attend to minor matters that you had put to one side. This will occupy you and give you time to recover while some of the bigger issues begin to resolve themselves. You might have felt threatened by what's happened. There's no point in building up resentment, as this could trigger a destructive process and everyone will suffer. If you retire with dignity and keep your distance, the wounds will heal with time. Allow nature to take its course, step back a little and gather your strength for another day.

Messages

1 Without knowing it, you may have become close to a competitor. You are at risk of stepping over the line. Consider your options carefully, and calm things down if you can. It's too late to try to reverse things – they've gone too far.

2 You won't have the right opportunity to withdraw completely from the current situation. There's no room for manoeuvre, so you may need the help of someone else to guide you out of the predicament.

3 You may have been dragged into the middle of something you wanted to avoid. Don't listen to those acting only in their own self-interest; their motives are shallow. Value the opinions of those closest to you.

4 There should be no regrets about pulling out of a commitment. You didn't invite it anyway, but couldn't get out of it. You can escape with a clear conscience; dismiss any misgivings, or you will be dragged back in again.

5 Don't let others distract you from your decision. Their views are not relevant and you don't need to reconsider anything. If your motives remain sincere, then everything will work out fine.

6 You can get out of responsibility without any guilt or remorse. You've done your bit for all concerned. Announce what you intend to do publicly and no one will attach any blame to you – and you'll be free to go your own way.

No. 34

YANG • POWER AND INFLUENCE

DAZHUANG

At the moment you are blessed with great power and the ability to influence others. Once unleashed, this power can act like a flash of lightning, providing energy, enthusiasm and passion. Unfortunately, this could lead to resistance and hostility if not handled correctly. It's how you use this power that is the real test. Don't let it corrupt your sense of perspective.

You will become the centre of attention in social circles and can use this to enhance your prospects tremendously. Be aware, however, that being too aggressive will provoke others to seek revenge. You've been dealt a good hand, so play it carefully – power should be a means to an end, rather than an end in itself.

Messages

1 Even though the force is with you, you must hold off for now. You're in a precarious position on a knife edge. If you go for it now, you could regret it.

2 Calm yourself and don't be over-confident, otherwise you'll trip up and lose everything. Enjoy your influence with modesty, and be prepared to make slow progress by taking small steps, one at a time.

3 Showing off often stems from an inferiority complex. Resist it if you want to make progress; be patient and cautious. There's potential disaster lurking around the corner.

4 Everything is in your favour to achieve a major breakthrough without the opposition you might have expected. An opportunity is there for you now – just try to take one thing at a time. Caution is the key.

5 Climb down from your entrenched position. You don't have to prove anything to anyone but yourself. The odds are stacked against you if you attempt new ventures.

6 You've reached stalemate and complications are multiplying, and it could become bewildering. This could exhaust your patience and lead to an explosion of some kind, which you need to control. Step back, take a deep breath and let the issues resolve themselves with time, then make progress slowly.

No. 34

YIN • TIME TO ENGAGE

DAZHUANG

You need not be constrained by convention or the rule book, as your creative instincts are at their peak. Your leadership skills will come to the fore and give you an advantage over the competition. This requires self-restraint, as it would be easy to become boisterous and go over the edge as your success repeats itself time and again. Remember to weigh the pros and cons of the situation, and don't lose your sense of what's right and wrong. If you can contain your excitement, it will make your victories last much longer; if you can't, they will be short-lived and you will be back where you started. A humble attitude is called for; use your power with careful judgement and discretion.

Messages

1 Everything is in place and you're feeling positive. However, the time is not right for making a major decision. If you do it now, it could all collapse in a heap. Collect more information and wait.

2 Too much success can lead to over-confidence. Everything you are doing at the moment turns out just fine, but remember your true intentions and don't get sidelined by the trappings of material success. Otherwise, you could turn from hunter to prey.

3 Those who boast too loudly are usually the ones lacking self-confidence. Restrain any inclination to enjoy the limelight. Conceal your true feelings, as you may irritate someone today and it will backfire. Bite your lip, if necessary.

4 Take a restrained approach to deal with what's at issue and you will find all opposition melts away. It will surprise you how simply matters can be resolved. You've been worrying more than you need to.

5 You don't need to prove anything to anyone, so let go of things and they will fade with memory. You don't even have to try hard any more. Just switch your strategy and things will fall in your lap.

6 You've been pushing hard recently and have reached a point where you could feel trapped. Be patient, and a deadlock will unblock itself without your help. Give things time to find their proper place and let nature take its course – then you can carry on.

No. 35
YANG • RAPID PROGRESS

CHIN

晉

You're ready to make great advances in a whole range of situations. Your communication skills are at their peak and your capabilities are becoming more evident to others. You will be successful not just in areas of study and investment, but also in close relationships. Your unbridled curiosity has driven you to this point. A new growing phase has taken hold, but co-operating with others will become more important, otherwise this will put a brake on your progress and jeopardize everything. You're now on a plane of higher understanding, so get your timing right and the benefits could be enormous. Don't fritter them away.

Messages

1 Others lack confidence in you, but don't force the pace or become angry because you need their support. Be especially careful and pay attention to detail in your work and personal life, and they will come round to your viewpoint.

2 Someone in authority could appear to be hindering your progress. You'll just have to suffer this for the time being, but you will get help from an unexpected source which was there all the time.

3 With the help of others you will make great strides and develop a mutual trust, so accept their offer of help and embrace the changes. You are fortunate to have a strong circle of friends and now is the time to resort to their help.

4 You've been fortunate recently and sometimes it's been undeserved, but it's made you more popular. Don't stick your neck out today, as danger is approaching. This could lead to disagreements and conflict.

5 Despite your clear success, and reaching a position of significant influence, you need to keep your feet firmly on the ground. If you do this, you can go much further without generating resentment and misunderstanding.

6 Only adopt aggressive measures with yourself to keep on the straight and narrow. You face a risky situation, so you must retain your discipline or you will be alienated from others. Hold your nerve, because the balance of probability is on your side; you are going to make it.

No. 35
YIN • UNBOUNDED SUCCESS

 CHIN

晉

Executive powers are within your grasp. This will put you in a position where you can choose to bestow benefits upon others. You're about to be entrusted with real responsibility, and this will place you right at the centre of the action. This is what you've been waiting for and you've earned the contentment that this promotion will deliver. Your decision-making skills have come to the attention of those in strong positions. They will come to recognize the interdependence between them and you. If you let it, your influence can now radiate like bright sunshine throughout your career prospects, and this will serve to accelerate your progress beyond your own expectations.

Messages

1   A major advance is imminent, but you may feel others are getting in the way. Work at convincing someone. Gain their confidence and support, and you will win the arguments and accumulate dramatic gains.

2   You are about to receive unexpected good fortune. You deserve it, and have the blessing of someone in authority who will come to recognize your real value. This will please you, in particular, as you will feel your personal beliefs are vindicated.

3   Don't feel any remorse for what's coming your way; you've done enough to deserve a bit of luck. You've secured the faith and trust of others and this is now bearing fruit. Accept any gifts given to you.

4   Caution is the key today. You've taken credit for something to which you may not have been entitled. Unless you deal with it and come clean it could backfire, and you'll be embarrassed publicly.

5   You can influence the outcome today, as you are blessed with an unusual authority. Act with modesty and restraint but ignore any impediments put in your way. Your decisions today will bear remarkable fruit. Press ahead.

6   Aggressive discipline should be applied to your own conduct as an example to others. Don't expect those around you to get the message first, or this will breed resentment. They don't have your feel for what's needed. Lead by example and others will follow.

157

No. 36

YANG • POWER THROUGH CAUTION

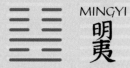

MINGYI

明
夷

This time in your life will test your personal convictions and ambitions to the limit. A mist has descended. It's not a good time to explore new things or travel, as darkness is embracing everything you do. It would be easy to give up the ghost and surrender to the surrounding gloom. People just won't listen to you, and you need time to recover both your health and composure. What is clearly not working should be left alone until the fog of indecision clears. But don't worry – it's always darkest just before the dawn. There's a glimmer of hope shining a light on all the aspects of your current situation and great things are on the horizon. Just be cautious for now – things will turn around.

Messages

1   You're trying your best but being thwarted at every turn. People just don't understand you at the moment. There's nothing you can do but wait for matters to settle down. Don't be fooled into the wrong actions by woolly thinking.

2   You thought that a recent setback had handicapped you, but it hasn't. In fact, you've been strengthened by it, and you should now go for it with confidence.

3   You're confronted by someone with weird ideas and you're unsure how to proceed. There's no need to rush things. Be careful or you will be corrupted and misled. You will suffer – they won't.

4   It's crystal clear to you what needs to be done and you cannot do any more for someone. If the situation is hopeless, just get out of it. You may need to put some distance between you and another's problems to work things out.

5   Although you have the power to make decisions, you're not comfortable with a particular situation that's developed. You may be imagining problems; you don't need to, as the real ones are enough in themselves. Leave it alone and keep your options open for now.

6   A recent period of turmoil is coming to a close and those who were trying to obstruct you will go away. This will be a great relief, and free you up to make progress on your own. But stay alert to the needs of others.

No. 36

YIN • RECOVERY NEEDED

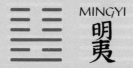

MINGYI

明夷

Wounded animals slink away somewhere safe in order to recover. This best describes your circumstances at the moment. A period of rest and reparation is called for. You could feel downhearted by recent events, and it would be easy to feel sorry for yourself. Don't let this shake your self-belief; just let things go. Nature never abandons hope – it just sleeps through the winter and returns stronger than ever when the conditions are right. You may have to suffer three times before you get the chance to return to the fight. Take guidance from the support you will be offered by someone in a position of authority. They will help you to identify a clear path to recovery.

Messages

1   Any attempt to distance yourself will backfire, and you could become the target. It won't be easy, but it's time to face up to reality and take the consequences. There's no alternative.

2   Regard a recent setback as a test of your resilience. Let it motivate you to renew your energy and determination. Push ahead – there's nothing further to discuss; someone's had their chance and wasted it.

3   You may be confronted by someone with confused thinking. Don't be fooled by their overtures or their promises. Stick to your own beliefs, but don't try to change their mind – they must do this for themselves. If they don't, then let them go their own way and suffer the consequences.

4   Your head is clear and you possess remarkable foresight at the moment. What you are confronting is real, and you can see that someone else is just getting nowhere. Keep your distance and observe events unfolding – they need to learn a lesson.

5   You can see what's wrong with the current situation, but you're not in a position to intervene. You have to ignore it; keep your powder dry and get involved later, when you will be really needed. Someone else needs to go through their own pain in order to reach the right decision.

6   There's an end in sight. Certain people are about to be found out and they won't enjoy the consequences. Don't get involved – let matters unfold at their own pace. You will be the main beneficiary.

No. 37

YANG ● FAMILY RELATIONSHIPS

JIAREN
家人

It's family matters which currently take centre stage, and all decisions should be heavily influenced by what's right for your immediate and extended family. In matters of career and personal relationships, attempts at social-climbing and fake affection could backfire. You have an intense understanding of what's right and wrong, and a respect for tradition. There is a natural position for you in your family and social circle with which you have become comfortable, and it's taken a long time for others to recognize this. Try to mirror this in your working relationships and you will succeed. Identify what binds people to a common purpose and adopt the role of orchestrator. If you try to exceed this role, you could fail to reach the high standards you set for yourself, and cause chaos.

Messages

1 As you commence a new challenge you need to get the balance right at the outset. It's a female characteristic to adopt different roles and act as a reconciler; this comes naturally to some but not others. You need this now.

2 Don't give in to sudden impulses. Concede your personal needs to the interests of a wider group, just to feel that you belong. This will benefit both the group and yourself.

3 You can't say yes but you shouldn't say no. This could upset someone, but you just don't have the skill-set. You've got to steer a course between the two, but you'll end up doing the opposite of what's needed if you aren't careful.

4 Concentrate on the details of your private life, which must take priority at the moment. This will provide you with greater insight to benefit you more widely. Your luck will improve if you do – remember: the harder you work at it, the luckier you'll get.

5 Stop being aloof and acting as if you're too good for the others. You must become one of them with sincerity in order to be taken seriously, and matters will improve. You might be offered a position of responsibility you've been looking for.

6 Your character and decision-making skills will be strengthened today, and this produces excellent results. You assume responsibility, which benefits your friends and colleagues, and you will express surprising insights, which will impress others. It's time for your reputation to spread.

No. 37
YIN • DETACHING

JIAREN

家人

The family unit is the basis of a common unbreakable bond that binds people together through mutual love and understanding. But, while living in a confined space with others provides warmth and comfort, it could become suffocating if it limits your freedom. Don't allow family or household commitments to dictate your conduct at the moment, or let those who depend on you limit your ambitions too much, or you risk your self-esteem. You may need to seriously consider shaking off the shackles of the past. You are bound to others by a shared habitat and history, but nothing lasts for ever. You've gone through a period of dependence and need now to assume responsibility and go your own way, especially in family matters. Search for a common theme for everyone, but don't over-stretch yourself or it could damage your health.

Messages

1 Going it alone at the moment will not work. You need to firm up on your exact role and play your part in a team. Submit yourself to the greater good and you will be pleased with the result.

2 It's best to focus on the needs of others right now. Restrain yourself from pursuing your own preferred objectives; they can wait. Your family relationships should then improve.

3 Prudence is the key today. Don't over-indulge or push things too far, or you won't be forgiven. You need to tread a careful path between self-discipline and going over the top. If you don't strike the balance, you will suffer a loss.

4 You need to be more economic in your use of limited resources. Be cautious and don't take unnecessary risks. Calculate carefully and consider the options before you. This will prove profitable indeed.

5 You can follow someone's lead today with confidence. Your relationship is strong and beneficial to you both. Get off your high horse and submit to the relationship and you will enjoy the outcome.

6 Your character will become more rounded as a result of a recent experience. This has improved your chances of being chosen for a particular job, but you'll need the support of your family to pursue it. Don't be afraid – you are up to it.

No. 38

YANG • CONTRADICTIONS

KUI

睽

There are contradictions and conflicts around at the moment, suggesting a negative tone to most situations. You're going to have to refrain from responding in kind and use all your diplomatic skills, as tensions in various relationships abound. Family and personal relationships may become strained, and this won't help your career and social prospects, either. Don't make things worse by provoking confrontation. Be open-minded, and allow new ideas to settle and find reconciliation. Divert your attention by engaging in side-issues and let others calm down. It's the small victories which lead to lasting success. It is also not the time to act in haste or to conclude a deal; there will be better times.

Messages

1 A surprising confrontation arises from a normally sound relationship, but you can just shrug it off. Don't worry about it, but don't provoke the other party, either, as they could get upset. It will soon pass, so distract yourself for now.

2 An accidental encounter will provide an opportunity and a natural attraction becomes evident. You won't see it coming, but enjoy it when it does. Your networking skills are at their peak.

3 Many setbacks confront you. Don't be disheartened; just take your time and they'll resolve themselves into a happy outcome. Take heart from the experience – all it's done is expose a fallacy.

4 Everything around you appears against you, with one notable exception. You could become disorientated but you won't be thwarted. The trust of someone close is crucial to resolving a problem, so be open to suggestions from them.

5 Despite disagreements, you need to listen to the other side of the argument. You've nothing to lose, so go ahead and you'll be surprised at the result. Keep working at it.

6 You're becoming paranoid and could be distracted by unqualified and uninvited opinions. Just because others don't agree doesn't mean they don't care. Agree to differ and focus on mutual benefits, and you'll be amazed at the outcome.

No. 38

YIN • UNKNOWN SIDE EFFECTS

KUI

睽

Opinions are polarizing at the moment and this is leading to tension that could create a rift between you and another. Fire and water do not mix, and you will have to navigate carefully to find a solution to the current impasse. Something you did recently has created a division, though this wasn't intentional. You're going to have to put yourself in someone's shoes to try to appreciate their point of view. If you run after a horse, it just runs further away; the best strategy is to let it go, and it will return of its own accord. Forcing things through won't work, as the divide will just widen. The way to resolve an issue has not yet presented itself, so patience is called for. What looks like a conflict today will just become a minor difference of opinion tomorrow. Then the conflict will evaporate.

Messages

1 Something has gone out of your reach and you are keen to get back to where you once were. A sign will appear when you see something that is not quite right and seems out of place. Don't try too hard; your predicament will resolve itself.

2 An accidental meeting will generate a new lead. This will change your approach and identify a different route. A natural attraction between two parties is driving them together – and you are one of them.

3 Things seem to be getting in the way and you feel you are not making much progress. But each step towards the mountain takes you closer, even though the view appears the same. Be patient – you are getting there.

4 After contradictory signals you're being driven closer to an agreement with someone. You may need to make a concession, but it will turn out to have been a great investment. This will allow you to avoid the embarrassment of revealing something awkward.

5 Sometimes what appears to be an opposition or completely different viewpoint sparks new ideas. A conciliatory gesture will bring hostilities to an end and create a co-operative environment where all the issues will get sorted out.

6 You may retreat into your shell if you let recent misunderstandings get to you. Your friends are still your friends – you can't agree on everything. It's difficult to admit an error, but if you do it will reinforce your friendship and release you from bitterness.

No. 39

YANG • WITHOUT FEAR

JIAN

蹇

You need to prepare yourself thoroughly for the obstacles which will be put in your path. Some situations could be dangerous, so you need to be very careful. Regard this as a process of discovery and self-improvement. You cannot continue along the same path and the pace of change will slow down, but don't be impatient, because there's a reason for it.

Don't look for scapegoats or assign blame to anyone, as it's your inner fortitude which is needed now. Take responsibility and be courageous. It's important to be at the right place at the right time and to consult others who can help you through their own experience. This gives you clarity of vision and a feeling of release – but it won't be easy.

Messages

1 Things don't look too good. You may hit a brick wall. Don't try to run through it; step back and think carefully – there will be a way around it.

2 It's not your fault that there are obstacles in your way. If you overcome them, everyone will benefit, both in your career and then your personal life. However, it could prove expensive in terms of time as well as money.

3 Wait until the mist clears before struggling with a problem. You will have time to stop and think, so use it profitably. If you try to make progress too quickly, it could turn out to be a costly mistake.

4 There is someone who can help you and you need them now. It may be that a recent wrangle appears impossible to overcome. Unite; if you go it alone, you'll fail.

5 It's not the time to give up or lose hope, but there's a lot of opposition to your plans in the offing. The obstacles will be overcome, as someone from a surprising direction comes to your rescue.

6 There's no avoiding it. Your problems will come to a head no matter how you try to sidestep them. Consult someone close and prepare to reveal to them what's really eating you, and they'll help you resolve the issues.

No. 39

YIN • BACK ON TRACK

JIAN

蹇

The only way you can make any progress at the moment will be in fits and starts. Just when you think you've sorted out one matter, a new problem will come to light. This means you need to redirect your efforts and go straight to the heart of an issue you had put to the back of your mind; it was more important than you thought. Pause and think about things; confronting adversity will make you stronger. There's no need to blame anyone else. It may be that you just need to show an unexpected kindness to someone you'd neglected. Once this happens it will have a transforming effect on your prospects. The world will turn, a new pattern of possibilities will be revealed, and the barrier to your progress will have gone.

Messages

1 At first, you may need to recover from an early setback. Don't try to resolve an issue that doesn't really matter; sidestep the problem, let it ride, and it will sort itself out. Then, you can carry on as you were.

2 You could hide yourself away and then avoid all the issues, but this would be self-defeating. Widen your ambitions and take more responsibility. This will assist those you care about and they will reciprocate. You can't lose.

3 There's no point getting downhearted about a recent shock – it's over now, anyway. Don't jeopardize the progress you've made by abandoning hope. You're just being tested again. Wait for things to turn around; they will.

4 Things are beginning to be clear. Use someone close to take advice, now that you know what needs to be done – but you must heed it. Whatever you may think, you just can't do this on your own.

5 Only co-operation will resolve matters. You need your friends and colleagues now, as there's no way to progress without them. The obstacles are just too high and you're not equipped to scale them. If you go it alone, you will fail.

6 If you ignore all that's going on around you and bury your head in the sand you will just be kicked in the backside. Deal with the first item on your list – you may find it's more important than you thought. A brilliant success is then in prospect.

No. 40
YANG • BECOMING FREE

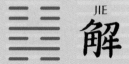

JIE

解

It's like the season is changing. It's time to clear the air and break free from a number of constraints that have been hindering your progress for some time. The ice is melting and a sense of liberation pervades everything. What's happened is in the past, and you can do nothing about it now. Let things go, changing your behaviour and your attitude, and begin a new stimulating phase in your working and personal relationships. It's time to forgive and forget, otherwise the baggage of the past will weigh you down. The problems you've experienced recently are now receding and unnecessary delays will evaporate, but you must act quickly in order to take advantage of the opportunities before you.

Messages

1 Let go of the past, find a solution and act now – your position will strengthen and you'll then move on to a new and gratifying phase of personal discovery. A new addition to your life is in the offing.

2 The time is ripe for a decision, but you have to be straight with another person, as they've tried to influence you unjustly. Forgive them for their contradictory behaviour. Listen to them courteously, but follow your own instincts.

3 You've begun to believe in your own ego. Don't let it rule you or you'll end up regretting it, since others are ready to step into your shoes. Bide your time and the situation will improve.

4 You're becoming too attached to someone else and this will only breed dependence. You have others to think about as well, so back off from them and widen your ambitions. Stick to those you trust.

5 You may have to give some ground in order to re-establish control over your situation. This will generate respect for you, and you'll assume extraordinary powers and influence. You will recover from a recent conflict or setback, so now is your chance to take risks.

6 You are going to get the chance to do something unusual, but you won't be sure which way to go. Take the opportunity and you will succeed, against all the odds. This is a great time for career, travel and making money; don't hold back.

No. 40
YIN • SOLUTION REVEALED

JIE

解

What was a tricky situation is now unravelling to your benefit. You can recover your composure and your health will improve as well. You may have to retrace your steps and review something you thought had already been dealt with – some of it was incomplete. You will spot a weakness in someone's attitude, but you're just going to have to forgive them their transgressions. They have limitations, and you will have to accept it. If you can come to some arrangement or understanding today, then this will accelerate your progress towards a treasured objective. You will snap the shackles, break free from the restraints and plough ahead with renewed confidence and enthusiasm. You will be back where you want to be.

Messages

1 A tough period is coming to an end and you can now see a clear path to progress. Get rid of the old material, jettison your old ideas and re-create yourself. The time is right.

2 You may be required to dismiss the efforts of others as ill thought through and counterproductive. It's time to get tough. You may need to denounce someone publicly. Take this chance to establish yourself; it won't come your way again.

3 You've assumed a position of influence and may feel to some extent you don't deserve it. No matter. Just don't believe in your own PR too much, or others may conspire against you. This could destroy what you achieved.

4 You've attracted unwelcome attention and you should try to shake this off. Someone's becoming too dependent on you and this won't do you, or them, any good. Distance yourself before it's too late.

5 You've got to become more determined to figure out your true motives, otherwise this comes across as indecisiveness. Liberate your inner thoughts and find a way to express them – releasing denial will transform your well-being.

6 Get rid of those who oppose your views. Plan it carefully and choose the time to act, but don't compromise or be deflected by their arguments – yours are sincere, theirs are not.

No. 41

YANG • STRONG OPINIONS

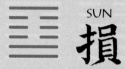

SUN

損

The pendulum is swinging away from you at the moment, and you face a radical decline in your immediate outlook. You could suffer a financial loss and personal relationships could become strained through lack of communication. It's how you react to this which is important. It's time to take stock and learn from recent setbacks, but you must initiate change in order to do so. You need to make sacrifices and conserve energy until the pendulum swings back again. Personal relationships may seem to have become more ordinary, but don't worry, as they'll blossom once more. Regard this period as a catalyst for change and turn negative events into positive outcomes.

Messages

1 Giving or taking too much will cause an imbalance in your life by creating uneasiness in your career or relationships, so think carefully before making a decision. This is a time to be cautious and not make financial commitments.

2 Don't make ridiculous sacrifices just to please someone in authority. Only if you show your inner strength will your contribution be appreciated, and this will improve your future position. Lie low and spend less time socializing for a while.

3 Two heads are better than one, so work with someone to resolve a problem – but don't include a third person, as three's a crowd. After a testing time you'll recover your composure, with the help of others.

4 Recent tension will now diminish and help will come from family and close friends. Don't expect rapid developments, but it's time to make a move, as things are looking good.

5 Have no fear and be brave. You're going to benefit unexpectedly but you won't know why. The forces of chance have shifted in your favour after a period of uncertainty, so go for it now.

6 Your social standing is about to improve, as you help others unselfishly. They will recognize your contribution to their lives and show their appreciation. This will transform your prospects and put you back on your feet.

No. 41

YIN • SHIFTING FOCUS

SUN

損

You need to withdraw completely in order for your current situation to improve. Take refuge from the problem by changing direction entirely. You're not responsible for the pattern of events which developed, but you couldn't help getting involved. Now it's time to get back to basics and return to looking after those who need you the most. Simplicity is the key.

You may have to work out how to transfer power or wealth to someone else. This redistribution will quell mistrust – then you can raise your head again once the storm has passed. Allow the distance between you and someone else to diminish at its own pace and bring you together once more. As your discomfort recedes, your appetite and enthusiasm will recover.

Messages

1 You could be asked to give someone a hand. Try to do just enough, or you'll take over the full responsibility. Equally, if you feel you need help, then by all means ask for it, but be careful that the person you consult doesn't commandeer the whole job and leave you stranded.

2 By all means make your contribution when asked, but don't sacrifice your own principles or it will backfire. Once the weight of the argument moves in favour of one direction or the other, you won't be able to shift it back again and you will be compromised.

3 You can get closer to someone now, but you'll need to exclude a third party to do so. Three just won't work, as the balance is wrong – better to do things by yourself instead. Then you might find unexpected help arrives to restore the balance.

4 Face the music now and recognize your shortcomings, but be quick. You won't be alone, as others will come to help you – even those you don't expect to. The tension will then disappear and you will feel comfortable with your position.

5 It's an astonishing time, and future profit is on the cards. Have no fear and roll the dice. Lady luck is with you, and trading terms are in your favour. Act now.

6 Widen your ambitions at this point and others will join in to help you. Your social standing is about to be enhanced and a long-held ambition will be achieved. Remember those who've helped you to get there; you may need them to catch you when you fall.

No. 42

YANG • ENRICHMENT

YI

There's a gathering momentum in your life, from which you can reap rich rewards. Recent storm-clouds have cleared and a sense of calm has returned. Collect all the evidence you'll need to take advantage of a developing situation. There's a breakthrough coming after an extraordinary busy period for you. You don't have to do a great deal to make tremendous progress because the wind is behind you, so don't try to do too many things at the same time. Don't get worked up about your problems and they will resolve themselves. Be open-minded and allow events beyond your control to unfold. You will learn from the experience and it will benefit you greatly in the future.

Messages

1 You'll shortly be given opportunities you didn't expect, but they may prove to be a tall order. You may even think that the challenges lie beyond your capabilities. Lower your expectations and they will be exceeded beyond your imagination.

2 You've got to give in order to receive, but a single gesture won't be enough. You're due for exceptionally good luck and events are about to turn in your favour, but don't get over-confident.

3 You need to surmount a few obstacles at the moment. Something that seems at first to be bad news, however, turns out to be to your advantage. Use it to make progress, but keep quiet about it.

4 You may be called upon to resolve a dispute. Take the responsibility and everyone will benefit, especially you. There's a rare and spectacular success on the cards.

5 You helped someone out recently and didn't give it any more thought. Well done; this will now reap handsome rewards, as you gain recognition and assume a great responsibility.

6 Don't get carried away by something you recently achieved, otherwise you'll be knocked off your perch and laughed at. There's a hidden agenda developing, so you'll need to be on your guard to protect yourself.

No. 42
YIN • FORWARD WITH CONFIDENCE

YI

The period of stillness has ended. The moment for reflection and calm consideration is over and you are ready for action. It's time to get involved in a big way, as you've sat on the sidelines for too long. Your situation could not be more positive. You can cross rivers and conquer mountains, if you want to. In fact, anything physical is within your grasp and will reap success. But don't forget the sacrifices made by others which enabled you to get to this point. You should reciprocate if you can. You cannot fail, as nature's path is driving you on. Listen to advice from those who've been there before. There is a way to enjoy success without upsetting others; learn from those who know better and adopt their ethical standpoint. It's time to embark on a great journey that will test you to your limit – but you will succeed.

Messages

1 You're now equipped to meet the task you had thought was beyond you, but it is only by ensuring you share the proceeds that you will get it right. Be generous to others and take less for yourself – you'll reap the rewards of self-satisfaction.

2 Keep things going as they are – don't change direction. Act sincerely and give it your best shot; that's all you can do. You'll be surprised how successful you are today. Something tangible and valuable is within your reach.

3 Something's about to turn to your great benefit, and you may wonder why you deserved it. But you have persevered through the setbacks and come out stronger for it. This is not a stroke of luck – it's payback for your persistence.

4 You may be asked to mediate between those you represent and a higher authority. You've found yourself in a position of influence because both sides value your opinion. Keep your feet on the ground and share the benefits with everyone.

5 You seem to have acted in kindness recently without thinking of your own interests. This charity will reap rich rewards, as you are about to multiply the return on the investment you made. Don't ask any questions about what's coming your way; it's well deserved.

6 You may need to hold firm to strike a bargain. This involves changing tactics in connection with a tricky problem that's suddenly surfaced. Although a collision is on the cards, it may be necessary to resolve an issue.

No. 43

YANG • GETTING YOUR ACT TOGETHER

JUE

夬

It's the culmination of a period of frustration that is coming to a head now. It's taken some time for matters to crystallize, and the wind of change has picked up momentum. You need to give yourself a good talking-to and experiment with new ideas. Things will then begin to fall into their natural place.

You have to address the basis of the issues you're dealing with, however, not just their evident consequences. Don't stand by any longer and just let things happen; denounce things that you don't believe in and let everyone know about it – but don't be too forceful. Try to be subtle, or you'll upset others.

Messages

1 Start as you mean to go on. You may have to go back a few steps to recover your composure, since you could lose your way by acting too hastily. Be more measured in what you're doing and the right decisions will become more apparent.

2 Events are moving in your favour, but you must remain cautious. Don't be tempted to invent problems that aren't there – you've enough real ones on your plate as it is.

3 Don't respond in kind, as this may lead to misunderstandings. Let others go their own way and you will win through by following your own gut feeling. This will make you feel that your chosen course of action is vindicated.

4 It seems to be just one problem after another at the moment. But the climate is changing in your favour. It's time to go it alone. Don't trust others; your chance is coming, so strike as soon as you see it.

5 It's time to get off the fence if you want to resolve the issues now confronting you. You've thought about things for long enough. Don't worry about the risks – the outlook is favourable and things will come good.

6 You may have been deluding yourself recently. If you don't go for it now, you won't get another chance. Holding back is not an option, so speak out or act without delay. You won't regret it.

No. 43

YIN • CHANGING TACTICS

JUE

A gate is about to open and a period of pent-up emotion will be released. You've been absorbed by an incident which made you stop in your tracks, and been forced to face up to something that's been at the back of your mind. But you cannot compromise: the way to defeat a wrongdoing is not by responding in kind but to do something positive to redress the balance. Give notice to those involved that you are about to sort things out. Use your objectivity and moral compass to your best advantage. By keeping your distance from someone, you will not become deflected by their activities. Others will see you sharpen your skills and help confront an issue on your behalf. This will allow everyone connected to you to make progress. All it takes for the rot to set in is for those with the right intentions do nothing. It's time to act.

Messages

1 Despite recent progress you need to be very careful. The next decision is the big one, as you won't be able to unravel the consequences if you get it wrong. Before you start a race, you need to be fit and prepared with a strategy worked out. Step back and take this on board.

2 Sharpen your awareness and treat everything as a test of your doggedness and determination. You need to be on your toes to cope with what's coming; keep your eyes and ears open or a sudden major setback could take you by surprise.

3 You need to go it alone at the moment, as the spotlight has fallen on you and it's entirely your responsibility. Choose carefully the time and place for a confrontation. You were not to blame for causing the issue, but you can't escape dealing with it now. Be positive.

4 It's not the time to trust others' guidance and decisions. You're on your own. Be patient and consider all the options. The right course of action will then reveal itself to you – then, just follow your instincts.

5 You're having to cope with things that have gone wrong. It wasn't your fault, but you are where you are. You need to make a choice now; don't hesitate, as the circumstances have shifted in your favour. You will win through, despite the odds.

6 You could be deluding yourself right now. Maybe you've just been lucky recently, but have decided it was skill. Self-deception can be dangerous, and is a way of kidding yourself. Change tack or your efforts will all go to waste.

No. 44

YANG • MEETING CHALLENGES

GOU

姤

Something's eating you at the moment, and an encounter of true significance is on the cards – but there's a threat around that could become unsettling and wreck your plans. The atmosphere is contentious, and a certain feminine attraction brings with it dramatic consequences. This all happened while you were preoccupied with something else, and you can't avoid it now. You have been burying your head in the sand, but the problem is coming to a crescendo and you've got to deal with it instantly or it will destroy your dreams. Confrontations are unavoidable, so meet them head-on. It's not the best time to take on a new position and, on the personal front, you may need to make some long overdue and difficult choices.

Messages

1 In certain relationships close to you, a female influence wears the trousers. If you let this persist it will be unfortunate, as this is a real mistake and everyone will lose out. Sometimes you need to cut ties to feel renewed.

2 If you come across something you know to be fundamentally wrong today, avoid it like the plague or it will drag you down with it. Remain cool under pressure and aloof, if at all possible.

3 Small disputes have had a tendency to escalate of late. Don't get too close to someone; carefully weigh up the advantages and disadvantages, and communicate your views. This will help you limit the damage.

4 You may be dismissing others' opinions too readily. Get real and look behind you. It's the hidden problems that will sink you, not the obvious ones. If you aren't decisive, then your confidence – and even your health – could suffer.

5 Keep quiet about your plans, as there are others looking to nip them in the bud. Don't let them pose a threat, and your plans will succeed unhindered. Someone of the opposite sex could unexpectedly come to the rescue.

6 A real test is coming, so be prepared, since it's not going to go away. Emotional problems could resurface if you don't focus on what's important. Look for the early signs and act quickly to address the problem, and you won't be blamed by anyone.

No. 44
YIN • FORCED TO DECIDE

GOU

姤

You are being gripped by an invisible hand over which you have no control, and it's propelling you towards a dramatic encounter. Something female is exerting a powerful influence over your destiny. If left uncontested, this could cause irreparable damage to both your close personal relationships and your career. Listen to the signals you are receiving and take the deeper meaning on board. You have no choice but to meet halfway, as circumstances are driving you there. You will be given the authority to spread the news everywhere, and publicizing your concerns may be your best defence. Unless you take the initiative in a critical meeting, you may be forced to suffer the consequences.

Messages

1 If you allow things to continue, this could be a disaster. There's something or someone getting in the way, and you need to circumvent an issue by identifying it and negotiating your way around it. Don't hesitate; do it now.

2 You need to keep tight control of a situation or it will run away from you. Certain matters are best kept secret, as they may become misconstrued and annoy someone and cause a reaction. It might be best to walk away completely.

3 You're not sure at the moment. You're tempted to get involved because something on offer looks easy, but you're not convinced. You need more information and proof before you can make that informed decision. Take your time and gather more evidence.

4 You seem to have forgotten those lower down the chain who have helped you before. Keep them sweet – you will need them later. If you don't make the effort to get their support, it could all go pear-shaped.

5 Keep your head and take a deep breath before engaging in a debate. Analyse the elements you need to understand before giving advice to someone. Your position will strengthen and others will then be convinced and follow you where you want to go.

6 You could be put in the unenviable position of having to expose someone publicly. This won't be easy, and could be hazardous. But you need to do it, or you will lose strength and regret it in the long run, as it won't go away of its own accord.

No. 45

YANG • GATHERING AND LEADING

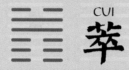

CUI

萃

Currently you're encouraged to concentrate on a common goal or one relationship. A reunion or get-together with colleagues or loved ones is in the air. If you've been working hard on a particularly difficult project, then you should persevere, as a celebration is on its way. You will make great progress by giving problems more direct attention – especially if you work co-operatively with others. As part of a group, you will achieve far more with the right leadership. The forces of chance and luck are not the same: taking a chance is the first step you take, whereas luck is an unexpected outcome. You may need to swallow your pride just now and accept your limitations – but this will stop you wasting effort and bring you closer to someone in a position of authority.

Messages

1 You need to go back to stage one, as you've reached a point of indecision and you don't have enough information to work on. So, start again with the guidance of those you can trust; if you ask for help, you will receive it.

2 You've only got so much time and energy available. Focus your attention and allow yourself to be drawn into a common purpose with others. Don't waste your time on unimportant things, or try to go it alone.

3 You're feeling like an outsider at the moment and things seem to be happening frustratingly slowly. There's a wider perspective than you currently realize, so open your eyes. A solution is staring you in the face.

4 Resist your natural urge to go it alone, as you feel you are on a roll, but you could take on too much if you're not careful. You can achieve anything if you just work with others, so give it a chance and see what happens.

5 You might be unsure where you fit in, or whether your credibility is taken seriously by others. Take time to assess their contributions and decide what role you can usefully play. Assemble your thoughts and others will agree with your strategy, which could surprise you.

6 You like to think of yourself as a natural leader, but you may have felt a little rejected lately. Events could bring a halt to recent progress and even create a personal health setback. Until you realize that others have strengths too, you cannot make progress.

No. 45

YIN • STICKING WITH IT

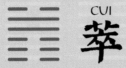

CUI

萃

Sticking with it is important today. It's not the time to go it alone, as the climate is in favour of forming alliances with others to combine your respective strengths. You must play your part in the team, despite the temptation to take all the glory for yourself. Harvesting is a collective pursuit; so is praying and open government. There's a large gathering of people taking place, and this will present management issues that only strong leadership can resolve. Turn the negative arguments into positive spin and bring the sometimes aggressive disagreement of others to your advantage. You will be strong as a unit as a result. You'll need to take precautions, but don't alert the opposition to your intentions.

Messages

1 You may have been too hesitant in a recent commitment or decision, and others have decided you are half-hearted. You've got to get to the core of an issue, and this may require going backwards and starting again. This is what's needed to convince others.

2 You may be inexorably drawn in a direction you hadn't considered before, like a moth is drawn to the light. It's OK to submit to your impulse, but you only have so much energy to go around. Reassess what you've got before making a commitment.

3 There's a lot of flak around and you are about to get your fair share. You might be excluded from a group or kept waiting, and this could upset you. Be realistic and bide your time. Things will turn around.

4 Sometimes we have to make a personal sacrifice for the greater good. This currently applies to you. Put the team first and you will achieve more success than going it alone.

5 Authority and power has to be won by commanding the support of others in your circle of contacts. This is at the forefront right now. You could be chosen to lead a group, but don't despair if your role is different – it's just as important.

6 A reconciliation you hoped for is not going to happen. Look inside yourself and explore the role you played. You won't like what you see and it could unsettle you. Don't despair; sometimes self-discovery is painful but necessary.

No. 46
YANG • FIRM PROGRESS

SHENG
升

You now need to recognize that things which take time to become deeply rooted last longer. Everything – from plants to buildings – needs a solid base and tender care to establish itself firmly, so make time to plan carefully for the future, which may have appeared uncertain lately. If you don't take advantage of the opportunities on offer, you can hardly complain if they pass you by. Friendships and close personal relationships should be fostered but not chased too quickly. Patience and endurance are the key. You are loved no matter what you've done in the past. Take a small step to plant a seed and then consult others with more experience about how to pace your relationships. The benefits will be permanent.

Messages

1 You can scale new heights today without worry of resistance. Progress and promotion are on the cards because the time is right. This is a very fruitful period, and new growth or a new addition is likely.

2 Gather the necessary arguments to convince others, and their misgivings will evaporate. Don't worry about giving something away in the process – no one will blame you for it. It will help you provide better balance in your life at this time.

3 So you've received a setback. Take a deep breath and revisit the problem with renewed strength. Great advances are forecast, especially in your career and personal development.

4 Forget about yourself for the moment and concentrate on others' needs. Don't ask for anything in exchange and you'll be surprised at the benefits. This is a time to be ambitious, but don't sell yourself short or you'll come to regret it. You'll enjoy the journey and it'll be worth it in the end.

5 You're not naturally over-cautious, but you should take one small step at a time and progress more slowly to your goal. It's definitely within your grasp now, even though the perspective appears not to change.

6 Keep pushing ahead, even if you're not sure where you'll end up. You may think that you're going up a blind alley but you'll benefit greatly from the learning process anyway.

No. 46
YIN • FORCING THE PACE

SHENG

升

This is your moment to move up the ladder. A distillation of your own efforts is about to bear fruit. Nourishing someone who needs it is called for, and they will grow with your support. Shed your inhibitions; there's nothing to hold you back. You may be required to contact someone who could be intimidating. Don't be afraid – events are moving in your favour and there's an unstoppable momentum under way. Your life is about to move on to a higher plateau. You will need to employ certain tactics to go all the way, however, such as being modest about your skills in front of others. It's the small victories which will allow you to win over others; then, there will be no holding back.

Messages

1 Advancement is on the cards, as you've made a great impression on people in important positions. A great challenge or expedition is in prospect. Don't hesitate to grasp the nettle – the wind of change is in your favour.

2 You might think you're a square peg in a round hole, but that's a mistake. Base your decisions on facts, not assumptions, and keep quiet about your misgivings regarding your own capabilities. You can't see through the eyes of others, but they will see the benefits of getting closer to you.

3 Things are going to come easily to you at the moment, but set something aside for a rainy day – it may come sooner than you think. Don't be afraid to say yes to accepting responsibility; you're up to it.

4 A magnificent result is around the corner. You could even reach the top of the pile and assume real power. No ambition is beyond you, but try to benefit others on the way up, as you may need them some day.

5 Success is coming easily right now, but this could lead to over-confidence and complacency. You need to graduate a step at a time, otherwise you could trip up and the whole edifice will come tumbling down.

6 Re-evaluate how you got to where you are, or you might make some dangerous mistakes. Continue to make progress but keep looking behind you. When the mist descends and a time of uncertainty and indecisiveness appears, use your experience; it will allow you to stay on the right track.

No. 47

YANG • CONSERVING ENERGY

KUN

You could become isolated at the moment, and feel exhausted by recent events. Nothing lasts for ever, and rejuvenation is needed. You're facing a number of difficulties, and may be beginning to wonder whether it's worth it. Dangers and conflicts abound, and personal and financial pressures have built up. You have been swimming against the tide for a while, and now it's time to resist no more – there's nothing you can do to alter your current circumstances. Jettison your long-held beliefs, exit your old haunts and resort to your own intuition; this is the only way you can deal with the current adversity and recover your self-esteem – by the changing landscape of your life.

Messages

1 You've lost your way for the time being and it's primarily of your own making. You need to allow time for the mist to clear – but it could take a while, so try to be patient. Just drift along and don't make any sudden impulsive decisions.

2 You may feel that you should do nothing. No one is fooled by your deliberate distractions. Just get real and face the music, and this will enable you to move on. Only you will know whether it's worth it.

3 You may have become distracted by matters which aren't important. You might feel you have lost something and that you are rudderless, but you're still impatient to make progress. Unless you begin to learn from your mistakes, you're destined to repeat them.

4 Don't be lectured at by others; no one can stand in your shoes. There will be a chance to wriggle out of their influence now, so take it and do your own thing. It may well be that you should do nothing at all and just sit on your hands.

5 Don't be discouraged. It doesn't matter whether others agree with you or not; so long as you are convinced in your decisions, they will just follow your example. You will overcome an impediment this way, but it could involve making a personal sacrifice.

6 Throw off your old restraints, as they are holding you back; you won't regret it. You've tried the standard solutions and they just haven't worked. It's time to try new things without a second thought, because the future looks rosy right now. Your luck has changed.

No. 47

YIN ● RECOVERY FROM SHOCK

 KUN

困

A period of confinement is on the cards. You may begin to feel disheartened and weary from what's been going on, and you could become exhausted. The wheat needs to be separated from the chaff, and the only way for this to happen is by going through the pain barrier of detachment. You've heard something you can't quite believe and it's damaged your spirit.

Meet the adversity by remaining cheerful. You are where you are. This will make you stronger, and you can draw a line in the sand and muster all your personal discipline to make that difficult decision. It's the end of the natural cycle in life, and you won't shrug off the feeling of being isolated until you face the truth. Don't hold any grudges – it won't do you any good.

Messages

1 You've been discouraged by recent events. You did contribute to this outcome, but don't fall into the trap of thinking you've failed. You just need some time out. This may take longer to sort out than you would like, but you don't have control of the timescale.

2 Lack of focus and pressure to deliver has left you feeling bored and distracted. Get involved with a new pursuit and pay attention to the multitude of contracts and arrangements, but don't stray from your skill-set. This will give you the focus that's missing.

3 You're not looking in the right direction. Trivial matters are distracting you from what really matters. Because you're impatient you've repeated the same mistakes, and may suffer the same consequences as a result. Keep your focus.

4 You may be about to suffer an embarrassing revelation – but it wasn't your fault. Your intentions are sincere but your actions missed the target. Take it on the chin, control your temper and move on.

5 There's a blockage in the way. A set of rules and regulations keeps thwarting your progress. Now's the time to demonstrate maturity by assuming a detached and considered position. This will slowly set you free from the constraints and you can get on with things.

6 Sometimes it's difficult not to let recent experience poison your attitude and make you cynical. Resist this and shrug off past mistakes. You may stumble on the way, but you're about to make real progress from now on.

No. 48
YANG • INNER DEPTHS

JING

井

You need to let your subconscious, innermost thoughts come to the fore, since the time is right to take advantage of your natural attributes. There's a struggle taking place between your daily life – which is totally preoccupying – and your heartfelt ambitions. The source of your strength is your deep-seated conviction that you are right and honourable in your intentions. You can either be a source of inspiration and nourishment to others, enriching their lives and breeding contentment, or you can allow things to regress, and the rot could set in and poison your relationships. Concentrate on simple pursuits which relax you and let you dream. This is how you unlock the solution – by unearthing your own inherent wisdom.

Messages

1 You've used up all your ammunition, your ideas have dried up and you no longer feel in tune with those closest to you. Seek new inspiration by stepping back from the situation. This will allow you to repair things and rebuild.

2 Going for short-term gain at the expense of the long run could leave you high and dry and empty-handed. Your talents need to be brought to the attention of a wider audience, because you're stuck in a rut and going nowhere.

3 You can see what needs to be done but you don't know where to start. Everything might appear like an uphill struggle. Stop what you're doing and think about what's really most important to you. The way will then become clearer and you can proceed.

4 Don't be distracted by what others are doing – try to distance yourself. Only you are in touch with your core strengths; they have their own agenda. Learn at your own pace; this will prepare you for what's coming.

5 You have the inner potential to achieve what you want because you have learned to see the issues from different perspectives. Let your own views prevail above others, but don't push it beyond what's familiar to you. The outcome will be surprisingly impressive.

6 We often have premonitions about what's going to happen, and this capacity in you is at its peak. Let your intuition make your decisions, and don't listen to others. The time is ripe for exceptionally good fortune that will last longer than you expect.

No. 48

YIN ● CLEAR THINKING

JING

井

The source of your strength is your absolute conviction that you've done all you can. You've amassed a great depth of knowledge and experience and you won't lose this just because you're being tested and aren't sure of the outcome. Don't allow others to obscure issues or muddy the water. Keep your head clear and don't do anything that could be misconstrued, as this could backfire. Just as a well is a source of nourishment, so education allows access to eternal knowledge and wisdom. Draw on this inner strength and you can build a relationship and career that will last. Pick those topics you most enjoy and give it your best shot. If you let others make decisions for you, the rot could set in and everything could stagnate, as they can't stand in your shoes. So, stand your ground and be brave today. This may pleasantly surprise some people.

Messages

1 You may have got above yourself in expressing your opinions too freely to someone close. This was unhelpful when they needed you to listen to them rather than talk. Now it's going to be hard for you to inspire that person for a while, so keep your own counsel and let matters settle down.

2 It could be frustrating for you at the moment, as you think no one's listening to you. Revisit your motivation – maybe it's misdirected and that's why others won't co-operate. Change something. Things don't look too good, so you may need to sacrifice short-term gain for a longer-term goal.

3 An opportunity presents itself but you can't see it, even though it's staring you in the face. Others around you can, but they're not recognizing your talents as the solution. Try to canvas their help, and they will allow you to see the light.

4 Maybe it's time to recognize that you can't make a contribution any more. Best to get out of the situation and revise your plans, otherwise you'll become exhausted and your health and welfare could suffer. You'll feel better once the decision is made and you're free of a responsibility. Then you will recover.

5 You can still be a source of inspiration and motivation to others, so grab the limelight while it shines on you. Drink the success that's coming to you, but don't try to spice things up too much or you could spoil the enjoyment. Put a limit on things.

6 It's a cracking time to enhance your career and get closer to someone in authority who is important. There's a clear path to promotion before you, so don't be deflected by others' caution. Go in head first; the time is right and you can't fail.

No. 49

YANG • TRANSFORMATION

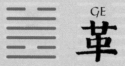 GE 革

Fundamental and difficult changes are in the air for you right now. Fire and water don't mix, and there is currently a struggle on the cards. The culmination of this struggle means you have to learn to let go. Be sensitive to other people's shifting attitudes and opinions. Open your mind to new experiences, don't rail against them, because what is happening is unavoidable and natural. Success is about your relationships, not money and power. You are receiving a warning here. Timing, however, is everything, so choose your moment to act. You'll be greatly strengthened by the experience but won't recognize this until the process has reached its conclusion, which could take longer than you'd like.

Messages

1 Don't do anything new for now, because the time may not be right. Keep your head down and assume a position of humility. Just see how things develop, and react to events rather than initiating them.

2 In the natural order of things we are reborn and move on. To do this you must be decisive and absolutely committed when the time comes to act. Take one step at a time; small victories are what you need at the moment. The big picture will then become clear.

3 If you continue to hold your stubborn position, this will cause conflict and send you backwards. Learn to be both patient and flexible, but don't use this as an excuse to hesitate, or you'll lose out. Try to be calm and remain unruffled by the tests before you.

4 These are radical times. You're shedding your old ties and moving on. Don't look back any more – leave them behind and look only to the future. You may end up leader of the pack, or very close to it.

5 Something's coming to a head. You can't do anything about it; don't dither any more, and stop assessing your options. Just choose the most obvious route and get on with it.

6 Only by bringing others with you can you move forward. Your patience and persistence, with their help, will be rewarded. If you drag up old problems this will cause conflicts to resurface and set you back where you started – so forgive and forget, and move on.

No. 49
YIN • NEW CHALLENGES

GE

Renewal is in the air. In nature, things transform themselves by peeling away the old and undergoing a remarkable transformation. This is happening to you at the moment. The whole cycle of change is being compressed into a short time period. You need to plan things so they take place in the correct sequence. Don't let things become confused – a revolution needs a focal point. You will know when everything is in its proper place; then, you are ready to move. This applies to taking a decision but also to your location and occupation. While it's an exciting time, there will be risks; when a situation changes this fast, it can spin out of control. Don't try to do too many things at once. Think of the reason you are doing something, not just the outcome. If you're sincere, it will work out fine.

Messages

1 Don't push it. The circumstances are not favourable and you could mess things up if you don't ease off. You don't have enough information to make a decision, so you should wait.

2 Things have begun to clear. The critical issues have come to the fore and crystallized themselves. Jettison old habits, because it's time for something completely new – but you must remain fully focused and committed.

3 You can't resist the changes now taking place, so there's no point in attempting to. Try not to be obstinate, as this could turn out to be harmful to your prospects. Go with the flow and accept what's coming. There's a test on its way, but you can cope with it.

4 There's a dramatic change about to take place. Look to the future and prepare yourself for a change in location or position. You won't see it coming, but it could transform your life.

5 You may be surprised that others support your position. There's no need to be cautious any more. Burn your bridges and get on with it – you're now heading in the right direction and the wind is behind you.

6 You've already achieved a lot, so don't try to wring too much out of the current situation. You can never sell at the top; always leave some profit for somebody else. Be satisfied with what you've achieved and take it. If you push it any further, you could lose everything.

No. 50
YANG • NOURISHING LIGHT

DING

Things are developing on a much higher plane and there's a cosmic balance in all that you are doing at the moment. Today you should become chastened by an unusual and unexpected experience. There isn't enough darkness in the world to extinguish the light of hope; nevertheless, sometimes we have to suffer pain and disappointment in order to become strengthened and changed by it. This is just realignment taking place in your life. In the background there's a tremendous cauldron of activity developing, creating an energy which is about to shed light on everything. Prepare for an initial setback, but try to use it positively to see what's important. If you do this, it will improve your inner strength and make you a warmer character to be around – and will benefit others close to you, too.

Messages

1 Unless you decide to change your attitude you can't make progress, because the ways you've tried to resolve matters in the past are getting nowhere. You may need to reflect on this and endure the anguish before continuing. It'll turn out right in the end, but only after a period of suffering.

2 There's a great prospect on the horizon and you may need to detach yourself from others, as they could become envious and try to distract you. Don't let anyone put you off; you're solely responsible for your choices, and you can go it alone if you have to.

3 Your colleagues are not convinced of your qualities, so you can't get help from that direction just yet. Don't overreact to dissent and disagreements. Hang around, and things will change in your favour. Persistence is the key right now.

4 You need to concentrate on your health and close relationships, as they're currently working against you and are out of balance. You've bitten off more than you can chew and will be out of your depth if you're not careful. Pull the plug on some things, or you'll come to regret it.

5 When the challenge is presented, just accept it. The time is right for change and you've known for some time it was coming. Watch out for signs, because they will now reveal themselves. Be receptive and it will work out.

6 Don't be disheartened; you will make progress, and a sign will give you encouragement soon. A new level of attainment stands before you, taking you to a higher level. If you manage your expectations, this will energize you even more.

No. 50
YIN • GUIDING OTHERS

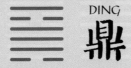

DING

Your wise words are about to provide nourishment to others. A cauldron of emotions has been boiling for some time, and others around you have looked for guidance as to their fate. You've been chosen for this purpose, and today you possess the authority to distil all the arguments in a cogent way and present a clear path of progress. But you will need to make some sacrifices. Detractors will try to deflect you from your purpose; burn them off and leave them in your wake. It's also a time for you to prosper. Your decisions will be correct, and the widespread benefits will surprise even you. Your confidence will then improve, as a result.

Messages

1 You've made a mistake and may have to start over again. It's been like watching an accident in slow motion. Take a different route. Be unconventional, and you won't regret it.

2 Don't be discouraged by the failures of others. They can't see the wood from the trees – but you can. Learn by their mistakes. You're about to get a pleasant surprise.

3 You might feel you're banging your head against a brick wall. You've not yet managed to convince someone that you were right all along. Don't give up. While in the short term this could upset you, in the long run it will turn out fine.

4 It's time to recognize your limitations and withdraw. You need to repair the damage done. If you don't try to recover the position quickly, you will lose the chance and fail to make any progress. You need to act now.

5 You have to keep on learning, at the same time being modest and open-minded to the ideas of those who work and live with you. Accept the challenges presented to you and you will surprise yourself with the rapid progress you make.

6 The way forward is now crystal clear. Some people are strengthened by adversity, while others never recover. You've been through setbacks and come out stronger and more purposeful. Set your sights higher, as today is one of startling success.

No. 51

YANG ● SHOCK AND AWE

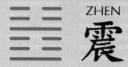

ZHEN

震

The only thing for certain at the moment is shocking unpredictability. A thunderous climate has developed and you'll be shaken awake as something comes to a head. It could go either way. This will test you to the limit. You may have laboured under an illusion for too long and now you're going to find out the truth. Your plans could be dashed, with everything you've planned for collapsing in a heap. The sudden forces about to be unleashed will act like a lightning strike, bringing great changes all around it. It will, however, clear the air. The good news is that the limelight will turn to face you – and this is just what you wanted. Use this as a severe warning, see it for what it is and invite change, and you can become even stronger in all you do.

Messages

1 If you can get through this time, you will be strengthened by the experience. It won't be a comfortable ride and you could well be frightened by an unexpected event. But you will get through it.

2 A cataclysmic upheaval is around the corner. Just let problems go and don't worry about them. You couldn't influence events anyway, and if you can just ignore the side effects you'll recover more quickly.

3 A person without substance has nothing to lose; neither have you, at the moment, so carry on regardless. Maintain your composure in the face of unwelcome pressure from new friends and acquaintances, and you'll be strengthened by the experience.

4 Don't let things you can't control have an effect on you. Keep the problems at arm's length and they'll just pass you by. If you let them get to you, you'll be reduced to a heap; be bored, not frightened.

5 Something won't go away no matter how you try, so you may as well just drop it. You've coped with these problems before, so there's no point in worrying any more. You've got more important things to attend to; get on with them instead.

6 Others seem to panic, whereas you know better how to cope. But others' problems are not yours, and you cannot put yourself in their shoes. Don't give them advice, as it will backfire – just keep an eye on them for now, and follow your own instincts.

No. 51

YIN • BOLT FROM THE BLUE

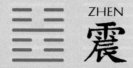

ZHEN

震

It's as if the ground underneath you is shaking. There's a powerful, thunderous energy rising from below and driving all opposition out of its way. This will cause surprise and a degree of concern in those you come into contact with. They may feel uncomfortable, and those who are scared will need calming down. Apprehension has spread far and wide, like distant thunder. Regard this as an omen that things have to change, but don't be fearful, as you can relieve the anxiety and use this to strengthen your hand. You will need to examine something very closely to get to the core issues and sort out some confusion. Then, like a bolt of lightning, your situation will be dramatically transformed.

Messages

1 An unexpected turn of events could look frightening at first. Take it as a warning not to overstretch yourself, and remember to employ caution now. Then you'll calm down and your mood will change.

2 It may be time to make yourself scarce. It could take a week before the storm passes. If you hang around, your losses can only deepen, so make a quick exit now while you have the chance.

3 Keep your wits about you, as you may need to dodge an issue. You can watch the problem bypass you, if you just step to one side – but do it quickly, as it's heading in your direction right now.

4 A shock wave is travelling towards you and you're not properly prepared. When it arrives, it could cause you to stop in your tracks and you may have to work hard to trudge through the quicksand trying to engulf you. Try to learn from the experience.

5 Once the initial impact of a recent shaking has worn off, other surprises may follow like aftershocks. You will become immune to their effects, however, and take them in your stride. Stay focused and the storm will pass.

6 Turmoil seems to be all around you. Relatives are unhelpful and there's a fear of impending disharmony. It's time to sit this one out, despite the grumbling from others. Wait until the storm passes before continuing with a project.

No. 52

YANG • STILLNESS

GEN

You've reached stalemate and aren't sure which way to turn. It's a time of reflection and introspection, when you need to contemplate your true objectives. Allow yourself time to think before you speak, and don't try to achieve fame, as its flame will be soon extinguished. You need to change course, as you can't progress in the same way as before. It's not a time to make fresh commitments, as you cannot keep to them. The problems that you face are caused by you and no one else. You must meditate and decide what's important now in your life, before you can go any further. This will crystallize the issues and renew both your mind and body, and bring a more lasting sense of fulfilment.

Messages

1 The issues confronting you are warning signs, not problems to resolve. The threats are more apparent than real. You're being given a chance to recognize the real issues and act now. Take notice of them, or else disaster could follow.

2 You can see that others are tipping over the edge and this hurts. You could be physically weary and unable to do anything about it, so look the other way and let them get on with it. The bad news is that you may have unwittingly contributed to all this.

3 You don't need to take any action at all. Keeping busy won't work as a distraction, so don't bother. Try to address the important issues and do what's right, but be more meticulous than usual; speed could backfire on you.

4 You just can't help it, but sometimes your efforts are misunderstood as interference. This just ensures the same problems will arise again and again unless you stop it. It's time for self-restraint.

5 Controlling what you say is sometimes very difficult. This outspokenness could cause you problems if you're not careful. If you can just take a deep breath instead, many of your difficulties will be resolved and you'll achieve that breakthrough.

6 Clear your mind of the clutter and calm yourself down. Once you are composed, your perspective will change. The issues will then become crystal clear and you'll reap the handsome rewards from your previous investment.

No. 52

YIN • TAKING A DEEP BREATH

GEN

It's the end of a natural cycle and your world is about to move on, into another phase of transition. But there's a space in between where you can take time out to think and also listen to another's views. Use the time to reflect on what's brought you to this position. Consider the distractions which have hampered your progress in the past and try to learn from the experience. The way you've seen things previously has held you back; wisdom comes from experience and learning from past mistakes, after exploring your inner world to discern your true motivation. Amassing possessions may just be a distraction from seeking the painful truth. Let go of something and reorganize your life. The new perspective will put you on the right path to self-discovery.

Messages

1 It's not clear whether a matter which was totally absorbing you is really over. You need more time. Don't rush into something just yet; just stay on your toes for now.

2 You're being swept along on the tide of change and you're enjoying the ride. But you don't know whether there's a ravine around the corner. Step off the gas and think more about where you are going. This will prepare you better for what's coming.

3 A restless situation did not arise as a result of your actions. Nevertheless, you may feel the urge to get more involved. It's not the time to; resist, or you may come to regret it.

4 You'll be in the right frame of mind to think things through once matters are more settled. Meditate on your own and don't be rushed by others; they can't see the wood from the trees, but you can.

5 You'll be exposed if you jump right in and start shouting the odds. Exercise your self-restraint and be careful what you say. This will save embarrassment – and it wouldn't have helped you, in any case.

6 Stop and think, and an inner composure will develop – which may surprise you. You may have wondered why people take relaxation classes and try to achieve a state of grace. You're about to find out why.

No. 53
YANG ● TAKING YOUR TIME

JIAN

漸

It's not a time to rush into things. There's a natural ordering of events unfolding which dictate their own pace. You need to slow things down. When things happen too fast, then the foundations of a career or relationship are not given their proper time to form naturally, and become weakened. If you can sit quietly and allow others to express themselves honestly, the roots of your relationships will be strengthened, making them longer-lasting. If you jump the gun you run the risk of jeopardizing everything, and things will drift out of your reach. Patience and perseverance are called for, and these will help you through the process.

Messages

1 You've only just begun, so relationships may be fragile and not yet properly formed. This is like the springtime in nature, where things need to take root but are at risk from external threats that are beyond control. Give it time and you'll see how much stronger you become.

2 You're now even more convinced that your time is coming. You are right. Give it just a little longer, and then form that new relationship or alliance. It will be beneficial for all concerned.

3 Stick to what's familiar or you'll be out of your depth. Failure can arise suddenly and unexpectedly. Don't risk anything; protect what you've got and events will turn in your favour.

4 Don't look for trouble – just sidestep a career or professional issue. Carefully assess your options; don't push it, and you'll be certain to succeed. The climate is favourable, so stop worrying.

5 Pushing ahead with your career could have consequences for your private life, if you let it. There's a window opening which will give you three chances, and it's time to take advantage. Attach priorities, and this will protect you from any threats.

6 Dispense with all the excess baggage and jettison what's not important, and this will elevate you above others. Adaptability is what you need to demonstrate right now. Then go for it – the time is right.

No. 53

YIN • SOLID PROGRESS

JIAN

漸

Just as water shapes most things on earth, today you need to submit yourself to the forces of nature. Constant attention to a particular matter has been preoccupying you recently, and you can't get it out of your head. A gradual and steady progress is on the cards, like a long-term building project or a series of small steps to fulfil a performance. This is the only way you can proceed. In the same way a mountain still appears distant even when you know you've travelled towards it, sometimes it's difficult to measure your progress. Don't let this dishearten you; an improvement in your situation is on its way. Those close to you will become more supportive, as they can see the way forward better than you. Domestic arrangements will benefit from a female influence. A cautious optimism will develop in you; you don't need to rush things.

Messages

1 Teething problems are quite typical when a new challenge is presented. Don't be downbeat if you take a couple of early hits which appear to hamper your progress. It's all quite normal.

2 Your security is uppermost at the moment, but your position is not under threat. There's no need to travel far to achieve what you want. Arrange a celebration and enjoy another's company; you're quite safe.

3 Consolidating your position should be the focus of attention. There's no need to go off at a tangent or take any risks. Secure what you have – cash something in, if necessary – and reduce your exposure to risk.

4 Safety first will ensure that a crowd around you can settle down and avoid a defeat. This will require some reorganization and it will test your patience, as others question your motives. But it will be worth doing, so you may as well get on with it.

5 Visible success always puts someone in the firing line. It could now be your turn. Take it on the chin, but try to confine the consequences to your career and not your private life. Steer a course between the two.

6 Hitting new heights is in prospect, and you may even develop a wider set of admirers. A spectacular and colourful event is about to take place, and you are at the heart of the arrangement. Enjoy it and relax – there are more challenges ahead.

No. 54

YANG • LOYALTY

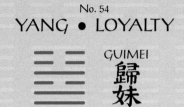

GUIMEI

歸妹

You could end up going around in circles at the moment. You're being led in completely the wrong direction, and it's largely your own fault because you didn't take time to assess the situation properly. You may be allowing someone or something to dominate you, but you believe it's worth it. Someone's intentions may not be sincere, and complying with them may appear to make you happy, but it's an illusion. If you are in a new situation, then it's best to keep your head down. Don't exceed your remit or you'll make mistakes, and don't push it in your personal relationships or it could backfire. Take time to get to know how an organization or group of people function; understand where the real authority lies.

Messages

1 You could be being taken for granted. Don't be pushed around or allow yourself to be blamed when you made no contribution to the current situation. Defend your principles, as no one is going to do it for you. You'll be surprised how people back off.

2 Don't worry about playing second fiddle at the moment. It won't affect you in the long run; just chill out for now, and let things float over your head. There's nothing you can contribute and nothing to gain at this point.

3 Remain steadfast in your intentions and don't be deflected by others. If you settle for less now, you will achieve much greater things later. You need to compromise, but don't take advice from fair-weather friends, who can be a bigger problem than you may think.

4 It's not too late to make amends. You need to stop taking action, however, and wait for a better moment, even though you are impatient. Stalling now will yield benefits.

5 Just because you really want something now doesn't mean it's the most important thing in the long run. The situation is serious, so think cautiously and be prepared to play second fiddle. You can expect a high-profile outcome soon, if you show some patience.

6 You've lost sight of what's most important, and the situation has now become difficult to manage. Let it go; nothing positive is going to come from it. Something better will come along later.

No. 54
YIN • LEARNING BY MISTAKES

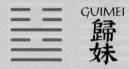

GUIMEI

歸妹

You need to renew your sense of direction today. A completely new situation has arisen, and it's as though you need to come of age. Sometimes sticking to a task requires a reassessment of previous well-entrenched beliefs. This is happening to you now. Recognize that you will never stop learning, and try to keep an open mind, despite the pain this might cause. Sometimes a change of direction or allowing a third party to get involved can calm things down and foster greater harmony. To get the best out of your predicament, don't try to enforce your will or impose a direction on events; you cannot control them. In any case, there are too many strands to deal with and you may need to cut out some responsibilities to allow you to focus on the main objective. This will enable you to gather support from others and alleviate matters.

Messages

1 There are times when you need to accept a subordinate role. Allow someone to take you into their confidence, and be supportive. Use tactfulness to influence their decisions. You can only benefit.

2 Maybe your expectations need revising. This will release you from a disappointment which is on its way. Set your sights lower for now; you still have lots to learn.

3 You may not like it, but your principles could be put to the test. Don't allow yourself to be compromised. Stick to your own rules, but try to learn from a mistake you made recently.

4 The world will not pass you by just because you've stepped back to think again. You've earned the chance to have second thoughts. An opportunity you thought had gone will come back around. When it does, grab it.

5 A degree of modesty can be useful in convincing someone you've got what it takes. Take an issue more seriously, because it could affect others more than you imagined. Then you'll get the appointment you always wanted.

6 You may have tried something new and it failed. It's just the inexorable power of nature, and you can't always influence the outcome. You're going to have to bite your lip and put up with the situation, but it will turn around quicker than you think.

No. 55

YANG • SUCCESS WITH CAUTION

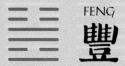

FENG

豐

You are reaching the zenith of your effectiveness and you should be pleased with yourself. Like a lightning strike, all about you will become illuminated and electric. But you need to harness all this creative energy to take advantage of what's coming, because it could be short-lived. You deserve success, and this wind of change pushes you beyond your wildest dreams. Just don't let it go to your head, or your friends will begin to see you in a different light and might not like what they see – and neither will you. Maintain your composure, even when enjoying the applause. In order to reap permanent benefit from the current situation, you need to assess what's really important to you and do without some of the trappings of success. Others will then be really impressed.

Messages

1 Take advantage of another's skills to grab what's there for the taking, even though you weren't aware of what they had to offer. A combined effort will reap rich rewards, but there's still a threat in the background that hasn't gone away.

2 Don't push it – there are some not yet convinced, and this could hinder your progress. Work hard to win someone over and others will follow. You may have been disappointed recently but things are about to turn in your favour.

3 You can't make progress without the co-operation of others – and they will block your progress if you don't change your attitude. It's time to let things lie, because this is not your lucky time. But it wasn't your fault in any case, so don't blame yourself.

4 There are so many opportunities available, you don't know which to choose. You need to consult someone who has already done it – they will help you. But don't try to make progress too quickly or you could trip up. Take your time.

5 At last, it's coming together. An elevation or promotion is on the cards. You can now have everything you've ever wanted, but you need to act with modesty or this could spoil things for you.

6 Success is on the cards. You're rightly proud of recent achievements, but be very careful not to peak too early. Don't let success go to your head or forget what others did for you. If they drop you, you'll be very unhappy, for your friends and loved ones are your greatest possession.

No. 55

YIN • ENJOYING THE LIMELIGHT

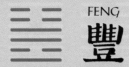

FENG

You've hit the peak and the view is breathtaking. Your talent is being recognized and the benefits are moving into view. You will also develop as a person – in fact, you need to, in order to keep a lid on the excitement. A sunny period is in prospect, and you could now be at the end of a phase of confusion or trial. A decision reached recently was just what you wanted and you feel vindicated in your approach.

A wise person will recognize that such periods of euphoria are very brief, however; a profusion of everything in nature usually precedes a change in the seasons and a reversal. You deserve the accolades, but contain the noise of your celebration, as the world will turn full circle and deflation will become inevitable. If you limit the upside, then you won't have too far to fall.

Messages

1 A mutually beneficial partnership is forming. Two heads are better than one, and the synergy will move you into a higher gear. Hold tight for an exciting ride – this is an exhilarating time.

2 Going it alone with a high-visibility strategy won't work. There's too much to do, and you could invite scathing comments – which might cause you stress. Avoid it, and contain your enthusiasm.

3 A mist has descended and it's difficult to know which way to turn. You need help from someone to give guidance and shed light on something that's just come up. Listen carefully, but don't act now; just wait for things to become clearer.

4 Try to retain your enthusiasm, even though some things are not working out as you'd hoped. Revise your plans and ask someone you trust if they agree with you. Then have another go.

5 Once you've taken advice, move ahead at full speed. It's time to harvest the crop you've been growing. It will then be a time of abundance; enjoy the fruits of success, but put something aside for a rainy day.

6 Enjoy your recent success but try not to over-indulge. Remember to appreciate the contribution made by others. If you don't, then they will disappear and won't come back when you might need them most.

No. 56
YANG • TRAVELLING

LU

It's time to test new horizons and experience what the whole world has to offer. Your life is going through clear changes, but you must remain true to yourself and your principles. Distance yourself from the pressure others are trying to exert, and make decisions with a cool head. You're about to alter some long-held beliefs and revise your views. Don't become a moving target just because you want to try something new. The vicious circle of stress can only be broken in your current situation if you step back and take time to assess what's going on. You're being tested to see whether your innate beliefs and principles will survive intact and protect you from adversity, but at times it could be a lonely journey.

Messages

1 You're getting nowhere and it could sap your energy and willpower. Decide what you want, rather than what you think you need. You're being distracted by trivial things, so retain your composure and persevere. You will benefit once more from help close at hand.

2 There's an opportunity now to take a break from the mundane and put some distance between you and others. Take advantage of it and you'll benefit from an unlikely source of comfort, as someone unlikely appears ready to help you.

3 You're not absolutely convinced, and this weakens your position and has made you careless. You may have interfered or gone too far when you shouldn't. You cannot be helped by others until you're sure of your stance; things don't look good, however, so lie low.

4 You're pleased with what you've achieved. but it's not really enough and you haven't arrived yet, so this may have left you feeling uneasy. Don't settle for a result other than the one you really want. This could involve moving or, indeed, going back to where you've come from.

5 Don't be distracted on the way. This is a fantastic opportunity for you, and you'll exceed all expectations. Keep your focus on the endgame; it'll work out and, at last, you'll get what you deserve.

6 You're faking it and got involved with matters you probably should have left alone. Open your eyes and stop being gullible. If you don't change your course, it could end in disaster.

No. 56
YIN • NEW FRONTIERS

LU

旅

Experiencing a different context is called for. Travel broadens the mind, but wandering aimlessly can bring danger. You need to consult widely before embarking on an expedition, and this could take some time. There was something holding you back from testing new horizons, but it's gone now and you're free of it. Refer to those with experience and look into the minutiae; the devil is in the details. Jettison your old habits and – especially – your second thoughts. You really are capable of taking on the challenge and should be free from doubt. That way, you'll embrace the new experience and extract the maximum benefit. The pressure will then be off – and away you go.

Messages

1   An unwelcome visitor may be on their way. Deflect them if you can, and send them travelling in the opposite direction. You've got enough on your plate as it is – you don't need any more hassle.

2   You'll get help now to plot a route. Use this both to escape a current predicament and to explore new frontiers. You've been waiting for this. A new world beckons.

3   A temporary association might lead to you burn your fingers. This is because you made yourself vulnerable by believing a story without the evidence to support it. This could place you in a weakened position and you're going to have to work hard to get out of it.

4   Some say it's better to travel than to arrive, but that's not the case with you today. You need the security of knowing your achievements have been recognized as genuine and valuable. Ask the question, and your self-confidence will benefit.

5   The greatest gifts you have are your time and trust. When venturing afar, you must be selective how you apportion these attributes. Give a little, and you will get a far greater return; be stingy, and you'll get nothing back.

6   Don't allow a new location to alter your moral compass. You're still the same. If you let your views change at the whim of what you just learned from a journey, you run the chance of becoming rudderless. You could then sink without trace, so step back and consider what you really want.

No. 57

YANG • GENTLE PERSUASION

XUN

巽

You can be as carefree as the wind now, as matters change course in your favour. But remain adaptable, as you are fundamental to effecting changes in those close to you. You'll confront all your recent problems and scatter them to the winds. You're willing to submit yourself to the gentle influence of others, and this brings with it clarity of vision which sharpens your perspective. Try not to force things, as this only brings out resistance; you must develop humility. The wind of change is about to be expressed through your actions. You may need to appear not to care too much in order to help someone close, and both your emotional and physical health will be tested and then improve. This way, your apparent indifference will become a strength from which you can both only benefit, as you become the catalyst for unfolding and dramatic changes.

Messages

1 You've got to be flexible and sparing with how you use your energy; it's not inexhaustible, and you're not sure which way to go, as the signals are mixed. You can't win people over by constantly nagging them; instead, you must be decisive and stick to your decisions.

2 There are certain things you can't control and they're taking over events. Just as some seed scattered is wasted, some great ideas don't see the light of day. Review where you stand, unearth the critical issues and ask someone who's not involved what they think. Don't be afraid to ask for help.

3 Take it easy and stop prevaricating – it's only causing problems with others. If you don't stop, others will back off completely and leave you to grapple with your indecisiveness. This could cause you an unexpected lack of confidence, or worse.

4 You've set off on the right course but now need to take your foot off the pedal. When you start again, the way forward will become clearer, as problems get out of your way. Whatever you're about to embark upon will succeed.

5 It's time to draw a line under your achievements and think about what you've got. Only then should you reveal something to someone close, and, after early setbacks, you can make progress. You will have to rise to the challenge in order to do so, and there will be risks on the way.

6 You may have become over-exposed and over-stretched. This could create some suffering and even jeopardize your health, if you're not careful. Limit your exposure and you can limit the damage; otherwise, someone below you in the chain of life could cause you grief.

No. 57
YIN • STRENGTHENING TIES

XUN

巽

It takes time for strong relationships to form. They need to be anchored in trust, co-operation and a mutual give and take. This is how nature operates, and you will currently be feeling the full force of the natural cycle, as events beyond your control gather pace. You now need to reap a harvest and offer to share the benefits with others – even those you haven't always agreed with. This will test your character, and runs the risk of shaking your convictions to their roots. A gradual change of emphasis will penetrate the minds of others, and this will have lasting consequences. Only by testing the strength of a friendship will you know it's well established and worthwhile, allowing the cycle of change to continue unhindered, driving you towards a stronger partnership.

Messages

1 It's not a time to dither. You might think that changing your mind could look thoughtful, but to most it speaks of indecision. It's make-your-mind-up time. Toss a coin if you need to – your decision will be the correct one, anyway.

2 There are influences around that are confusing the situation. Get to the core of an issue today; be forceful, as you could have the most to lose. Opposition will then melt away.

3 You run the risk of over-cooking a problem if you carry on as you are. Be realistic about who is doing what, allocate responsibilities using your own interpretation and make an instant judgement.

4 The way forward is about to reveal itself to you. When this happens, throw yourself into it with both feet. Don't worry about splash-back or upsetting someone – it can't be helped, and was necessary to bring someone into line.

5 If you really want to change things around, first off, finish what you've started. Then, when you're ready, change direction. You will find you've already done most of it, and the rest will be easy.

6 You could spread yourself too thinly if you carry on as you are. Don't commit yourself. Learn to say no, and then you will have the time and energy to exert the maximum influence and achieve the result you want.

No. 58
YANG • INNER CONTENTEDNESS

DUI

兑

This is a time of great encouragement for you and it will infect those around you, but you must continue to co-operate with others. You'll find true fulfilment today, as opposed to merely temporary pleasure. This stems from knowing what's really important to you, rather than from the accumulation of material things. You have a natural charisma which can be employed to teach others the right way to improve their lives. You've learned that material possessions can be an illusion. Get rid of the trappings of transient success, don't be distracted by a piece of good luck and you'll feel deeply contented by finding the thread of truth in all things. It's time to let yourself blossom.

Messages

1 What more do you want? You should be thankful for what you have achieved already. Relationships are stronger than they may at first have appeared. Settle for what you have and more things will turn out right.

2 If you try to behave as others want you to, it won't work, as this will distract you from the real issues and you'll come to regret it. Follow your own path and things will work out. You were born with an unusual clarity of vision and it's now at its peak.

3 Distracting yourself with short-term highs won't work. The more you do it, the deeper your problems will become, so extricate yourself now before it's too late. There's usually a payback time, after going over the top in enjoying yourself.

4 Be positive and don't just react to uncertainties or go with the flow, as this comes across as dithering to others and devalues you. You need to decide what's most important and act decisively. Don't trust everyone you meet – just those you know.

5 You feel uneasy about confronting your feelings and changing your circumstances. A series of half-truths are in circulation and you can't figure out the source. A relationship or new association is on the horizon, but the timing just isn't right – avoid it like the plague.

6 Things have turned against you and uncomfortable truths have been unearthed. You're not yet sure what to do and matters are currently beyond your control, so leave it alone for a while or you'll be making a big mistake.

No. 58

YIN • CLEAR COMMUNICATION

DUI

A meeting of minds is in the offing. You should remain open to others' ideas and engage in clear communication; a frank exchange of views is about to take place. You may be invited to address an audience and capture the attention of the wider public. Your communication skills will enrich those who listen – including a partner – and something which had gone out of joint will click back into place. Knowledge and education are paramount now. This brings you a clear vision and an infectiousness which enthuses those who come into contact with you. It's rare that the natural cycle brings all the patterns of experience in balance together in one place, but this is happening to you now. Your confidence and self-belief will improve as a result.

Messages

1 The time is auspicious. You may find it difficult to accept just how lucky you've been. It was your attitude and frame of mind which produced a great result. Remember this and learn from it.

2 You could regret it if you take unnecessary risks. You're having a great run of luck, but don't push it – you're already over-burdened with benefits. Just count your blessings, sit back and enjoy it.

3 You may be tempted to become distracted by an opportunity presenting itself today. This will involve straying outside your comfort zone, where your knowledge and experience are paramount. Don't do it, or you may come to regret it.

4 A choice presents itself. Should you go high or low? It's best to stick to what you know and understand; you don't need to take risks you can't calculate. Then, what you choose will yield a great result.

5 An enjoyable time will produce encounters with new people who have different ideas. One of them lies beneath your dignity. Despite the obvious attraction, shun them and stick to your close circle of friends and loved ones, or you may come to regret it.

6 Why risk what you've got? You're having an enjoyable period, and refreshing entertainment is coming from the most unexpected directions. Embrace it, but don't over-indulge. Use the experience to develop an inner peace and calm; this is where your true contentment lies.

No. 59

YANG • RECONCILING

HUAN

渙

In nature and all of physical existence, the process of dying performs a pivotal role in renewal. This is a time for the reforming of ideas and rebuilding personal and family ties. To do so, you may need to let go of some things and get back to your roots. Matters will only become clearer for you at the moment if you allow things to come to a head. You need to broaden your vision, as you've become preoccupied with old problems and this has narrowed your outlook. Let go, widen your personal horizons, alter your perspective, and regain your creativity and enthusiasm for life. The important matters will crystallize, while the insignificant ones will simply disappear from view.

Messages

1 News of an offer or proposal is about to arrive. If you wait for things to develop at their own pace, you could be overwhelmed. Sort things out, now that you have identified the issues, take control and you'll be better prepared for what's coming.

2 Stop trying to deal with problems on your own. Step back and give yourself time to think things through, because there are opportunities coming to a head from unexpected directions you may not recognize. Enlist the support of others or you'll fail.

3 Don't try to get one over on others or take more than you deserve, because you may need their help in the near future. There's something much more important about to happen to you.

4 Put some distance between you and the wrong people. This is the only way you can be rid of your past and share your future with those who are like-minded. Trust your own judgement.

5 Something's got to give, and you need to overcome certain feelings that have made you feel alienated. The issue can be resolved if you concentrate on it to the exclusion of everything else. Only you can sort the problem out, so you had better get on with it now.

6 Your situation could look dire, but at least you've recognized the issues in time. This is lucky, as you can nip problems in the bud. There's no gain without pain – you can't avoid it, and it wasn't your fault anyway.

No. 59

YIN • CLEARING AWAY

HUAN

渙

It takes sunshine to disperse mist, and the wind to clear the skies. This is a time when the fog of confusion is lifted and you see things for what they are. You can now make that important decision. In doing so, you need to find a common theme that will bind people together, reminding everyone that all creatures form part of the same universe. Acquire the property, travel the distance or change vocation if you need to. Whatever was holding you back has released its grip; a problem has been resolved and you can cope with the consequences. The wheel has turned full circle and you're free to jettison certain relationships – but you won't forget them. It's just nature's process; renewal always follows clearing away the old.

Messages

1 You need to fix something before it gets any worse, otherwise it will take longer to heal or resolve. Deal with it now and disperse the crowd, which is creating a suffocating atmosphere.

2 Peace of mind will only come by getting your head straight. You probably need to debate something so you can expose all the arguments on both sides. Then, you can decide what you really believe and identify a common purpose before acting.

3 In order to sort things out, you need to be more selfish. It's not that you don't care about the others – it's just that you need to immerse yourself more with the issue at hand. That way, you won't be distracted and you can push harder to resolve a nagging problem.

4 It really is time to resolve a dispute. You have the vision to assess the consequences for all parties involved. You're not entirely independent or objective, but that won't matter, as you find common ground for everyone. Spread the benefits around as best you can.

5 Others will look to you to come up with a penetrating idea. Only you have the attributes necessary to secure a breakthrough. Once you do this, others will join you and set aside their differences. That's the way forward.

6 They say there's no gain without pain. The problem is how widely that pain has spread, and your caring nature wants to spare the consequences for others close to you. You won't be blamed if you try to avoid responsibility completely and escape the situation.

No. 60
YANG • AVOIDING EXTREMES

JIE

節

Everything has its limits and you may be reaching yours. Grasping what you can is all well and good until you become over-stretched, then problems can set in. You need to make sure that you don't overdose; you can have too much of a good thing, so stop and think. Limit your expenditure and your ambitions, but don't be over-cautious; if you go from one extreme to the other you'll really regret it, because now is not the time to hide from taking calculated risks. You don't always think before you speak, but you need to now. Try to set limits on your personal conduct and an inner calm will develop in you.

Messages

1 Restrain your inclinations and don't act now, because the test ahead of you could be overwhelming. There will be a better time to pursue your ambition, so sit tight and gather your strengths.

2 Don't be afraid to step out from the past if you want to make progress. Good luck is usually the result of turning chance to your advantage. An opportunity with great potential is on its way in your life, but you mustn't hesitate; grab it, otherwise it may pass you by.

3 Put a stop to things now or you'll regret it later, because you may have gone too far in your recent behaviour. Some of your associates aren't helping the situation. Get your act together by not blaming others, take the responsibility on the chin and move on.

4 Don't push yourself too far. If you try too hard, the success will be temporary, so take a deep breath, accept your limitations, be cautious and the benefits will be lasting. Be happy with what you've got.

5 Make progress discreetly – don't make a song and dance about it, and you'll achieve your goals more quickly. Others will be turned off if you blow your own trumpet too often. Enjoy your good fortune quietly.

6 You could feel weary after recent pressures. If you push too hard now, you could lose everything, because you may push others too far and they can't cope as well as you can. Let things lie, try to ignore others' limitations and success will arrive anyway.

No. 60

YIN • KEEPING YOUR NERVE

JIE

節

What's happening at the moment requires you to remain diligent and inspect something very closely indeed. Only you have the equipment to investigate a difficult matter. You need to cut through the fat and get to the core of the issues – then the weaknesses in the current situation will be exposed, and you will be able to avoid difficulties. Setting personal limits in conduct is not easy, but it's critical in restricting the abuse of scarce resources and corrupting our position in society. You're like a surgeon about to perform before students: everyone is waiting to observe your professionalism in action and to learn by your example. In some senses this role was thrust upon you by circumstance. Keep focused on the job and know when to stop; if you were to stray along the way, the consequences for all could be dramatic.

Messages

1 You'd like to push forward in one direction now, but this could be a mistake. Recognize your limitations – it's time for second thoughts and a reinspection. Are you sure you've got everything you need?

2 When you've got everything together, then it will be time to drive on. If you remain confined to your present location or circumstances because it's comfortable, this may cause you to miss the opportunity. So, get on with it – you need to change things around.

3 A decision you made earlier may have backfired. You didn't read that situation correctly, so it's time to collect your thoughts and reconsider. Accept responsibility for the error, put it in the past and move on.

4 If the consequences of a mistake are painful, you will heal the pain by coming clean on an issue and revealing your role. This will secure your position and allow things to improve at their own pace. Don't create further aggravation by sitting on your principles.

5 Accept your limitations. You are at a juncture and need to decide which route to take; knowing what you're good at should drive your decision. Don't take the chance that you can learn what you need to know quickly enough – you can't.

6 Just because you can't do something, don't stop others attempting the same. Step back and watch the show. You'll need all your self-restraint not to get involved, but they have to learn their own way, not yours. Limiting your participation will benefit everyone.

No. 61
YANG • INNER TRUTH

ZHONGFU

中孚

Some people possess a natural inner strength that enables them to absorb everything life throws at them. They turn misfortune to their advantage and never give up. Your inner strength is inspiring others, and creating lasting friendships and strengthening family ties. When given the chance to speak openly about your heartfelt beliefs, do so with confidence, because you have developed an insight which enables you to see from others' perspectives. Don't hide your deepest emotions, or you could become ill. Let the truth speak. Contain your ego and you'll know when the moment is right to reveal your views and act on the basis of the valuable things you have learned. Everyone will benefit.

Messages

1 Take a deep breath, let events unfold and try not to stand out from the crowd. Don't worry about what others think; follow your innermost feelings – they're right. You won't regret it.

2 You have lasting relationships that can withstand any test. Let these relationships guide your decisions and you'll succeed. This could be your finest hour, with a new arrival on the horizon.

3 Don't become too dependent on others' views, as this will obscure your innermost beliefs and distract you from your goals. You need to decide what you need to do for yourself and then act on it. Great changes are in prospect, but their outcome will remain uncertain.

4 Detach yourself to some extent from those you've got a little too close to, since things have become strained. This won't be a mistake, as it will allow you to learn from experience. You'll find this will strengthen your relationships, not weaken them.

5 Find a way to speak out openly about what you believe. You have the capability to lead others into a better place. Those who agree with you will be inspired and driven by your words, and this will lead to career enhancement and wider recognition.

6 Although you've expressed your views, your perspective on reality is slightly adrift and could have been influenced by someone new on the scene. Change your attitude, or you could lose your real friends and your self-confidence.

No. 61

YIN • SHARED FEELINGS

ZHONGFU

中孚

You'll be expected to pull things together that have drifted apart. Others will rely on you, and believe in your judgement and sincerity. This power brings with it responsibility, and this will require you to reveal your true feelings to someone. This might be risky, but you have to do it to measure their reaction. Only then will an inner truth reveal itself. The strongest bond that holds people together is more than a common objective; there must also be a shared interest in truth and forgiveness. You need to find this out now, and there is no time like the present. This will separate the wheat from the chaff and, after a trial period, you can get your act together again and restore balance and harmony. Everyone will thank you.

Messages

1 It's time to get back to basics. You know what drives you and the principles which operate your moral compass. If you depart from your core values you'll come to regret it, so start a debate now.

2 Speak to another about why you feel as you do. Your words will comfort more than one person, and will resonate with them all. This will enhance your status and sphere of influence, and allow everyone to come to a common view.

3 Don't let a malign influence determine what you do, otherwise you'll be pulled in one direction, then another. This will confuse matters and deepen the uncertainty. Keep away from them.

4 Detach yourself from certain people and go your own way. You need to clear your head in order to analyse a problem more closely. Start with the detail and build from there – you will then discover a consensus.

5 The levers of power operate in different ways. You have a special gift of communication at the moment, and what you say today will exert more influence over others than you think. This will bring added responsibility and authority. Be careful how you use this power.

6 You could be driven to asking for help in public. This outward display would be inappropriate and could backfire. Keep your thoughts, and your weaknesses, to yourself, as this will only expose differences and cause a rift.

No. 62

YANG • HOLDING BACK

XIAOGUO

Circumstances have worked in your favour recently, but self-restraint and paying attention to detail are now called for. Something's telling you not to push things too far. A weakness has been exposed. You need to revise your expectations and set your sights lower, as you're trying to fly too high and could be in danger of a great fall to earth. The signs are there – just think about it. Don't pursue fantastic gains, and keep a careful eye on all financial matters by studying things carefully and exercising caution. Avoid being arrogant; instead, try to be humble and prudent, and then your shortcomings will be forgiven. If you don't take action now, you will be severely disappointed.

Messages

1 After a decent run of good luck, things don't look too good at the moment. Don't get involved with what you don't understand. You may be deceiving yourself – it's too early for you, and everything could go pear-shaped.

2 If you can just settle for second best, then this won't push you too far in the wrong direction and you'll be satisfied. Relationships should be nurtured carefully, as you'll need them, particularly for career advancement.

3 There's no need to run the risks you are taking. You've become over-confident and this could be bad news, as you may be betrayed by false friends. Stop now, or you'll come to regret it.

4 It's not good enough just to sit back and wait to see what's coming. You need to recognize the mistakes you've already made and address them in detail in order to make progress. Things can't be swept under the carpet, so don't even try.

5 It's not turning out as you've anticipated, so change your expectations and adopt different tactics by consulting others. Only then can you achieve what you want. If you continue as you are, you will only make things worse.

6 If you go for it now aggressively, you'll fail, as you've set yourself impossible objectives. Take a break from things and forget about your problems for a while. Once you stop deluding yourself, you'll be pleasantly surprised at the outcome.

No. 62

YIN • TIME TO WITHDRAW

XIAOGUO

小過

You could become a prisoner of your own success, if you're not careful. A recent run of good fortune has set you up a treat, but you could have more on your plate than you asked for. Others envy your achievements and are placing demands on you that they wouldn't dream of attempting themselves. It's a way of testing your mettle, to see if you're as good as you think you are. See through this, and focus on what really matters to you rather than to others. Concentrate on helping those less fortunate than yourself, even though there's no obvious material benefit. As you watch the effect this has on the lives of others, it brings a sobering influence and an inner calm. That way, the pressure on you will subside, as others recognize your unselfishness. Then they can go their way and you can go yours with confidence.

Messages

1 If you were thinking about taking a risk, avoid it. Everything is stacked against you. Occupy yourself by going through the motions; spend time attending to those jobs you've been putting off. Keep a low profile.

2 Use your connections to find common ground. You're going to have to be content with what you already have today and give something away. If you try to go off in a new direction you could fail, so hold off for now.

3 If you're travelling a new route, be very wary. This may be new ground and you don't know what might be waiting on the sidelines, as you may not have experienced this before. Keep your wits about you and watch your back.

4 Best to stay where you are at the moment and stick to what you know. This is not the time to push ahead, because a barrier has come down. Wait for another chance; there will be a better opportunity and it will be less risky.

5 There's a glimmer of hope on the horizon but, despite some positive news, it is still not the time to forge ahead. Be flexible, and ask someone you trust for their opinion – then take more time than usual to think about it.

6 Try not to become over-ambitious. If you fly too close to the sun, your wings could get singed and you'll fall down to earth with a bump. Restrain yourself; it's just not the right time to reach for the sky. Try to be patient.

No. 63

YANG • SAFE HARBOUR

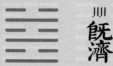

You can find the right balance with patience and through concentrating on small, mundane tasks you normally find boring. Don't force matters, as you don't need to achieve great changes to maintain a successful balance in your life. The time is right for enjoying success, but keep on your guard or it will all change again. It's like being becalmed in the eye of a storm – as if you've just finished a great meal and are taking time out to relax. But the universe is never static; use the time to contemplate the really important matters in your life. You're at the apex of your career opportunities and personal relationships, but when the storm moves on, sometimes cataclysmic events can ensue.

Messages

1 Things keep going wrong. You won't feel like you're going in the right direction but you are – it's just that your perspective hasn't detected it yet. It could be a rough ride and you're bound to have second thoughts, but press ahead anyway.

2 Don't get desperate if you're not sure of things. The problems are not of your making; they will pass, and you'll get back on track. Patience and perseverance provide the key to success.

3 The worst is over, but don't let ignorant people spoil what you have achieved. Your ambitious goals are certainly attainable but it will exhaust all your energy. So, take a break, concentrate on family matters and come back refreshed.

4 Be very careful. Don't do something you don't want to do just for the sake of others. Use your own common sense – you need it now. Attack any problems head-on and don't be distracted.

5 Sometimes it's better to make less effort to get what you want. Others don't necessarily see things the way you do. Resist being ostentatious, as this could backfire at the moment.

6 You've achieved great things lately, but this has brought with it new responsibilities. Don't get too comfortable or blasé, or you'll be back where you started. Travel is tricky at this time, and could bring problems.

No. 63
YIN • TAKING SHELTER

You've made progress already and need to keep on the same course. You may have to handle rifts within the family and you might discover that your career is less secure than you thought. It's like being caught in the eye of a storm. You feel becalmed, as if there's no threat around and all is peaceful; it appears as though you've reached a safe harbour. In fact, there's turmoil in the outer realms of your circumstances; you must maintain a careful balance between competing energies. Be cautious, so you don't tip this balance one way or the other. As things move on you will experience a period of turbulence, and your comfortable position will be shaken and tested. You may have to confront someone who is distressed and come to their defence. You can't avoid this and have to see it through in order to restore things to where they were.

Messages

1 The process of change you're going through is bringing with it more pressure than you'd imagined. Interconnections you hadn't anticipated now come to the surface, and frustrations could boil over. The way forward is not clear, but you need to carry on anyway, as you can't do anything about it.

2 A sudden weakness has been exposed. Don't try to cover it up, but let it come to the fore. You haven't lost your way – you're just suffering a delay. Wait, and the situation will resolve itself.

3 It's worth hanging in there, despite the trials and the pain. Persistence will pay off. You've achieved more than you may have thought and you're nearer your goal than is apparent, so carry on regardless – you will get there.

4 It's time to watch your step. Something was hidden from you and it disguises a bigger problem. Keep your eyes wide open today and prepare to react quickly. You won't see it coming.

5 If things turn out as you hope, you can feel comfortable in enjoying the limelight today. Another issue you've been grappling with can be put in its box and dealt with separately. Choose the best way to celebrate a victory with close friends.

6 You were forced to kick off a process which is now racing ahead at full speed and is out of control. You couldn't have predicted the course things would take and have no idea what the consequences might be. Brace yourself – things could turn nasty.

No. 64

YANG • ALMOST THERE

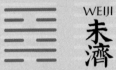

WEIJI

未
濟

You have survived a period of uncertainty, but it's still not the time to be bold. There is a culmination of events or climax coming, and you've worked very hard to enjoy a rich experience. However, there's something missing that you can't put your finger on. If you try to rush things now, it could backfire. A successful outcome often brings with it the fear and emptiness of what to do next – like winning a marathon or gaining a degree qualification. This is the time to brace yourself for a result which could be very positive if you prepare correctly. Don't take anything at face value. Check your facts carefully before making a decision; it's far better to be slow and right than quick and wrong.

Messages

1   You could end up in a one-way street if you press ahead without thinking carefully. There are matters you are unaware of coming to the surface. All the issues have yet to reveal themselves, so you shouldn't make a decision yet.

2   Be patient. Don't rush to a decision, even though you think you may know the solution. It's not the right time yet, so hold off for now. Savour small victories for the time being; the big ones are on the horizon.

3   Your objective is in sight, but approach it slowly; be patient, or it could disappear. You need encouragement and the insight brought by new associations. You may have to travel to accelerate matters.

4   Don't think you've solved your problems – you haven't. You need to sort something out before you'll get what you want; there are conflicting views around which need resolving first. Once you do this, you will move ahead rapidly.

5   You're getting there already, so you don't need to push it further. Relax and enjoy your success – you're about to become the centre of attention and others will follow you. A project will see a successful outcome and you can use this to help someone else.

6   Be proud of your achievements and enjoy them, but don't wallow too much in your success. You're reaping the rewards of months of endeavour, but if you're not careful it could all disappear. This may well be a turning point in both your career and personal relationships.

No. 64
YIN • UNEXPECTED DELAY

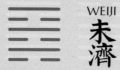

WEIJI

未
濟

Just like a fox that has cornered its prey but gets stuck in the mud, you're on the brink of success but you're not yet there. Your objectives were within sight but you've stumbled across unexpected problems. You need to build a framework to understand the issues confronting you. Without a secure footing you will not be able to scramble out of the rut you're in, and you'll make no further progress. You may have to accept something is beyond your grasp and just not worth the risk. There are natural laws which require caution and deliberation before the completion of something which brings abundance and good fortune. This is how true leaders should conduct themselves. Focus on dealing with mundane issues, one at a time, and proceed cautiously. Tick off your duties one by one, and you'll escape a dilemma and come out on top.

Messages

1 You may be keen to see an end to something and get it resolved, but this is not the time to push it. If you jump in with both feet, you could find the water is deeper than you thought, and you won't like the consequences.

2 Set a trap or organize a challenge to someone. This is the only way you will find out whether they are sincere. If they don't respond, then don't push it – the delay itself will tell you something important. Then you will know the truth.

3 It's not a great time to forge ahead with a delayed project. Things are just not right yet, although you may think a solution is in sight. If you really must proceed, then change the team of people around you first. This could be the solution.

4 There's a struggle or confrontation in prospect. Unfortunately, you'll have to get through it or you won't make any progress. You will then overcome opposition more easily than you think, and the rewards will follow quickly and exceed your expectations.

5 A decision you just made is going to prove correct. It could take some time for the evidence to reveal itself and you may be castigated, but it's because you stuck to your principles and didn't shout about it that you will win through. Enjoy the outcome.

6 If what you've just done produces the right result, don't feel you're invincible. You are entitled to celebrate and take the deserved plaudits, but pride often comes before a fall. Just don't let this go to your head, or you could be embarrassed by your own conduct.

The future is a fabric of interlacing possibilities, some of which gradually become probabilities, and a few of which become inevitabilities, but there are surprises sewn into the warp and the [weft], which can tear it apart.

The Witching Hour ANNE RICE

CHAPTER SIX
The Power of Numbers

For those interested in exploring the mythology behind Chinese oracle reading in more detail, this chapter delves deeper into the remarkable revelations contained within The Yellow River Map. We also take a closer look at the origins of Yin and Yang and the hexagrams, plus the significance of numbers in the universal code.

The Yellow River Map and ancient Chinese philosophy

In Chapter One we discovered how, according to Chinese folklore, the trigrams were delivered to Fu Xi on a map from the Yellow River – a map borne on the back of a dragon horse. As this inscription on a tomb-shrine from the second century CE (detailed in a Chinese Imperial Encyclopedia in the British Library) proclaims:

Dragon-bodied Fu Xi first established Kingly rule, drew the 8 trigrams, devised the knotted cords (for reckoning) in order to govern all within the four seas.

Fu Xi is a mythical version of a charismatic leader. His story represents a further development of the original Chinese creation myth, known as The Great Beginning. Chinese children are taught that the universe was created from the empty cosmos; that heaven and earth resulted from a collision of forces in which light matter drifted up to heaven (Yang) and heavy material solidified and sank to form Mother Earth (Yin) – much like an egg is separated into the white and the yolk and yet they combine in one

◀ *A depiction of the 'Dragon Horse', or 'Lung-ma', which delivered The Yellow River Map to Fu Xi.*

living organism. This concept is represented in the Yin-Yang symbol, familiar to billions of people around the world.

The agent of The Great Beginning was a spirit called Pan Gu, a giant who straddles the earth and reaches up to the sky. Myths carry our truths through time, and it's clear that Yin (female) and Yang (male) have come to play a fundamental role in understanding how creation and order are governed in the universe. They function as the representation of balance and harmony which lies at the core of Chinese natural philosophy. Ancient Chinese philosophy focuses on the natural function of everything that exists in the universe, rather than on its detailed constituents.

Contrast this with the Western scientific method, where we draw conclusions from a set of observations in a controlled environment and then make statements about how the world works. We make judgements about what we don't or cannot know as if we have evidence we can always rely upon. Yet time and again throughout history it is clear that it's what we don't know, or can't observe, which drives major events and produces turning points in the fortunes of civilizations, like the First World War or 9/11. The ancient Chinese, on the other hand, would seek to detect a misalignment through divination and prepare themselves for a dynastic collapse or major geological event and take the appropriate action.

The critical importance of the Yellow River basin itself for the earliest Chinese civilizations should never be underestimated:

The first inhabitants of the Yellow River came to see themselves as members of a vast order of living things … This profound sense of reciprocity found expression in the ancient theory of Yin-Yang, which has remained a basic concept of the Chinese mind.

Tao of Chaos: DNA and the I Ching K. WALTER

Early attempts at consistent measurement, philosophical teaching, cooking and rapid agricultural progress can all be traced to this 'middle kingdom'. The Qin (Chin) dynasty was established there circa 220 BCE in Shaanxi province, which is how the name 'China' originated.

Each civilization on earth tends to have its own creation myth which is passed on from ancient times to offer an explanation for our existence. Fu Xi is credited with creating order by teaching the population to fish with nets and how to cook, and establishing social order and regulatory prin-

▶ *The Yellow River is regarded as the cradle of Chinese civilization. The section shown here is taken from a detailed geographical map comprising manuscript on silk, produced circa 1750, and shows part of the lower portion of the river in Jiangsu province (north is to the bottom, according to standard Chinese practice).*

ciples; in other words, he is principally responsible for Chinese civilization rather than the earth's creation. He is supposed to have devised the eight trigrams in order to help humanity gain better control over daily life, and to describe for everyone in a simple way how the universe functions.

Since Fu Xi is said to have physically witnessed this message carried by a dragon horse from the Yellow River, its depiction has not unreasonably become known as The Yellow River Map. This Map was reproduced in ancient Chinese encyclopedias for the general public to observe, and an early version is set out in the Appendix (*see page 250*). It is still used today to demonstrate to children the principles of natural philosophy, measurement and mathematics, and to explain how early patterns of Chinese thought developed. The renowned nineteenth-century Sinologist James Legge believed the Map really did exist, and that it surfaced around 3300 BCE. He claimed it was last seen in its original form around 1100 BCE, when it 'afterwards perished'. If it did exist and were ever discovered, it would undoubtedly be beyond value.

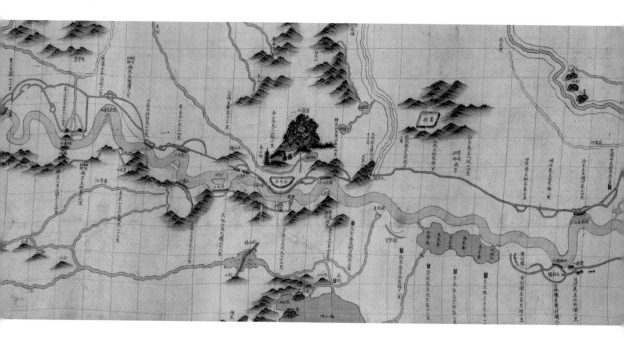

Dot to dot

Before any formal numbering system was developed in China, counting was symbolized in early documents (often on bamboo strips) by a series of solid and hollow circles, or dots. The earliest representation of counting was through a series of knots on pieces of string, the same as in early Mayan culture.

The Map became the basis of later geomantic charts, which explained how the sky was divided up and could be used to locate the seasons and all points on the compass. These allowed the determination of the summer and winter solstices with accuracy, and indicated when crops should be planted, harvested and stored. For example, the chart depicted in the Appendix on pages 248–9 explains that rice should be planted when the swallows arrive. In some rural districts, it's still the tradition today to prepare a box inside the house for swallows to nest, so that there's no misunderstanding about the timing of crop-planting. Their arrival and departure acts as nature's timekeeper.

But the original Yellow River Map went beyond this and, on closer examination, contains further revelations. It displays the five Chinese elements of nature at its centre and counts to ten.* Even numbers are female and depicted as black dots, while the odd numbers are hollowed and male (*see Appendix, pages 250–51*). The external numbers are fixed as 6, 7, 8 and 9 and they link the five elements to our daily lives. These are the oracle numbers which drive the Hon-Shō daily consultation process.†

Anyone who knows of the Kabala, an esoteric Jewish mysticism, will note the parallels with The River Map. The Kabala became very popular from the twelfth century CE. It seeks to interpret much of the Old Testament through numbers and has at its root the number ten. This number is regarded as the Tree of Life (Sephiroth Tree) and all the numbers to ten are connected. The Kabala shows these connections in the twenty-two letters of the Hebrew alphabet. Tracing this cosmic structure links us to God, and using this to guide one's life provides the route to God.

---

* The five elements according to China's early literature are water, fire, wood, metal and earth. Contrast this with the four forces identified by the Greek philosophers: water, fire, earth and wind. Interestingly, Agrippa, writing in later Roman times, decided that there was a fifth element – that which binds all of humankind together.

† I devised the Hon-Shō oracle process before learning about the Map. The software engineers and I discovered through trial and

error that these four numbers, and only these numbers, generated a reliable and suitable reading. How, or whether, the architects of The Yellow River Map knew this before formal number and writing systems were developed is a mystery. But I think the answer lies in the ancient lunar calendar. This calendar dictated the actions of civilizations from China to the ancient Middle East. Its influence carries through to today in the Christian religious calendar, where 6, 7, 8 and 9 are still used to calculate important dates from Easter Day.

The Map appears to fulfil a similar purpose in Chinese mythology.

A recent book by Xu Kun (*see bibliography, no. 8*) sets the Map and the trigrams into context (*see diagram below*), while author Frank J. Swetz, in his book about magic squares and the roots of Chinese numerology, succinctly links The Yellow River Map to the familiar Yin-Yang symbol by simply dividing up the Map into its solid (Yin) and empty (Yang) circles. This leads us convincingly to the Yin-Yang image (*see bibliography, no. 27*).

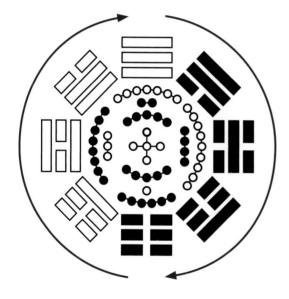

▲ *The Yellow River Map and the trigrams in context.*

Even in today's fast-developing modern China there remains a temple dedicated to Fu Xi, located in the Jiuzhaigou Valley Nature Reserve at the southern end of the Minshan Mountains in northern Sichuan province. The photograph in the Appendix (*see page 251*) provides a glimpse of the ceiling inside the temple, which illustrates the clear link between The Yellow River Map, the eight trigrams and the sixty-four hexagrams which Hon-Shō uses to deliver daily oracle readings. The square root of sixty-four is, of course, the number eight. It's also the number of squares along the sides of a chessboard. This number is always associated with good luck and is embedded in the Chinese psyche. Let's explore the reasons.

The mystery of number eight

The opening of the Beijing Olympic Games in the summer of 2008 revealed the rich inheritance of Chinese culture for the first time to many throughout the world. This single continuous culture can be traced back more than 5,000 years (at least), and it's no accident that the timing of the opening of the Games was eight o'clock on the eighth day of the eighth month in 2008. The number eight enjoys special status in Chinese tradition. But why? And where does this superstition come from?

As with Western civilizations, the history of China reflects the progression of humans from hunter-gatherers to managing the land and then industrialization. The greatest transformation in ancient Chinese society came when humankind ceased to rely on foraging for food and began to manage its relationship with nature. This provoked a thorough appraisal of the workings of the natural world and a deep questioning of humankind's existence and its role in the cosmos. All this was pulled together in the early creation myths and stories about the adventures of the earliest emperors in conquering adversity and delivering knowledge to the people of China. The outcomes of some of the earlier myths and stories are captured in The Yellow River Map and predate Confucius and his teachings by thousands of years. The Map also leads us directly to the number eight.

As we know, the dragon horse which appeared to the emperor Fu Xi from the Yellow River displayed a set of eight symbols on its back (*see page 217*). Since time immemorial these have been recognized by all Chinese as the trigrams (Bagua) and are

▲ *Fu Xi, with the eight trigrams and a turtle (signifying longevity), by the thirteenth-century Song painter Ma Lin.*

associated with ancient divination. Fu Xi, as we have learned, was responsible for teaching humankind what was required to understand the universal principles, work with nature and advance Chinese society. He is often depicted alongside his wife, Nuwa (also described as his sister), in an 'Adam and Eve'-type arrangement, to reinforce this message (*see Appendix, page 252*). This imagery has been discovered at many archaeological sites. A thirteenth-century depiction of Fu Xi with the eight trigrams is shown to the left.

We know that the basic three lines of a trigram represent heaven above and earth below, with humanity in the middle. Change and the cycle of life is represented in the opening and closing of all the lines depicted in each of the eight trigrams in sequence – like a gate, widening and then shutting. Each line changes in succession until a cycle is completed, when the process starts all over again. There are eight points in this cycle, just like there are eight notes in a musical octave. Balance, harmony and wholeness come about for us all in the fulfilment of a complete cycle, reflecting the circle of life and nature, through which heaven, earth and humankind are reconciled. We all have the universe operating inside us, and the succession of the eight trigrams captures this movement like a universal mechanical timepiece.

This opening and closing sequence is a universal principle we in the West depict with binary notation. It forms the basis of our own number system and lies at the heart of our science and civilization. The Chinese call this universal truth Yin and Yang. Acting like an ancient clock, the number eight sits at the root of everything, managing nature's progression. As a result, it is regarded as the most auspicious number. It is one of the oracle numbers set on the outside of The Yellow River Map and it represents the ultimate power of Mother Earth or a stable female authority. It represents the Taoist state of grace and is known as 'The Way' of the universe.

In Chinese tradition, if you add the first male number, 3, to the first female number, 2, this gives 5, the number for marriage.* The combination of marriage (5) with the male number 3 creates 8, which represents balanced human relationships.

It implies the continuity of the blood line and the enduring family. The number eight therefore represents love binding a family together, the most important thing in the world. The number contains both man and woman embedded and entwined within it. Interestingly, the Greek followers of Pythagoras in 550 BCE agreed with this philosophy and developed it further (see bibliography, no. 24, for more on this topic).

Therefore, only through the number eight is wholeness achieved. Other numbers are allocated important roles, but none has the deep-rooted psychic influence of the number eight. For example, nine is the ultimate male power number, which is why every door in the Forbidden City in Beijing displays exactly 81 rivets (9 x 9 is 81). Nine is also an oracle number. It represents the male and is associated with powerful changes. The various emperors inhabiting the Forbidden City wanted to associate with this power number, since this is the ultimate male Yang number. However, if left unrestrained by humility, it can be associated with disaster – and anyone visiting the City is made only too aware of the tragic events which regularly unfolded inside it. Even today, no visitors are allowed in the Forbidden City during the night-time, when the spirits of those emperors are said to return.

The subsequent conversion of the original eight trigrams into the sixty-four hexagrams of the Book of Changes during the Zhou dynasty

* You may wonder where 0 and 1 have got to. The number 1 is reserved for the originator or, if you prefer, God. The cosmos, or void, from which everything was created is represented as a circle or zero.

(1027–224 BCE) preserved the importance of the number eight. As we know, these sixty-four hexagrams are used to represent all the different things that could happen to us in our lives, and this is brought about by multiplying 8 by 8. The opening and closing of the lines in each hexagram represent changes in our personal circumstances, and this is driven by a synchronicity over which we have no control. But we *can* assess our location in the firmament and nature's influences upon us at a particular point in time, to guide us in our decision-making. This is what reading the oracle can achieve for us all.

A sister to the Yellow River is the Luo River, which also runs through Shaanxi province. This river is said to be the source of another set of numbers known as the Luo Writing or 'Hong Fan'. These numbers are said to have appeared on the back of a turtle and set the laws of nature alongside the laws of the universe reflected in The Yellow River Map (note the turtle's presence in the painting on page 222). The Luo Writing complements The Yellow River Map and allows the deduction and interpretation principles central to Taoist thinking and which still remain influential in traditional Chinese culture.

Magic squares

A fascination with the mystery of numbers is, of course, not confined to Chinese civilization. But an interesting feature of the Luo Writing is how it gave rise to the development of 'magic squares', said to contain eternal mysteries within them and captured by a variety of religions to display mystery and divinity. It is said to have influenced the numerology of the Pythagoreans and been adopted by many leading philosophers, mathematicians and artists throughout history.

The first documented magic square derived from the Luo Writing – the Magic Square of Order Three – is presented below. Note how the number 15 is always the sum of three numbers added together in any direction, whether horizontally, vertically or diagonally.

I found it revealing that the oracle numbers 6, 7, 8 and 9 are balanced when divided into their matching Yin-Yang combination: 6 (Yin) and 9 (Yang), and 8 (Yin) and 7 (Yang). They each total 15, in compliance with the magic square. Moreover, the numbers lying at the centre of The Yellow River Map also total 15. I believe that this number is used to link the Map to the Luo Writing, and the Magic Square of Order Three was devised to tie them together in a cosmogram or map of the universe. Others have reached the same conclusion (*see bibliography, no. 27*).

4	9	2
3	5	7
8	1	6

◄ *The Magic Square of Order Three. The numbers total 15 in each direction.*

A similar magic square – believed to be the first seen in European art – appeared in the engraving *Melencolia I* by Albrecht Dürer in 1514 (*see left*). Modern mathematicians have reputedly discovered the presence of 'mysterious intertwined hexagrams' in this image, connecting even and odd numbers (for more on this see bibliography, no. 24). More recently, the author Dan Brown, in his book *The Lost Symbol*, points to the mysteries contained in a similar magic square constructed by Benjamin Franklin in 1769. It's worth noting that there are sixty-four elements in Franklin's square, which of course is eight squared and equal to the number of hexagrams used in the Book of Changes and the Hon-Shō divination system. The number eight also retained its important position at the centre of many of his calculations (*see bibliography, no. 33*).

The core of existence

Whether the number eight's position as the most prophetic number lying at the core of our existence really did originate in China, or whether such wisdom was borrowed from other cultures, remains unresolved. The American physicist Murray Gell-Mann received a Nobel Prize in 1969 for his work on the theory of elementary particles. He coined the term the 'eightfold way'. The 'Noble Eightfold Path' describes the route to the end of the sufferings set out in the Siddhartha Gautama, a major text which lies at the centre of

▲ *Albrecht Dürer's* Melencolia I, *and the magic square contained within it* (right). *The numbers total 34 in each direction, as well as in the four quadrants, the central four squares, the corner squares – and more. The date Dürer completed the engraving occupies the two central squares in the bottom row.*

Buddhism and leads to truth in all things. It is used as a guide to personal development which frees the individual from attachment and delusions. In addition, some Christian teachers adopt the eight-step programme which is a 'ladder of virtues', taking believers from faith to love in eight stages. The eight-pointed Templar Cross also captures this imagery. The same process is embedded in The Yellow River Map. All these examples – and there are many more – reflect a remarkable synchronicity in unrelated events and discoveries throughout history and across civilizations.

The number eight may sit at the core of some long-forgotten communication device. It surfaces time and again in our lives to influence us. Of course, a case can be made to attach mystery to many different numbers, but only the number eight anchors the mechanics of the universe and humanity so firmly in the Chinese mind. It does this through the confluence of The Yellow River Map and the Book of Changes. Perhaps this is why the Chinese rate number eight so highly.

Yin, Yang and oracle reading

Yin and Yang represent the two polar opposites; think of binary notation (without which computer software would not exist) or male and female, or negative and positive energy or opposing magnetic poles.* Early Chinese sages recognized this dualism as the fundamental element

that is hard-wired into nature's processes, and built this into their teaching, their oracle reading and much of their early philosophy. The process reflects switching something on and off repeatedly and is represented in the West, as we touched on earlier, through the 0 and 1 of binary notation. It's instantaneous and is witnessed daily by all of us in the rapid-fire networks captured by our computer screens, from the study of biological processes using electron microscopes to the fluctuating prices on stock-market dealing screens.

As we've seen, representations of nature's basic processes were set out in ancient Chinese textbooks used as encyclopedias by teachers travelling the country to educate the population in the facts of life. Much earlier, Neolithic thinkers scratched marks on bones to capture and record their inherited knowledge. Very early evidence of Chinese mathematics is recorded in this way through different combinations of pluses and minuses, and through lists of digits tied on lengths of string.

---

* The man credited in the West with the invention of binary arithmetic, G. W. Leibniz, was said to be struck with awe when he learned about the hexagrams. The so-called Fu Xi sequence of arranging the sixty-four hexagrams turns out to be identical to Leibniz's binary numbers. Leibniz was writing around 1700 CE in Europe, while the Book of Changes was formalized 2,500 years earlier, from around 900 BCE onwards during the Zhou dynasty in China. (*See bibliography, nos. 7 and 34.*)

Like binary notation, what mattered to the earliest diviners was the alternation between odd and even numbers and not the numbers themselves. It's the process that matters. Nature's action is captured in the operation of the universe as it swings from Yin to Yang. This sequence of movements can be detected every day and captured in a score generated by coincidence which creates an observation about our lives. This is how Hon-Shō works.

Archaeological research has gathered reliable evidence to support the mechanism by which Hon-Shō accesses the oracle:

New evidence suggests the Bagua [eight trigrams] derived from a method of divination based on a game dating back to Neolithic times.

Chinese History: A Manual ENDYMION WILKINSON

These ancient equivalents of computer gamers gathered a bundle of sticks and asked each other to guess whether they were odd or even in number, then recorded the guesses according to whether they were correct or not. Perhaps if they were right they scored a plus, and if they were wrong, a minus, to create a series of digits. These were then assessed to confirm a result – and, later, to generate reading. Hon-Shō does the same; it converts the data recorded in your daily Hon-Shō box into a list of six Oracle Numbers.

These are used to locate your oracle reading and its associated hexagram for that day. It's personal to you because the outcome has been produced by your Digital-DNA and no one else's. This is a critical feature of Hon-Shō: its delivery system is uniquely personal. In all other respects the method is identical to ancient Chinese divination. Your oracle reading is not someone's invention – it's genuinely driven by your personal details and cannot be corrupted or manipulated.

Consulting the oracle can help us cope at momentous points in our lives. Some believe that, by forming an explanation in our minds from a series of apparently unrelated events, our brains are perpetrating a fallacy upon us. But the fact of the matter is that our conscious minds are driven to seek a simple convincing explanation for everything we witness in order to make sense out of chaos and help us to cope and give us hope. This is a basic human need and not something to be disparaged. We naturally recognize coincidences and take reassurance and comfort from them, and often share them with our friends. This is not the same as pretending to predict the future, which really is a fallacy. Entering the realms of prediction is where a simple fallacy becomes a fraud. Hon-Shō is never predictive. If anyone tells you they can predict your future, they are either a liar or taking you for a fool.

Yin, Yang and odd numbers

The solid and broken lines in a trigram have a long tradition which, some contend, came about by early humans overlapping their fingers and looking at the campfire through the lines they naturally created in between (*see bibliography, no. 28*). Whether this is true we can't be sure, but it's certainly believable and also entertaining.

Originally, in ancient China a straight line (▬▬▬) was used to denote an odd number. It is still used in Chinese today to represent the number one. It is believed that 'even' was originally written as an inverted 'v', but when written rapidly could be confused with the number 1 and was therefore later split into two lines (▬ ▬) for clear identification. Much later, in the Zhou period (1027–221 BCE), this method of recording outcomes was adopted by interpreters and practitioners of the Book of Changes and made to correspond with Yin and Yang. In this system Yin became a broken line, representing an even (female) number, whereas Yang became a full line, and always an odd (male) number.

There is an old Islamic saying, 'God loves the odd', and even Shakespeare's Falstaff recognized there was something special about odd numbers when he said, 'They say there is divinity in odd numbers, either in nativity, chance or death' (from *The Merry Wives of Windsor*). But it is the change in a number from odd to even, or vice versa, which is believed in some civilizations to produce dramatic outcomes. In Hon-Shō oracle reading, this mechanism is captured to deliver the daily pronouncements.

Some of the early Chinese texts clearly link specific numbers to heaven and earth. Even numbers are always born from the earth and linked to the feminine capacity to be rooted in common sense, with skills of reconciliation and facilitation. On the other hand, the odd numbers are always heavenly, possessing a striving for change and an explosive, controlling energy which, as Shakespeare said, reflects divine inspiration and drives major events. These are regarded as the principal features of the male character in ancient Chinese literature (although not always politically correct in the context of modern Western civilization).

So, the male (Yang) was always associated with a full or straight line (▬▬▬), while the female (Yin) aspect was a split or broken line (▬ ▬). The lines could also be used to represent yes (solid) and no (broken). Again, it is easy to register this mentally as a gate opening and closing. Both the early Eastern mystics and many Western physicists and biochemists have come to recognize that all particles in the world are constantly changing form and are interrelated in some way. The earliest Chinese philosophers decided to express this as a line changing from one shape to another – full to broken and back again, in a complete cycle represented by the eight trigrams we know as the Bagua.

These later developed into the sixty-four hexagrams, which, as we know, are constantly transforming themselves into one another, reflecting nature's changes unfolding and the effect of chance in producing coincidences in our lives:

The firm [━━━] and yielding [━━ ━━]
displace each other ... Thus the firm is
transformed, melts as it were, and becomes
the yielding: the yielding changes, coalesces ...
and becomes the firm.

The Original I Ching Oracle
R. RITSEMA AND S. A. SABBADINI

As these firm and yielding lines displace one another, they represent change and transformation taking place, much like molecules recombine to guide the proteins in our bodies, the recurrence of which has been described as the single most distinctive property of all living beings (*see bibliography, no. 29*).

It's clear to me now that the transmutation of the lines from one into the other was used as a metaphor to explain to the uneducated how nature worked. In our modern time we can look through a scanning electron microscope to witness biological processes at first hand. This ancient imagery, I believe, was used to represent the same molecular processes and link them to nature and ourselves through universal laws. The

two polar opposites, Yang and Yin, set the limits for change, and enable us to observe their transformations from one to the other continuously through time, much like particles are said to settle and reform in particle physics, thus producing all the things we observe and experience in our lives. What drives these processes and brings purpose to our lives remains open to debate and is certainly beyond my remit. But to the ancient Chinese scribes it was simply the operation of the forces of nature driven by universal truths.

I wasn't the first to notice this. Detailed analogies have been drawn by some writers between the molecular biology associated with DNA and the Book of Changes and also medicine and mathematics (*see bibliography, nos. 7 and 9*). The solid and broken lines are seen as always moving, never static, and transforming from one to another in continuous change, reflecting all the events which can happen in nature and our lives. Reading the oracle imposes a freeze-frame on this process and allows us to peek very briefly at how our current circumstances interact with chance. This process of continued change is set out starkly in the ancient texts, extracts from which are provided in the Appendix on pages 242–5. It's worth inspecting them closely. By consulting the oracle we're doing nothing new.

The Greek philosopher Heraclitus, who lived in the fourth century BCE, wrote about a cosmic 'reason' which connected all things together through some unseen mechanism. To him the universe was an interdependent system in which we all played our part. Daily events are not simple unrelated outcomes which operate in isolation, but had consequences across the entire fabric of our existence:

> *Heraclitus argued that it was humankind's task to discover and understand the principles that bound all living and inorganic things together in an overall common purpose.*
>
> The Sacred Books of China JAMES LEGGE

This train of thought reflects ancient Chinese philosophy precisely.

The concept of Yang and Yin can therefore be viewed as being at the fulcrum of nature's process of creation and destruction. Through their balance they convey symmetry in everything, a fundamental building-block in nature. We've discovered how they are used throughout Chinese ancient philosophy as an educational tool to link human activity to nature. Their role is deeply embedded in the Chinese psyche and remains there today despite the modernization of its society in imitation of the West. The ancient imperial Chinese emperors gave due regard to this concept of duality, balance and the link with heaven. And still, at the time of the third Ming dynasty around 1400 CE, the construction

of the Forbidden City faithfully carried its features in its architecture.

And, as if to reinforce that there's nothing new under the sun, take a look at the photographs on page 253 in the Appendix. The first image shows the interior of part of the Large Hadron Collider (the most advanced – and expensive – physics experiment on earth) at CERN in Switzerland; the second shows the ceiling inside the Temple of Heaven in Beijing, built during the Ming dynasty. Humankind's continuing search for patterns and symmetry in nature is reflected in their uncanny resemblance.

Change, hexagrams and Hon-Shō

So, the Book of Changes was the ancient Chinese attempt to capture the effects of coincidence on our lives. Hon-Shō now does the same. The hexagrams created daily to accompany your oracle reading are the most ancient form of Chinese symbolism and are accessed by adopting the earliest method of divination so far discovered.

As we've seen, Hon-Shō compresses our name and date of birth into a personal label. Its operation reflects the overriding power of the cosmos (heaven) and earth (nature) and their combined effect upon our lives. As we learned in Chapter One, the original reason the Chinese sages began with three lines in a trigram was because it reflected these three life-forces and because their influence was declared on The

Yellow River Map. It demonstrated that nature and the elements are the driving force behind all of our circumstances.

Some writers believe each line in a hexagram represents different character features: from line one (the bottom) upwards they are said to represent security, sex and reproduction, power, love, communication and mind (*see bibliography, no. 31*). But I believe this is just too simplistic. It lacks integrity and demeans the intellectual rigour inherent in the whole philosophy of the Book of Changes. Oracle reading is much more than consulting a daily horoscope.

More realistically, the hexagrams were designed to represent cosmic archetypes symbolizing all the potential events in nature and human existence, as shown in the image in the Appendix (*see pages 246–7*). This image represents the 'Canopy of Heaven' philosophy, where the earth is depicted as a square of hexagrams with the cosmos encircling it daily. The Hon-Shō oracle pronouncements simply reflect the collision of coincidences which connect events beyond our control to our daily experiences. We have the architects of The Yellow River Map to thank for this inheritance.

It was Richard Wilhelm who introduced me to the Book of Changes. He also personally introduced Carl Jung to its mysteries. In his book *Memories,* *Dreams, Reflections,* Jung wrote that one night he dreamt Wilhelm was standing over his bed dressed in ancient Chinese garb. He could feel his breath. He awoke startled and sweating. The next day he discovered that Wilhelm was dead.

Wilhelm directed my thinking when he said:

The process of consulting the oracle is brought into relation with the cosmic process ... *through the [Yellow River] Map.*
I Ching or Book of Changes RICHARD WILHELM

In keeping with the great tradition of Chinese natural philosophy, Hon-Shō treats us as being rooted on earth but surrounded by cosmic events. We can't control the events going on around us, yet no one can deny they all impinge critically upon our lives. You can still take responsibility for the direction your life will follow even though you are not in control of selecting the choices you face.

In the changes there are images to reveal, *there are judgements appended in order to* *interpret, good fortune and misfortune are* *determined in order to decide.*
I Ching or Book of Changes RICHARD WILHELM

This is Hon-Shō oracle reading in a nutshell.

By a single stroke it claimed to sweep away the tradition of a hundred thousand years, which had become one with human nature itself ... leaving nothing in place of that precious bond but an anxious quest in a frozen universe of solitude. With nothing to recommend it but a certain puritan arrogance, how could such an idea win acceptance? It did not; it still has not.

On Science JACQUES MONOD

Conclusion

After completing the development of Hon-Shō, I read Taleb's life-changing book *The Black Swan*. His philosophy of life is to conquer uncertainty through our own choices:

... you are exposed to the improbable only if you let it control you. You always control what you do; so make this your end.

The Black Swan NASSIM NICHOLAS TALEB

Consulting the oracle through Hon-Shō on any day enables you to engage in an ancient and mysterious process. Your reading and any associated messages inform you regarding where you stand in your life and where you could be heading. But you are the driver, so you have to decide! The Hon-Shō oracle method departs from the traditional Book of Changes by not over-emphasizing an uncontrollable fate or trying to be too predictive or needlessly mystical. We've now become all too rational for that. Most people born in the digital era have come to the view that their fate rests in their own hands, and will settle for guidance and reassurance in their decision-making. They treat reading the oracle as a form of personal counselling to enable them to take control of their lives, and are content with that.

Maximum benefit from the readings and messages delivered using Hon-Shō is gained through prolonged reflection and meditation. Its text is derived from the original pronouncements made by oracle-bone diviners in ancient China more than 3,000 years ago. Later, sages based their own commentaries on the judgements or decisions made by King Wen of Zhou (circa 700 BCE), who analysed the structure of the six lines in the hexagrams and studied their movements. He developed the sixty-four different hexagrams and came up with his own interpretations of what they meant. It's taken me five years to reinterpret them for the twenty-first century.

To the early Chinese, the purpose of oracle reading was to consult their destiny by seeking the advice of their ancestors. They recognized that men, animals and plants each have lives which pulsate to a different rhythm alongside nature. Because all creatures on earth possess different levels of consciousness, the only way to reconcile these differences was through the common denominator of numbers, by which all things may be expressed – even chance events. When we introduce the collision of chance with our unique digital label, this produces our oracle reading, or a revelation of our predicament at a point in time. But the Chinese knew that a slight change in the structure of an image or the words in a statement could radically alter its meaning. This is why each oracle reading is very personal to its recipient and provides unique solace to them.

Our own time appears to be one of the very few periods in human history when oracle reading is quite dormant and often ridiculed. There are a host of reasons for this, ranging from the power of organized religions to a misplaced faith in the omnipotence of modern science and technology. During the Shang period, the King would not make the smallest decision without consulting the oracle, especially with regard to religious matters, birth and marriage, illness or death, hunting, the weather, agriculture, political appointments and military campaigns – in fact, almost anything you can think of! This legacy lies at the heart of Hon-Shō oracle reading as a consultation device.

And still today there remain organizations whose purpose is fundamentally linked to the whole arena of researching the common themes in East–West philosophy and stimulating debate about the personal psyche and the process of self-discovery. One such is the Eranos Foundation. Residing at Ascona in Switzerland, on the beautiful Lake Maggiore, Eranos was founded in 1933 by one of the acolytes of Carl Jung, who gave enormous credence to the whole philosophy of the Book of Changes (*see bibliography, no. 1*). The Eranos Foundation provides courses and arranges discussion groups for those engaged in studying the psychology and philosophy of the process of change and self-discovery (see overleaf for an account of my own revelatory journey to visit the Foundation).

Let's give the final verdict to Carl Jung, who was both a highly qualified medical practitioner and a world-leading psychologist. He found the whole process of using the Book of Changes more than useful when engaging with patients in his psychoanalytical activities:

> *Time and again I encountered amazing coincidences ... (a synchronicity I later called it) ... When I often used to carry out the experiment with my patients, it became quite clear that a significant number of answers did indeed hit the mark.*

Memories, Dreams, Reflections C. G. JUNG

I created Hon-Shō in order to provide both an authentic divination technique for the digital generation and to enable easy access to the earliest oracle pronouncements recorded by the Chinese. It sheds light on our circumstances and the pressures which surround us at any given time, allowing us all to take counsel from our personal reading. By consulting the oracle we are tapping into silent evidence from a mysterious universal mechanism using the most advanced procedures currently available to us. This could enable us to restore our sense of community without taking away our free will and personal integrity. It's a small but important step in rebuilding our bridge with nature.

It is my great hope someday to see scientists and decision makers rediscover what the ancients have always known, namely that our highest currency is respect.

NASSIM NICHOLAS TALEB

EPILOGUE
Searching for the Self

The early midsummer sun mounts the Alpine range and cuts through the mist enveloping Lake Maggiore. From the hotel balcony I looked south along the lake, as the sun revealed the twin towns of Ascona and Locarno by its drenching light. A distant fishing boat carved its quiet wake through the still water. I was searching for Eranos.

Founded in 1933, after a chance meeting between Richard Wilhelm and Carl Jung, this curious educational institution has been sitting comfortably alongside Lake Maggiore for nearly eighty years. But why did these people get together in the first place? And why here? What possessed them to focus an academic institution on the study of the self and the Book of Changes? I was about to discover more than I bargained for.

The previous evening, at my hotel in Ascona, I ventured to ask if anybody knew where the Foundation was located, and whether it was possible to park there (it isn't!). An old man, somehow connected to the owner, interrupted me.

He grabbed my Google map and squinted at the address. In heavily accented Ticino, he warned me off: 'I know it. They talk about strange things up there. They live for the mountains and the seasons. Very strange. Keep away.' The owner then provided me with precisely the wrong directions. He was easier to understand, but was incredulous; after running his hotel for twenty years, he had never heard of Eranos and had no idea why it was there or what it did.

Despite this dispiriting conversation, I found it. Picking my way cautiously down the hill from the hotel, along Via Collinetta towards the lake, I hugged the dangerous road which snakes alongside the water heading in the direction of Italy. A small purple sign read 'Eranos' and an uncertain arrow had been chalked on the stone wall, indicating that access was downwards once more. Gripping the rusted handrail, I took the steep stone steps gingerly. Fronds of ferns obscured the route, discreet pathways and clearings bounded by rudbeckia, echinacea and geraniums in full bloom by the side of the crumbling path.

A levelled area appeared as if from nowhere. It came as a welcome relief and provided a breathtaking view of the lake and the small islands of Isole di Brissago, which looked close enough to touch. Tables were set for small groups. A stone plaque read in Latin 'Genio Loci Ignoto' ('to the unknown spirit of the place'). I had arrived at Casa Gabriella, home to the Eranos Foundation.

'Welcome to Eranos'

Like most Swiss Italians, the manager of the Foundation, Gertrude Brunner, spoke perfect English. Over a glass of Henniez she explained the fascinating history. The Foundation was established by Olga Fröbe-Kapteyn, who used her late father's house as a place for meditation and debate regarding the burning topics of the day relating to philosophy and psychology of the self. She knew both Jung and Wilhelm well, and they introduced her to the Book of Changes and its measured pronouncements. Driven by Jung and his acolytes, the focus of study gradually shifted more towards psychology, which became the enduring purpose of the Foundation – and still is today.

The Foundation hosts regular seminars devoted to the study of the process of self-discovery and lures participants from all over the world. It attracts not only academics, but also those who are just interested in seeking purpose or a new direction in their lives.

I was shown around the house. The musty library was just as it would have been in the 1930s. A longcase clock stood sentry by the bookcase, and hand-painted Bavarian furniture decorated the room. The Germanic influence was unmistakable. I was told it was just the same as it had been when Jung used the study. His picture, pipe in hand, hung on the wall. Two beds were made ready for student visitors. They like to preserve the ambience of the place, and it held a welcoming charm for me.

The house next door had for some time been adapted for use as a lecture theatre. Its walls displayed a selection of items of an esoteric nature relating to the psychology of the self, which Jung and his followers had collected from a variety of cultures created at different points in history. They reflected a bewildering range of mythical archetypes which ancient civilizations had used to communicate eternal truths to their offspring. I found it puzzling that none were Chinese.

When I asked the question, I discovered that the fascinating origins of the Book of Changes and its ancient heritage were not a matter which concerned those at Eranos any longer. Its teachings are taken as representations of universal truths in the process of human self-discovery. The fact that the ancient Chinese had developed a reliable mechanism for retrieving a set of pronouncements which stem from the relationship between nature and ourselves was neither here nor there.

Then it suddenly hit me: I was being driven to experience my own process of self-discovery. Receiving a revelation, along with my visit to Eranos, was part of that process. I had unwittingly become the vehicle through which the Book might reveal itself to those living in the digital era. That's what the Book of Changes can do to those exposed to it: it hijacks your senses and reorientates your thinking to a non-linear way.

Returning up the winding, overgrown path, I thanked my host for her hospitality. Turning towards the steps, I left her with the comment that I wished I had more time to study the sketches on the wall of the lecture theatre. I thought they presented an intriguing insight into humankind's early mythology and spiritual expression. The symbolism created by those civilizations forms part of the continuing search for a meaning to our existence.

'Oh, that's just a small selection,' she replied. 'If you want to see the full collection, they're in the Warburg Institute.' I asked where that was. They were in London – where I had just come from. So I headed back to England to find the Warburg Institute. As the plane lifted over Lake Geneva, I caught a glimpse of Mont Blanc through the window, backlit by the full moon. I imagined the Foundation at Eranos sheltering in the distance behind it – a comforting mist reaching around the lake once more, and wrapping the gardens in silence. As we banked towards the Jura Mountains the vision vanished, and I turned the page in my book once more, to Carl Jung's thoughts on the Book of Changes. He was writing about the Chinese preoccupation with chance and coincidence – how they decided that nature and our lives are so subject to chance that what we in the West call a scientific relationship should be regarded as a rare exception. As a result, Western science is incapable of explaining the nature of our existence satisfactorily. Knowing the mind of God through science is not going to happen.

Jung defined synchronicity to explain the unexplained and how, through sequences of simultaneous and unpredictable events, all living things can communicate with one another. I felt this was happening to me – a revelation was taking place, with me at the centre. Through a number of apparently unrelated and accidental events, I had been driven in a direction which I could influence but could not ultimately control – much like everyone's lives.

Once more, Jung's words lifted off the page before me:

The great achievement of the Book of Changes is that it creates a reaction which makes sense from a technique which apparently makes no sense.

Maybe he was right.

Appendix

The pages that follow provide vivid and compelling illustrations of the ancient Chinese wisdom that lies at the root of the Hon-Shō oracle system. Original artefacts, publications, temple ceilings, paintings and startling comparisons between the ancient and modern – all are evidence of the deep-seated provenance behind Hon-Shō. Many are available for public view, should you wish to investigate for yourself.

Note on the Book of Changes: One of the earliest complete copies of the Book of Changes I have come across in the UK is to be found in the John Rylands Library at the University of Manchester (*see illustrations on pages 242–50*). Dated 1596, written in Chinese and published in France, it was most likely procured by the early Jesuit missionaries to China. Other repositories of ancient Chinese knowledge also exist; for example, a different copy of the Book dated circa 1609 resides in the British Library. These volumes can be viewed in both libraries by special arrangement (*see bibliography, no. 11*). Modern-day versions, containing identical explanations, are now published in both Mandarin and English (*see bibliography, nos. 8 and 20*). The entire Book of Changes is captured on eleven stone steles (upright stone columns bearing commemorative inscriptions or designs) dating from 1090 CE onwards, on display at Beilin Museum in Xian, the ancient capital of China. The Chinese script, etched in stone, stands alongside the Confucian analects, as testimony to their enduring importance in Chinese culture.

Oracle bones

These oracle bones can be found in the British Library and date from the Shang dynasty (1600–1027 BCE).

The first scapula (figure **a**) indicates the early oracle method whereby a hot piece of metal was used to pierce the bone on one side, which caused cracks to appear on the reverse. These cracks were then interpreted (known as scapulomancy) and notes were made of the reading.

The second set of oracle bones (**b** and **c**) are thought to be later in the period, and are ox bones with symbols clearly set out on them. The divination would have been done using milfoil sticks, with the outcomes etched on the bone as a permanent record of the reading. On the bottom right-hand side of exhibit **b** it is believed to

say, 'There is uncertainty coming. Today the Emperor will make a comparison [about a person or location]. Someone is taking a boat downstream towards danger.'

Later oracle bones have now been unearthed which display references to the Book of Changes and the hexagrams. For further information regarding oracle bones visit the British Library website at www.bl.uk or download their *Treasures* application. The British Library also holds the reference book *A Journey into China's Antiquity*, compiled by the National Museum of China, published in 1997, which provides an extraordinarily rich display of oracle-bone photographs *(BL reference OIK951, Volume I, pages 170–76)*.

b

a

c

241

Creation and the family

Reading from right to left, the pages shown below indicate how the whole, or Great Extreme (heaven or eternity, denoted as number 1), gave rise to woman (Yin ▬▬ ▬▬, denoted number 2) and man (Yang ▬▬▬▬, denoted 3). This develops as a result of marriage (denoted as 5 in ancient China) in progression to four things (the parents and their first-born son and daughter), then eight trigrams in the typical ideal family unit. The eight original trigrams are clearly depicted, and eight is still regarded today as the luckiest number in China. The image reflects the ideal family unit of a man,

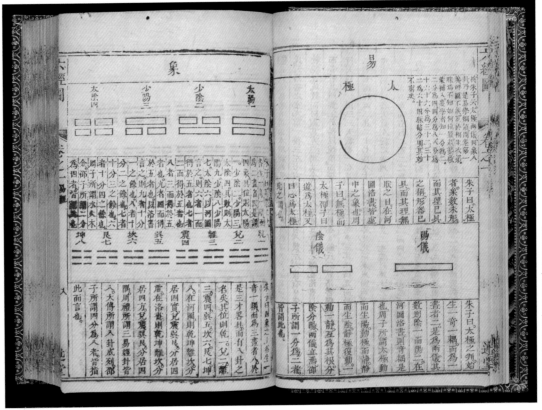

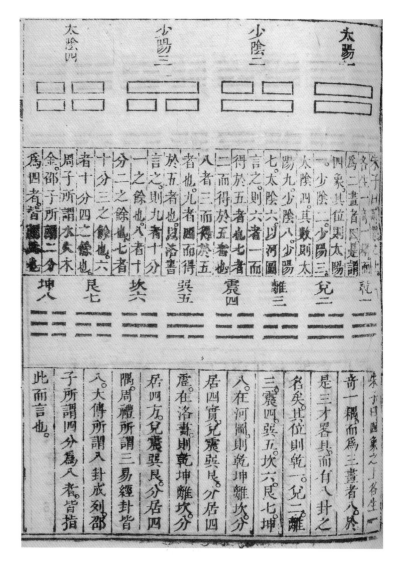

woman and their six children – three boys and three girls. These are the trigrams said to have been sent from the cosmos to Fu Xi. They form the basis of all things in nature and are driven by the natural laws of the universe, and combine to produce the hexagrams used in the Book of Changes and Hon-Shō oracle reading.

The trigrams become hexagrams

Here you can see how the two original trigrams for a man ☰ and a woman ☷ are manipulated in sequence to create the six children, giving a total of eight within the ideal family unit. These trigrams are then combined to create the hexagrams. Different hexagrams are shown with an explanation clearly written underneath (*see enlargement opposite*). What's remarkable is how a blocked (Yin, or broken) line is shown ascending the hexagrams (from right to left). This is a change or message being delivered, and could be a very early depiction of the relationship – now commonly accepted

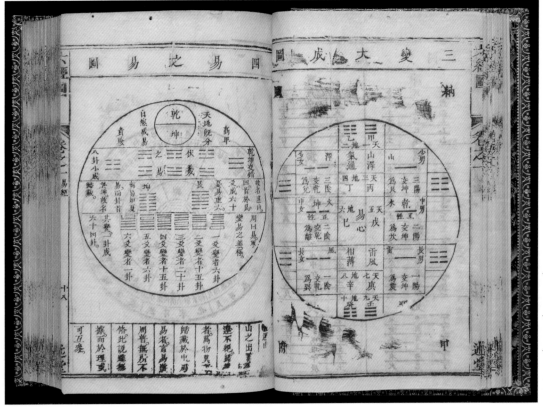

by Western physicists – between a particle and a wave.

According to Sinologist James Legge, from the combinations of odd and even numbers 'a knowledge of all the possible occurrences in nature may be previously known' (*see bibliography, no. 25, page 41*). This reflects the 'Canopy of Heaven' philosophy commonly accepted by the ancient Chinese as regulating the laws of the universe. This is believed to influence our lives, as we each possess the universe inside us. (For more on the Canopy of Heaven, see overleaf.)

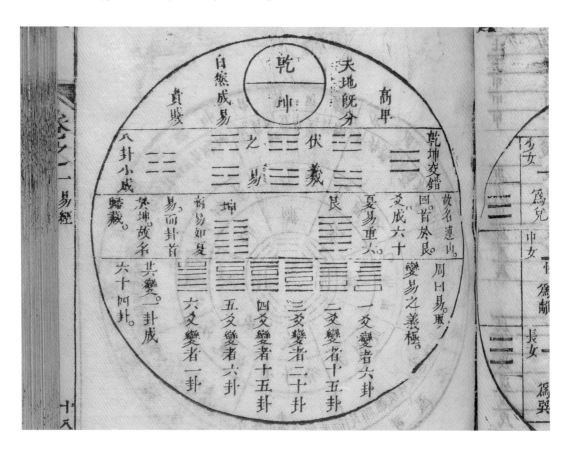

The Canopy of Heaven

The pages shown here set out the 'Canopy of Heaven' philosophy. Heaven is depicted as the circle of hexagrams, with earth on the inside in the shape of a square. Humankind stands on the earth and we look above us as the heavens rotate around us, changing our circumstances but regulated by natural laws. According to Richard Wilhelm (*see bibliography, no. 23*), the circle is set out in the Early Heaven sequence attributed to the mythical Fu Xi (supposedly around 3300 BCE). It is not surprising that, by close observation of the night sky and careful recording of the movement of the stars,

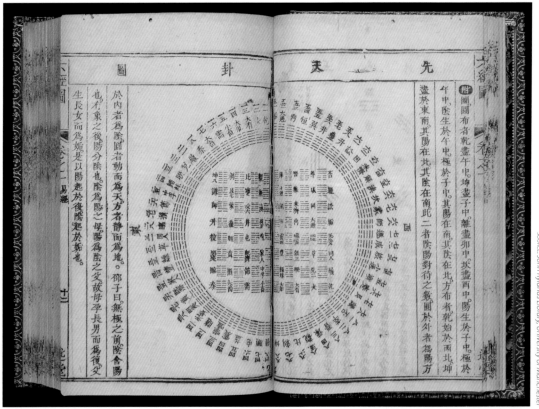

the ancient Chinese linked the progression of the seasons with star patterns and the sun and moon. They then used this information to guide their lives in what was then a predominantly agricultural society. But, as Wilhelm notes, they also associated all this with patterns in numbers: 'The square [arrangement of the hexagrams in the middle] corresponds to modern binary and decimal systems. Leibniz recognized this chart as his own binary system in reverse.' Yet Leibniz didn't 'invent' the binary system until around 1700 CE, thousands of years later.

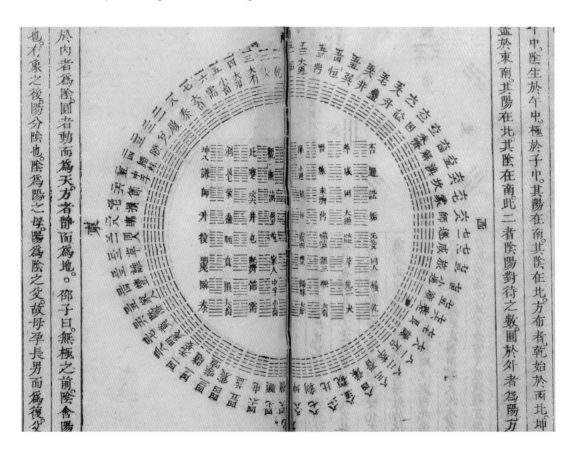

A geomantic compass

This chart places Yin and Yang at the centre, surrounded by the trigrams. It links the seasons to crop sowing, and the movement of animals (swallows are named) to changes in the weather. The outer ring show time elapsing and very precisely links this to astrological events. It's a truly cosmographical chart depicting the relationship between nature and human beings. It encompasses the immutable laws which regulate the universe and govern our daily existence. These charts, commonly used by Feng Shui specialists, were used by the Chinese to plant crops, wage wars, locate capital cities and bury emperors.

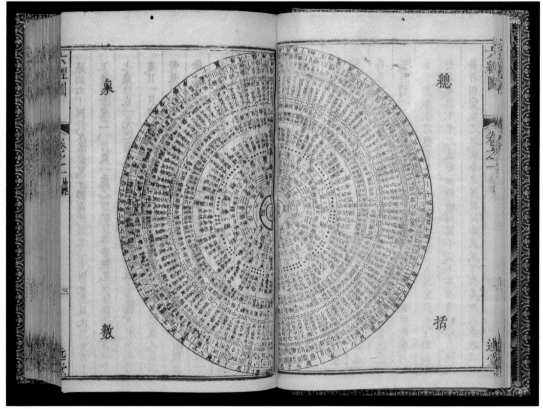

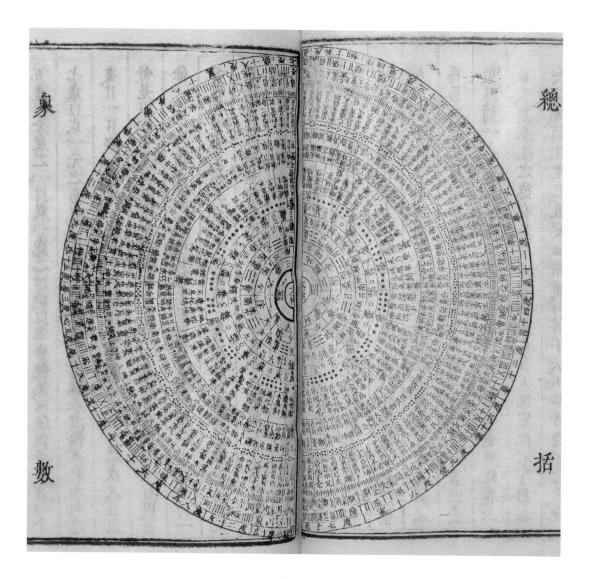

The Yellow River Map

This is a depiction of The Yellow River Map, supposedly revealed to Fu Xi from the Yellow River on the back of a 'dragon horse'. It is described here in Chinese as a map for counting, and detailed as coming from the river. It reads north to south then east to west, with north at the bottom, in accordance with Chinese tradition. The five Chinese primary elements are at the centre (wood, earth, fire, water and metal) and these are connected to each other and the points of the compass by the outer numbers 6, 7, 8 and 9. This is the Chinese Code which drives the Hon-Shō oracle readings. As we saw

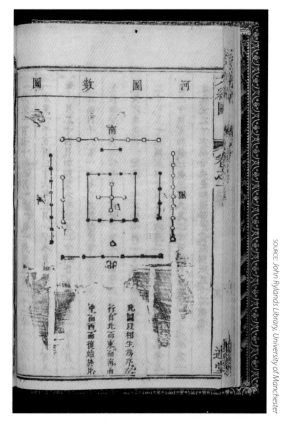

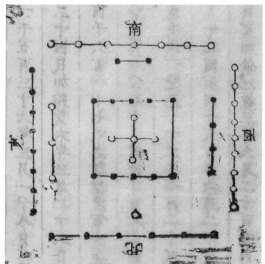

► *The numbers that correspond to the Map are set out here for easy identification* (see right). *The two outer 5s in the centre join together to make 10.*

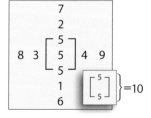

on page 242, the number 5 represents marriage (since a woman is 2 and a man is 3.

Ancient Chinese books advise that the numbers shown should always operate in this sequence in order for proper harmony and balance to be achieved. So 2 and 7 always go together, as do 4 and 9, 1 and 6, and 3 and 8, because they all lead to the five elements in the middle ($7-2 = 5$ / $9-4 = 5$ / $6-1 = 5$ / $8-3 = 5$). Odd numbers are always associated with heaven and even numbers with the earth, and, as we now know, odd numbers are shown as hollow dots, while even numbers are depicted as solid dots. It's interesting to note that the followers of Pythagoras in Greece, around 550 BCE, reached the same conclusions, but they could not have known about the ancient Chinese Yellow River Map – unless someone can prove otherwise. (To explore this theory further, see bibliography, no. 23.)

The Yellow River Map is regarded as a cosmic archetype. It connects all the elements of nature to the universe, and evidence linking the Map to the Book of Changes is incontestable. It strikes me as yet another coincidence that the Tree of Life (Sephiroth Tree) of the Kabala also depicts the creation process as involving ten divine numbers, which are mysteriously connected to each other through the twenty-two letters of the Hebrew alphabet. The Kabala gained credence in the first century CE and became popular during the Middle Ages, whereas The Yellow River Map was supposed to have been discovered before 3300 BCE.

▼ Fu Xi temple ceiling

This photograph shows the ceiling inside the Fu Xi temple in Tianshui. It depicts The Yellow River Map encircled by the trigrams (in the Early Heaven Sequence, because this is how they appeared to Fu Xi). The sixty-four hexagrams are then shown around the rest of the ceiling and walls, linking all three aspects – the Map, trigrams and hexagrams – together. In ancient China the three are therefore very firmly connected, and the Hon-Shō method of oracle reading faithfully reflects this relationship. Sixty-four cypress trees were also planted in the temple courtyard to symbolize the sixty-four hexagrams, though sadly only thirty-seven of the trees still remain today.

▶ **Fu Xi and Nuwa: the Chinese Adam and Eve**

Many texts and a variety of archaeological discoveries depict Fu Xi and Nuwa, the first 'married couple' of Chinese antiquity, known as the Chinese Adam and Eve. In this Wu Liang tomb-shrine relief, dating from the second century CE, Fu Xi (on the right) is shown holding a measuring device or set square, while Nuwa, his wife (also sometimes described as his sister), holds another device (a compass), which resembles a child. They are inseparable, as symbolized by their intertwined tails. They also represent the interconnectedness of Yin and Yang.

▶ **The Republic of South Korea flag**

The flag of The Republic of South Korea is unmistakably influenced by the trigrams and Taoist philosophy. At the centre is the well-known Yin-Yang emblem, representing balance and harmony in nature and all things in the universe. This is surrounded by four trigrams: the male three full lines signify energy and heaven, while the female three broken lines represent justice and the earth. The two trigrams in between depict wisdom and nourishment, and courtesy and radiance.

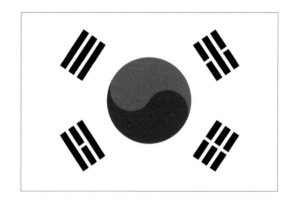

▼ Temple of Heaven / Large Hadron Collider

On a recent trip to CERN – the European Organization for Nuclear Research, and one of the world's largest and most respected centres for scientific research – I made an astonishing discovery. On seeing this image of the Large Hadron Collider's ATLAS experiment (*below*), I was at once struck by the fact that it seemed familiar. I was convinced I'd seen something just like it somewhere before. Then it hit me. On returning home, I consulted my reference books.

The structure of the Large Hadron Collider – a modern-day machine built to advance our understanding of the fundamental laws of nature – bears an uncanny resemblance to the ceiling of the Temple of Heaven in Beijing (*below right*), originally built over five hundred years ago during the Ming dynasty. Is the resemblance once more down to mere coincidence, or is this evidence of nature's forces at work? Are the patterns of the cosmos so integral to our existence that they pervade all we do, embedded in our conscious minds?

This discovery stopped me in my tracks. Maybe our brains are hard-wired to use such regular patterns to connect us to the universal laws which dictate our lives, as the ancient Chinese believed. You can, of course, make up your own mind. The choice is yours.

BIBLIOGRAPHY

Note: numbers refer to bibliography references included in the text.

1 *Memories, Dreams, Reflections* C. G. Jung, Fontana Press 1995.

2 *The Power of Coincidence: The Mysterious Role of Synchronicity in Shaping our Lives* Frank Joseph, Arcturus Publishing 2009.

3 *The Human Touch: Our Part in the Creation of a Universe* Michael Frayn, Faber and Faber 2006.

4 *A New Historical Relation of the Kingdom of Siam, Simon de la Loubere, Envoy Extraordinary from the French King to the King of Siam in the years 1687 and 1688.* Translated by A. P. Gent (London: Horne, Saunders and Bennet, 1693, from the French edition, Paris 1691). Biblioteca Apostolica Vaticana. Borgeani Cinesi collection 397.

5 *Zhouyi: The Book of Changes* Richard Rutt, Routledge 2002.

6 *Chinese History: A Manual* Endymion Wilkinson, Harvard University Asia Centre 2000.

7 *The Tao of Physics: An Exploration of the Parallels between Modern Physics and Eastern Mysticism* Fritjof Capra, Flamingo 1991. See also *DNA and the I Ching : The Tao of Life* J. F. Yan, North Atlantic Books 1991.

8 *Zhou Yi: Bagua* Xu Kun, Forecast Publishing 2004 (Mandarin only).

9 *The I Ching and the Genetic Code: The Hidden Key to Life* M. Schönberger, ASI Publishers 1979.

10 *Tao of Chaos: DNA and the I Ching – Unlocking the Code of the Universe* K. Walter, Element Books 1996.

11 See both *San Ts'ai T'u Hui: A Chinese Encyclopaedia* dated 1609 (British Library, shelf number 15024.a.1) and also *Graphic Illustrations of the VI Classic Books* by Liu Jing Zhou dated 1743 (John Rylands Library, Crawford collection, Chinese books 458). Finally, see *Le Y-King Des Tcheou* by Lun-Li, Introduction and 'text ancien', dated 1597 (Crawford collection, Chinese books 286).

12 *The Shorter Science & Civilisation in China: 2* Colin A. Ronan, Cambridge University Press 1978.

13 *The Philosopher's Stone: A Quest for the Secrets of Alchemy* Peter Marshall, Macmillan 2001.

14 *The Road to Delphi: The Life and Afterlife of Oracles* Michael Wood, Pimlico 2005.

15 *Finding Happiness: Monastic Steps for a Fulfilling Life* Abbot Christopher Jamison, Weidenfeld & Nicolson 2008.

16 *The Original I Ching Oracle* R. Ritsema and S. A. Sabbadini (Eranos Foundation), Watkins Publishing 2005.

17 *The Luck Factor* Richard Wiseman, Arrow 2004

18 *Lost Languages: The Enigma of the World's Undeciphered Scripts* Andrew Robinson, Thames and Hudson 2009.

19 *Oracle Bones: A Journey between China and the West* Peter Hessler, John Murray 2006.

20 *The Illustrated Book of Changes* Paul White, Dolphin Books 2006.

21 *The World Atlas of Divination* John Matthews (ed.), Headline Book Publishing 1992

22 *The Silk Road: Trade, Travel, War and Faith* Susan Whitfield, The British Library 2004.

23 *I Ching or Book of Changes* Richard Wilhelm, Penguin 1951.

24 *The Loom of God: Tapestries of Mathematics and Mysticism* Clifford A. Pickover, Sterling Publishing 2009.

25 *The Sacred Books of China: The I Ching* James Legge, Oxford 1899 (reprinted by Dover Publications 1963).

26 *The Early Civilization of China* Yong Yap and Arthur Cotterell, Weidenfield and Nicolson 1975.

27 *Legacy of Luoshu: the 4,000 Year Search for the Meaning of the Magic Square of Order Three* Frank J. Swetz, A. K. Peters 2008. See also *Fleeting Footsteps: Tracing the Conception of Arithmetic and Algebra in Ancient China* Lam Lay Yong and Ang Tian Se, World Scientific, 1992.

28 *The Early Heaven Oracle: Original Oriental Wisdom to Unlock the Power of Good Fortune* Ken Taylor, Random House 2002.

29 *Chance and Necessity* Jacques Monod, Penguin 1997.

30 *The Tao of Medicine* Stephen Fulder, Destiny Books 1982. See also 'The Mathematics of the I Ching' M. Gardner, *Scientific American*, Jan. 1974.

31 *The Astrology of I Ching* W. A. Sherrill (ed.), Routledge & Kegan Paul 1976. See also *Chinese Astrology* Derek Walters, Watkins Publishing 2002.

32 *The Black Swan: The Impact of the Highly Improbable* Nassim Nicholas Taleb, Penguin 2007.

33 *Benjamin Franklin's Numbers: An Unsung Mathematical Odyssey* Paul C. Pasles, Princeton University Press 2008.

34 *Writings on China* Gottfried Wilhelm Leibniz (Daniel J. Cook and Henry Rosemont Jr trans.), Open Court Publishing Company 1994

35 *The Memory Palace of Matteo Ricci* Jonathan Spence, Quercus 1978

FURTHER READING

For those who want to learn more about the rich history and philosophy of ancient China, the following are recommended:

The Cambridge History of China Denis Twitchett and John K. Fairbank, Cambridge University Press (ongoing series).

The Cambridge Illustrated History of China Patricia Buckley Ebrey, Cambridge University Press 2006.

China Edward L. Shaughnessy (ed.), Duncan Baird 2005.

China: A History John Keay, Harper Press 2008.

The Composition of the Zhou Yi Edward L. Shaughnessy, PhD thesis in the Joseph Needham Institute, Cambridge. He studied methods of divination, their timing and application to a range of subjects, from sickness and warfare through jobs, travel, dreams, crossing rivers, marriage, and more.

The Genius of China: 3,000 years of science, discovery and invention Robert Temple, Andre Deutsch 2007.

The Genius of China Exhibition held at the Royal Academy, London, 1973–74; catalogue published by Times Newspapers, 1973.

ABOUT THE AUTHOR

Kevin Wilson is a former investment banker and stockbroker who lectures internationally in finance. Given an hour to pack his bags on a cold Monday morning in 2002, he became a corporate casualty, as the office he ran was closed by new owners. This blew his world apart. He recovered by spending time working on a farm and walking in Pembrokeshire and Cyprus, determined to change his life. Trawling through a stack of old books on a market stall, he stumbled across a fascinating book about ancient Chinese philosophy and culture. His enthusiasm was further ignited by visiting both China and Japan. The rest is history. Hon-Shō was born.

ACKNOWLEDGEMENTS

It's taken many years to get a handle on the Book of Changes, and I'm still learning. Ploughing through hundreds of books and ancient manuscripts required the skills of those with much greater knowledge of China and its history than I, especially since I cannot read or speak Mandarin. My gratitude extends far and wide, commencing with Nick and Rosemary Hansell (now Wilson), who spent many months working with me on the technical aspects of the Hon-Shō oracle-delivery system.

I could have made no further progress without the patience and encouragement of Susan Whitfield and Graham Hutt, plus their colleagues at the British Library. After years of studying the techniques of oracle-bone divination, I will always treasure the moment I was allowed to hold the 3,300-year-old Shang oracle bones in my hand. I was speechless.

Dorothy Clayton, Anne Young and the team at The John Rylands University Library in Manchester helped guide my manuscript research, while Hong Liu and Minjie Xing at the University of Manchester dealt with my interminable enquiries about language, meaning and sources of information. Minjie also accompanied me to China, which renewed my energy and strengthened my ambitions for Hon-Shō. I returned reinforced in my conviction that the time is right, at this point in the twenty-first century, to use a digital mechanism to revisit the lessons learned by the ancient Chinese from their ancestors.

My visits to the Joseph Needham Institute in Cambridge were critical to understanding the methods of divination employed during the Shang dynasty and the rich history behind the oracle-bone procedures. John Moffatt and Susan Bennett deserve special thanks. My visit to the

Eranos Foundation at Ascona on Lake Maggiore was both rewarding and inspiring. Standing alone in the study used by Carl Jung, seeing his books untouched and his picture with pipe in hand, was another magical moment.

During his remarkable life, Jung became as fascinated with the Book of Changes as I have become. Following the trail of his discovery of the book and its meaning was like looking through a mirror in time. What happened to him was happening to me, except that his knowledge and understanding of complex human psychology and his gift for interpreting myths, dreams and the human psyche was way beyond my own capabilities.

Much of Jung's collection of universal archetypes resides now at the Warburg Institute in London. Many of the papers he gave at Eranos in the mid twentieth century on the subject of Chinese oracle reading and its meaning are particularly revealing. The files standing sentry on those dusty shelves in a library in London bear testimony to the huge contribution Jung and his colleagues made to the whole subject of psychoanalysis and the healing process of self-discovery.

Hundreds of years ago the Book of Changes had itself predicted that the art of oracle reading would be lost to China, and that it would find its way back through another route. Maybe this will prove to be the role of Hon-Shō. I certainly hope so. The new, young, dynamic and aspiring Chinese generation deserve to recapture this knowledge and, in my opinion, would benefit enormously from it. After all, they will simply be accessing the advice of their own ancestors.

There are dozens of 'guinea pigs' who suffered the consequences of my product testing and the constant refinement of the oracle pronouncements until the Hon-Shō divination procedure was both accurate and ready to unleash on a sceptical world. My colleagues at Zeus Capital deserve special praise for their patience, especially Caron O'Carroll and Sally Williams. Building the product's technological capability would be beyond the ability of most, but not the team at Square 1, especially Adam Voisey and Justin Keevill. Finally I should especially like to thank Karen George, Tessa Monina, and Audra and Chris Sheffield for all their support and encouragement, and Susan Clinton, who, as always, contributed beyond the call of duty.

Bath, 2012

Picture Credits With special thanks to the British Library, University of Manchester John Rylands Library and the Eranos Foundation for permission to reproduce material.

© page 21 shutterstock.com; page 217 British Library; page 219 Library of Congress; pages 222 and 225 Wikimedia; page 236 with courteous permission of the Eranos Foundation: page 241 British Library; pages 242–50 John Rylands Library, University of Manchester; page 251 Alex Dally MacFarlane; page 252 top right Wikimedia, bottom right shutterstock. com; page 253 bottom left CERN, bottom right Gail Mooney. Opener images pages 6, 12, 18, 34, 42, 76, 86, 216, 232 from shutterstock.com.

Hon-Shō logo designed by Kay Why Marketing.
Design advice from Trenjory Designs.

EDDISON•SADD EDITIONS

EDITORIAL DIRECTOR Ian Jackson • MANAGING EDITOR Tessa Monina • CREATIVE DIRECTOR Nick Eddison
DESIGNER Malcolm Smythe • PROOFREADER Nikky Twyman • PRODUCTION Sarah Rooney